The Only Son Offered for Sacrifice
ISAAC OR ISHMAEL

The Only Son Offered for Sacrifice

ISAAC

OR

ISHMAEL

Abdus Sattar Ghauri,
Ihsanur Rahman Ghauri

GYAN

The only Son Offered for Sacrifice Isaac or Ishmael

Rs. 750

ISBN: 978-81-212-1029-4

Published in 2010 in India by
Gyan Publishing House,
23, Main Ansari Road, Darya Ganj,
New Delhi-110002
Phones : 23282060, 23261060
Fax : 011-23285914
E-mail: books@gyanbooks.com
Website: www.gyanbooks.com

Lasser Type Setting by: Quick Media, Delhi
Printed at : **GIAN RIDHI OFFSET PRINTERS**

To

My Father Dīn Muḥammad Ghaurī
Who taught me how to read and write;

My Wife Mrs. Tasnīm Ghaurī
Who provided comfort and convenience to me
During my research and academic undertakings;

Sayyid Abu al-A'lā Mawdūdī
From whom I learnt the Logical Treatment
and Comely Presentation of a Theme in Polite Manner;

Mr. Javed Aḥmad Ghāmidī
At whose behest I undertook this huge project
and whose encouragement and guidance had been
a constant source of support throughout the work.

Gratitude

First of all, all praise and gratitude be to Almighty Allah, Who guided and made it convenient for His humble bondman, as the writer is, to undertake and accomplish such an important assignment. Whoso-ever helped the writer in this material world, was with the grace of Allah Almighty. It is really He Who implanted and infused in their minds the love and affection for the writer and his assignment. The writer owes a debt of gratitude to all of such benefactors:

The valuable moral support and encouragement of Lt. Col. (Rtd) 'Ābid Husayn 'Ābid; Mr Gul Muḥammad Iqbāl of Lohsar Sharfū; Mr. Muḥammad Jameel Baluch; my sister Mrs. Sa'eedah Yamin; Mr. Na`īm Durrānī, Chief Executive, Noor Durrani and Associates; Mr Nawāb Nayyar Iqbāl; Dr. Munīr Aḥmad; Mr. Shahzād Saleem; Mr Parvaiz Hāshimī; Ch. Altaf Maḥmood; Sufi Muḥammad Abdul Qayyum had been a source of strength to me.

I feel it my duty to extend my gratitude to Mr Azeem Ayyub, Mr. Muḥammad Sami' Mufti, and Mr. Sajid Ḥameed for their guidance towards comely presentation of the book.

I am particularly thankful to Dr Maḥmūd Aḥmad Ghāzī, International Islāmic Univ., Islāmābād; Prof Dr Muḥammad Tāufayl Hāshimī of Allamah Iqbal Open University and Prof Dr Safīr Akhtar, who had been very kind to extend guidance in research methodology whenever I approached them to seek it.

Finally, I am highly grateful to Messrs Gyan Publishing House, Delhi for their kind consent to publish the work from Delhi, which is really an honour for the writer.

Contents

Common Abbreviations

AD/CE	*anno domini* (*Latin*), in the year of the Lord, Common/ Christian Era.
Ar	Arab, Arabia, Arabian, Arabic.
B	Bible.
BC	Before Christ; Bible Commentary; Biblical Commentary.
BCE	Before Christian/Common Era.
BD	Bible Dictionary.
c/ca	About, approximately (Latin *circa*)
CB	Commentary of the Bible.
CE	Common Era: secular form of AD.
Cf	cónfer: compare.
Ch	Chapter.
DB	Dictionary of the Bible.
DSS	Dead Sea Scrolls.
E	East.
E	Elohist tradition of some books of the OT of the Bible.
Ed	Editor/edited by.
Edn	Edition.
e.g./eg	for example (Latin *exempli gratia*).
Enc	Encyclopedia/Encyclopaedia/Encyclopedic.
Esp	especially.
Heb	Hebrew.
i.e.	that is, that means, namely.
J	Jehovist or Yahwist tradition of some books of the OT of the Bible.

JE	Text of the OT based on the combination of the E & J Traditions of the Bible.
L	Latin.
LLX	Septuagint (70): Greek Tr. of the OT claimed to be accomplished by 70 scholars in Alexandria between 250 –150 BC.
MS/MSS	Manuscript/Manuscripts.
MT/Mt	Massoretic /Masoretic Text of the OT; Matthew; Mount.
N	North.
NT	New Testament of the Bible containing 27 books: 4 Gospels + Acts + 21 Epistles (letters) + Revelations. It was originally written in Greek, whereas Jesus Christ delivered his message in the Aramaic language.
op.cit.	in the work already quoted (Latin *opere citato*).
OT	Old Testament of the Bible Consists of 39 books: The first five are collectively called the Pentateuch or Torah. It was originally written in Heb.
p/pp	Page/pages.
P	Priestly tradition of the OT of the Bible.
Pbl/pblg	Publisher(s)/Publishing/.
Pbln	Publication(s)
Q	*Quelle* (a German word), i.e. source. A hypothetical common source of the gospels of Matthew and Luke.
q.v.	vide
Rvd	Revised.
S	South, southern.
Sic.	thus, so: used within brackets, [sic], to show that a quoted passage, esp. one containing some error or s.th. questionable, is precisely reproduced.
s.o.	Some one.
s.th.	Some thing.
St	Saint.

s.v.	Under the word or heading.
Tr.	Translator, translation, translated by.
Trad/Tradn	Tradition(s).
Uni./Univ.	University.
v/vv	Verse/verses (of the Bible).
V	Version (Tr.) of the Bible.
Vol.	Volume.
Vulg.	Vulgate, the Latin Tr. of the Bible accomplished by St Jerome in late 4th century AD.
W	West, western.
Y	Yahwist (Jehovist) tradition of the Bible.
(…)	It indicates that some word(s), sentence(s), or line(s) have been left over from the original quotation.
(….)	It shows that a sizeable text has been omitted from the original quotation.
[]	Square brackets are used to insert something by the Tr./Ed., which did not originally exist in the quotation.

Foreword

The relation of Umm al-Qurā [Makkah] with Abraham (pbuh) is a significant theme of the Qur'ānic Da'wah. The Prophet of Islām (pbuh) was raised from among Banī Ishmā'el, a branch of the descendants of Abraham (pbuh). They were settled in Makkah. Abraham (pbuh) had himself settled this branch of his descendants at this place. This is the site where he had offered his only son for sacrifice in the vicinity of al-Marwah. This son was Ishmā'el (pbuh) who was the ancestor of Allah's Last Prophet, Muḥammad (pbuh). The corruption made by the Jews in their scriptures had been mostly pertaining to these themes. They incorporated the name of Isaac (pbuh) in their scriptures as the only son offered for sacrifice in lieu of Ishmā'el (pbuh). They have created great confusion regarding the place of Ishmā'el's (pbuh) offering. They have also endeavoured to make the relation of Abraham (pbuh) with the sanctuary of Makkah doubtful in every respect.

It was essential to bring all these corruptions to light to establish the reality upon the Jews and Christians beyond any shadow of doubt. A renowned and great scholar of the present age, Imām Ḥamīd al-Dīn Farāhī, rendered this service. He wrote a booklet, *al-Ra'y al-Ṣaḥīḥ, fī man Huwa al-Dhabīḥ*, on this topic, in which he laid all the facts bare with most acceptable arguments.

Mr. Abdus Sattār Ghawrī is also a scholar of the same field of learning. He has devoted his life in the study of the prophecies regarding the Prophet of Islām (pbuh) in the scriptures of the Jews and the Christians. Keeping in view the significance of the theme and to promote the esteemed research of Imām Ḥamīd al-Dīn Farāhī, he undertook a further study on '*the Only Son Offered for Sacrifice Isaac or Ishmā'el?*'. He wrote such a book in English which will be welcomed by the scholars of the religio/historical learnings. In addition to thrashing out the main problem, Mr. Ghawrī has explored the mention of Makkah, Zamzam, and the mention of the pilgrimage of Makkah by King David and Isaiah in the Bible. He has included the following appendices as well, which provide useful and relevant information to the reader:

The Text of the Bible and Some Types of Corruption in It;

A Brief Account of the History of the Solomon's Temple; and

A Brief Account of the History of Jerusalem.

He has set forth such ideas in his specific scholarly style which are equally notable for the scholars of the Bible and its relevant sciences; and for the scholars of the religious learnings at large. One may differ with his views; and, being a student of these sciences, I also hold varying views in some of the themes, from this our scholar; but nobody would deny his sincerity, his painstaking efforts, and his scholarly style of research. He is a heedful explorer of this concern and knows the ins and outs of the course fully well. Discerning scholars will testify his deep insight in biblical sciences.

It is a matter of privilege for al-Mawrid to have such a scholar at its campus as a research fellow. We pray to Almighty Allah that he may work with this institution for long. May Allah shower His choicest blessings upon him for his valuable services.

Javed Ahmad Ghamidi,

President, al-Mawrid.

June 13, 2007.

Preface

To the Second (Revised) Edition (2007)

Initially the book was published in 2004. After that the writer received some suggestions. Valuable reviews have also been published in some esteemed national and international journals. The author tried to improve the book where required. The author is grateful to the authorities who had kindly undertaken the reviews and suggestions. The author himself went through the book a number of times and made some revisions where deemed fit.

'A Brief Account of the History of Jerusalem' has also been included as an Appendix in the book. The author asked his son, Iḥsanur Raḥman Ghauri, Lecturer, Isl. St. Dptt., Pb. Univ., Lahore to undertake the task. It is gratifying that he completed the task quite to the mark. The author thoroughly revised the work and recommended some updates that he properly incorporated therein. He has also prepared the index of the footnote entries, which has increased the utility of the book to a great extent. The writer is thankful to him for his scholarly contribution. He has submitted his Ph. D. Thesis. May Allah Almighty bless him with success!

Improvements have also been incorporated in the Appendix 'A Brief Account of the History of Solomon's Temple'. For the sake of propriety 'The Status of the Chronicles' has been shifted to the Appendix section of the book.

Generally the *Chicago Manual for Writers* has been followed in footnotes, references, etc; but sometimes it was considered useful to devise some style friendly to the user. Some observations and reviews have also been included in the preliminary pages of the book to apprise the reader of its usefulness.

Abdus Sattar Ghauri,

Lahore: Sept. 6, 2007.

Some Excerpts from
THE REVIEWS ON THE BOOK

An E-mail to the writer from Biju Abdul Qadir, Editor, Young Muslim Digest,

It (your book) left upon me the distinct impression of being a work that has been thoroughly researched for the subject that it deals with. Without exaggerating in the least, it may even be said that in the reading experiences of this writer, he has hardly come across a more diligent study on so crucial a subject as the identity of the son of Abraham who was offered for sacrifice.

Biju Abdul Qadir
Dated 07-06-05

****

Young Muslim Digest,
Bangalore (INDIA): September, 2005.

Isaac or Ishmael?

Author: *Abdus Sattar Ghawri*
Publisher: Al-Mawrid Institute of Islamic Sciences
Reviewer: *Biju Abdul Qadir*, ed., Y M D, Bangalore.

For a book that was intended to be an appendix to another one, namely *Paran prophecy of the Bible regarding the Prophet of Islam*, the writer's contention that *Isaac or Ishmael?* has instead become an attempt to solve a long addressed problem on the principles of objective research is, indeed, something of a humble understatement. Few Muslim scholars in the recent past have addressed the question of the identity of the actual son of the Prophet Abraham who was taken for the sacrifice with such vigour and tenacity as has been done by Abdus Sattar Ghawri in his Isaac or Ishmael? What makes Ghawri's work of particular relevance is his almost total, albeit deliberate, reliance on the Bible and the works of Biblical scholars to prove his point. Indeed, and as the author himself whole-heartedly admits, the question that he addresses in his book had been 'settled once forever' by the celebrated South Asian Muslim scholar, Imam Hamid al-Din Farahi in his masterly Arabic work, al-Ray al-Sahih fi man huwa al-dhabih, which was later translated into English (Who was offered for sacrifice?) by Nadir Aqeel Ansari while its Urdu version was produced by Amin Ahsan Islahi in 1975. Muslim scholarship on the subject that was based primarily on Muslim sources had, thus, probably effected a culmination with Farahi's work in the first quarter of the twentieth century. However, genuine Muslim scholarship on the same subject, based on Judeo-Christian sources, was not as forthcoming. It is, perhaps, into this genre of academic work on the topic that Isaac or Ishmael? categorically falls, and in which it has become something of a pioneering effort.

To say, today, that the work of an artist has an innate tendency to grow on him as he progresses with it, is to say something that is generally accepted as a matter of fact. Indeed, true art – and any effort worth its time can be rendered to the sublimities of a quintessential art form – presupposes an evolution of purpose within the artist in his work. True scholarship, too, is not beyond the pale of such artistic renditions. That much, at least, is in evidence as one reads through the path of discovery which Ghawri charts out for us in the progression, indeed, the evolution, of themes that center around the moot question: 'was it Isaac or Ishmael who was taken for the sacrifice by Abraham?' Doubtless, in this evolution of themes around the central point, there has been a broadening of the very scope of the book itself. Thus, it covers, and addresses a whole host of different, yet intimately related, incidents and issues that must necessarily be of the greatest interest to the genuine scholar, Muslim and non Muslim alike. Amongst others, it covers the relevant themes of the site of Makkah according to the Bible, pilgrimage to Makkah as described in the Bible, the site of Al-Marwah in the Bible, King David's visit and pilgrimage to Makkah and of his later yearning to be there, the offering of sacrifices at Makkah as mentioned in the Book of Isaiah, the well of Zamzam and a brief, yet significant, outline of the history of the Temple of Solomon in Jerusalem.

However, to go by the Biblical version of the identity of the son as being Isaac, would be to trust in the fleeting opinion of a redactor who penned down his wishful thinking, as presumably being part of the Divine word, a full one thousand years after the incident of the sacrifice. Evidently, serious historians would hardly take such naïve, or even pious, assumptions as genuine facts of history, particularly when the only instance in which the identity of the son is mentioned appears almost totally out of context, and in a manner which provides genuine grounds for suspicion. This, then, has been the methodology adopted by Ghawri throughout his presentation of the problem - a problem about which one observer noted very pertinently: 'Lying at the root of centuries old Judeo-Muslim differences, this controversy is all that the Judeo-Muslim relations stand for.' [It was the observation of Mr. Nadir Aqeel Ansari]

Ghawri's has been an effort to, among other things, present a logical appreciation of the statements, factual or otherwise, that appear in the Bible. In thus providing a logical context for the narratives in the Bible, and with his own sure-footed understanding of history and data handling, his has been a thorough study of the subject which owes its authentication not to Muslim scholarship, but to the opinions and considered judgements of some of the greatest names in modern Biblical scholarship within the Judeo-Christian world. It is in this connection that reference must be made to the remarkable number of books and authorities which the learned author has consulted in the making of this ground-breaking research. Indeed, the extensive footnotes to which the attention of the reader is constantly invited in almost every page of the book constitutes a significant, if not a major, part of the work itself. In fact, the footnotes and annotations form a parallel world that operates on the reader's understanding in tandem with the main body of the book. The end result, of course, has been an overwhelming body of evidence in favour of Ishmael having been the son who was offered for the sacrifice: a conclusion made even more relevant by the fact that it was derived almost in its entirety from the Bible, and from the works of renowned scholars of the Bible.

Of especial consideration, with regard to Ghawri's approach, must certainly be his eye for detail and his ability to go directly to the point; to the heart of the matter, as it were. While this approach has necessitated a seeming repetition of relevant aspects throughout the course of the study, when read in conjunction with the immediate context of the author's arguments, however, these repetitions almost never end in the dry monotony that would be otherwise expected of them. Contrariwise, they result in a further consolidation of the strength of the argument. One instance wherein the author's ability to go directly to the substance of the argument is seen quite early on in the work. A classical stance of the modern Judeo-Christian world with regard to the identity of the son taken for the sacrifice has been that while Ishmael was, indeed, the first born of Abraham, he need not be considered as such owing to his 'low' birth through Hagar, a mere bondservant of Abraham. As such, it must be Isaac, born through Sarah, the 'real' wife of Abraham, who needs to be considered as the first-born and the only son of Abraham. In a manner that amply illustrates the way in which he demolishes all such false, egotistic pretensions of the Judeo-Christian world, Ghawri quite simply brings the attention of the reader to the following passage from Deuteronomy:

> "If a man have two wives, one beloved, and another hated, and they have born children, both the beloved and the hated; and if the first born son be her's that was hated: then it shall be, when he maketh his son to inherit that which he hath, that he may not make the son of the beloved first born before the son of the hated, which is indeed the first-born: But he shall acknowledge the son of the hated for the first-born, by giving him a double portion of all that he hath: for he is the beginning of his strength; the right of the first born is his." (Deuteronomy xxi: 15-17, KJV, p.181)

It would not be too much to say that Ghawri has merely allowed facts, and aberrations, from the Bible to speak for themselves. The rest of the matter should be easily settled by the common sense and intellectual logic of the impartial seeker after truth. The author's committed labours lend credence to the fact that scriptural aberrations or corruptions, far from hiding the facts, actually leave, in their wake, a string of clues and trails which the real historian, working with the advantage of hindsight, can sift and reassemble to reconstruct a semblance of what might, indeed, be the real Truth.

The sections appended to the book as Appendix I, II and III (titled respectively as Beersheba: the 'Well of Seven' or the 'Well of Zamzam,' The Text of the Bible and Some Types of Corruptions in It, *and* A Brief Account of the History of the Temple of Solomon*) might very well have formed integral portions of the book, which, technicalities apart, they actually do. This is very much owing to the fact that they supplement the arguments in the core sections of the book, and the book would have been all the poorer for their absence from it. A useful index and a complete table of bibliographical references (which include 25 versions of the Bible, 39 commentaries on the Bible, 53 encyclopaedias and 16 other Biblical studies, all by Christian scholars) must further place the work of Ghawri amongst the top-most references on the subject today. Indeed, it is hardly an exaggeration to say that* Isaac or Ishmael? *has substantially altered the way in which the academic world must view the answer to the age-old question that it poses.*

A fellow of the prestigious Al-Mawrid Institute of Islamic Sciences, *Lahore, Abdus Sattar Ghawri is the author of a number of articles on the Biblical text that has special reference to the prophecies heralding the advent of Prophet Muhammad (pbuh). He has also lectured extensively on the subject. This robust experience in treating the subject at hand is fairly visible in Ghawri's* Isaac or Ishmael? *If the results of his honest labours are accepted in a spirit a impartiality and good-will within the community of Jews and Christians, it goes without saying that it will help in clearing the international atmosphere between the Muslims and the Judeo-Christian world so much vitiated by misunderstanding and hostility begotten of centuries of ignorance and mistrust. To this end has surely been the author's motivation, and in this end-result, most certainly lies, his higher reward. His highest reward, of course, must, like all other sincere efforts in the Islamic cause, find its expression in the presence of his Maker, Lord of all Creation.*

Quarterly Fikr-o-Nazar, Islamic Research Institute, Islamabad Vol. 42; No.3: 1-3/2005

Mr. Ghauri's book provides valuable information regarding the important topics like the 'Only Son' offered for sacrifice, Beersheba, and Bakkah. He has established his viewpoint with very convincing arguments. He has availed himself immensely of the existing works of the Western scholars on these themes. His style is that of a research scholar rather than polemical. (...). It is, of course, an esteemed scholastic effort. Mr. Ghauri genuinely deserves felicitation for it.

Quarterly Tahqeeqaat-e-Islami, Aligarh (India) Vol. 24; No.3: 7-9/2005

The style of the learned writer is objective, scientific, and research oriented. He has availed himself of different versions and translations of the Bible, its commentaries, dictionaries, concordances, atlases, and encyclopaedias in his works. This book is a valuable contribution on the theme. The learned writer deserves praise and felicitation for it.

Radiance Viewsweekly,
New Delhi: 16-22 January 2005

(...). Ghauri deals with this issue in a very systematic manner in 11 chapters with 3 important appendices (...).

The two main issues selected by Ghauri are: (a) which son of Prophet Ibrahim was offered for sacrifice? (Chapters I to IV), and (b) what was the place of sacrifice (Moriah or Al-Marwah) and related matters (Chapters V to XI).

Before moving further it is better to summarize the story of prophet Ibrahim. Prophet Ibrahim was a prophet of Allah. He had two wives – one, Sarah and the other Hagar (Hajirah). Noble Hajirah was an Egyptian princess, daughter of Pharaoh, who had offered her to Ibrahim. At that time Prophet Ibrahim was issueless. Hajirah gave birth to the first son of Prophet Ibrahim. His name was Ismail, to whose progeny last Prophet of Islam, Muhammad, (peace be upon him) came. Later another son of Prophet Ibrahim was born by noble Sarah. His name was Isaac, whose progeny includes Prophets like Moses, David, Solomon and Jesus. The Jews generally consider Prophet Ismail of inferior origin. As Ibrahim was a great Prophet whose life was full of sacrifices, God ordered him to sacrifice his 'only son' or 'beloved son' into the land of Moriah. But when finally he took the knife to slay his son, God stopped him. The Jews and Christians consider Prophet Isaac the 'only son' referred to above for the special sacrifice. For [most of the] Muslims, it was Prophet Ismail. The Hajj Pilgrimage is based on the traditions of Prophet Ibrahim, his son Ismail and noble Hajirah's faiths and sacrifices at Makkah.

The author's methodology is simple. First he would put forward the Bible story or the claims of the Biblical scholars directly and comment on its weaknesses in the footnotes or in the text as the growth of story demands. Second, he would show its contradictions by extensively citing the criticism of Jewish or Christian scholars on the story or the thesis. Third, he would also raise questions and answer them with utmost skill. He mostly did his construction or deconstruction by using the works of Jewish or Christian scholars.

In these discussions, the author has not claimed any superiority of Prophet Ismail over Prophet Isaac. He avers, 'The Biblical scholars have taken much liberties with the interpretations of Biblical themes while depicting the characters of Ibrahim, Ismail, Isaac … Sarah and Hagar. The writer of the present book holds all of these great personalities equally respectable, honourable and innocent.'

There is no doubt that the book has been written in 'vintage scholarly style'. I would like to make a suggesstion at the end. As most of us are not familiar with Biblical historiography [or 'chronology'?], it would be pertinent to add a chapter thereon in the beginning of the book. Without this full appreciation of the book is not possible [The Chronology has now been given in Appendix on 'A Brief Account of the History of Jerusalem']. (By Javed Ali)

Islamic Studies; Vol.44; No.1: Spring 2005

In the Second Appendix, Ghauri gives heaps of evidence about the different types of intentional and unintentional corruption in the text of both the Old and the New Testaments. This is followed by a brief account of the history of the Temple of Solomon in the Third Appendix. These appendices have added to the value of this scholarly work. (….), the book has been written in a scholarly manner and the author attempts to accumulate irrefutable arguments in support of his views.

The Daily Pakistan Observer, Islamabad: 07 August, 2004

Mr. Abdus Sattar Ghauri, the learned author of this well-researched work, must be complimented for the trmendous work he has done in documenting this important issue of religious history. This issue, of course, has direct bearing on the relationship of Prophet Muhammad (SAW) with Abraham (AS) and the land where the latter had settled his progeny, i.e. Arabia. Besides discussing the main issue, Mr. Ghauri has added some other related topics as well in the book.

These include the locations of Makkah, Al-Marwah and the well of Zamzam.

Here, it may be made clear that at some places the writer of this book had to reproduce some Biblical authorities, which implied the comparison between the Prophets. The Biblical sholars have taken much liberties with the interpretations of Biblical themes while depicting the cahracters of Abraham, Ishma'el and Isaac. Regrettably, noble Sarah has been depicted as a very cruel, jealous and revengeful woman, while dealing with noble Hajra and her son, Ishma'el.

Mr. Ghauri, however, differs with these Biblical scholars and holds all of these great personalities as equally respected, honourable and innocent. It is, indeed, a matter of great interest to note that this event of the offering for sacrifice was reduced to writing in the Bible more than a thousand years after its happening. It is quite unknown who its writer was and what his credentials were, but, of certain, he was not an eyewitness of the event.

Commenting on the book, Allama Javed Ahmad Ghamidi, the profound scholar of Islam, remarks that going deep into the ancient time, the learned author has conducted an incisive multidisciplinary analysis to bring out the truth. Marked by copious references, this book testifies that the author has an eye for the subtle and the penetrating details.

[Allama Ghamidi, continuing his observations, asserts:] The author has indeed, undertaken daunting task to gather and arrange all the scattered pieces of the facts that were also defaced by corruption and ignorance. Further, Allama Ghamidi asserts that many a time, textual corruption, far from hiding the truth, actually leaves behind bright clues and trails, which, in turn, help reconstruct the disjointed pieces of the picture.

To conclude: Mr. Ghauri has brought forth copious evidence to show that Abraham had offered Ishma'el for sacrifice. He has made an attempt to solve a long addressed problem on the principles of objective research. He has also tried to present the evidence faithfully and without any manipulations. A narrative par excellence, indeed!

(Reviewed by: Col. (R) Ghulam Sarwar.

Vidyajyoti Journal,

4-A, Raj Niwas Building, Delhi-110 054

This book is the fruit of a serious effort at studying a complex issue. The author has studied the problem not only by drawing on Islamic resource material but also by studying a wide selection of Christian scholarship. As such, it must be admitted that the book is a unique contribution in the field of Muslim-Christian scholarly dialogue. It is rare to see a Muslim scholar approach Christian scholarship to build his argument. Hence, as an effort in the area of Muslim-Christian dialogue, this work must be welcomed.

Reviewer: The Rev. Herman Roborgh, Research Scholar,

Aligarh Muslim University, Aligarh, India.

9934_ NRT_08_Bibliographie 14-03-2007 09:04 Page 336

****

BIBLIOGRAPHIE

Nouvelle Revue Theologique

GHAWRI, A.S., The Only Son offered for Sacrifice Isaac or Ishmael?, with Zamzamm Al-Marwah, and Makkah in the Bible, Lahore, Al-Mawrid, 2004, 22x15, xiv-310p., 15 $.

Un livre bien étrange que celui de ce chercheur Pakistanais qui déploie une érudition absolument étonnante et un esprit inquisiteur remarqablement ingénieux pour prouver que “le fils unique” que devait sacrifier Abraham au mont Moriah n’était pas Isaac (tradition Judéo-chrétienne), mais bien Ismaël (traduction musulmane). Mettant bout a bout des analyses de textes provenant de commentaires bibliques divers anciens et récents, des détails sur les processus de transmission des manuscrits et les erreurs qu’ils perpétuent, dans la tradition tant juive et chrétienne que musulmane, il en arrive à démontrer avec aplomb que l’interprétation musulmane est la seule objective. Il poursuit sa lancée en identifiant le Moriah à la Ka’bah, construite par Abraham et Ismaël (!), et il découvre que le pèlerinage à La Mecque (Mekkah) se trouverait mentionné dans la Bible par Isaïe 60 et dans les Psaumes, notamment Ps 84,7 (=vallée de Baka).

Beaucoup de notations intéressantes dans ce travail, surtout à propos de l'évolution de la double lecture des textes bibliques, mais malheureusement au service d'une cause fondamentaliste qui historicise le "sacrifice d' Abraham" sans y percevoir le message essentiel. Tout en admirant la sagacité et la patience de l'A., nous ne pouvons le suivre dans son raisonnement.—J.R.

Tome 129/ 2 (annee 2007)

de la part - et avec le merci - due secr. de la
Nouvelle Revue Théologique
Boulevard Saint-Michel, 24 **BE-1040 Bruxelles**
secretariat@nrt.be tel. 00 32 2739 34 80 http://www.iet.be

Its English translation

by

Dr. Mahmood Ahmad Ghazi:

Bibliographie

Nouvelle Revue Theologique

A very strange book by this Pakistani researcher who deploys an absolutely astonishing scholarship as well as an inquisitor spirit which is remarkably ingenious to prove that 'the only son' whom Abraham was to sacrifice on Mount Moriah was not Isaac (the Judeo-Christian tradition), but rather Ismael (Muslim interpretation). From beginning to end of the analysis of texts derived from various biblical commentaries, both ancient and recent, from details in the process of transmission of the manuscripts, and the errors which they perpetuate – in the Jewish and Christian as well as Muslim tradition – he finally shows with firmness that the Muslim interpretation is the only objective one. He continues his course by identifying Moriah with Ka' bah, built by Abraham and Ismael (!), and he discovers that the mention of the pilgrimage to Mecca (Makkah) is found in the Bible in Isiah 60 and the Psalms, in particular PS 84,7 (=valley of Baka).

There are many interesting notes and observations in this work, especially as regards the evolution of the double readings or versions of the Biblical texts, but unfortunately, in the service of a fundamentalist cause which historicises "Abraham's sacrifice" without perceiving the essential message here. While fully admiring the author's sagacity and patience, we cannot agree with him in his argumentation.

INDEX

OF THE FOOTNOTE ENTRIES

NOTE: *The Arabic numerals in the beginning stand for footnote Nos.*

The Essential Message

of the Offering

The essential message of the ACT OF OFFERING is total submission to God which has been indicated in the scriptures of all the Abrahamic religions–Islam, Christianity, and Judaism:

a) Hear, O Israel: The Lord our God is one Lord: And thou shalt love the Lord thy God with all thine heart, and with all thy soul, and with all thy might (Deu 6:4-5 KJV; Mark 12:31; Luke 10:27; Matt 22:37)–[Judo-Christian tradition].

b) God did tempt Abraham, (…). Take now thy son, thine only son Isaac, whom thou lovest, (…); and offer him there for a burnt offering (…). And Abraham rose up early in the morning, (…): for now I know that thou fearest God, seeing thou hast not withheld thy son, thine only son from me. (…); And in thy seed shall *all the nations of the earth [and not only one specific nation] be blessed* because thou hast obeyed my voice (Gen 22:1,2,3,12,18).

c) 'My son, I see in a dream that I shall sacrifice thee; consider, what thinkest thou?' He said, 'My father, do as thou art bidden; thou shalt find me, God willing, one of the steadfast.' When they had surrendered, and he flung him upon his brow, We called unto him, 'Abraham, thou hast confirmed the vision; even so We recompense the good-doers. This is indeed the manifest trial.' And We ransomed him with a mighty sacrifice, and left for him among the later folk '*Peace be upon Abraham*!' (Al-Qur'ān 37:102-109; tr. A.J.Arberry, p. 460) – [Muslims].

d) You can never attain righteousness until you spare, spend away, and consume of what you love (Al-Qur'ān 3::91)

Thus the essential message can be summed up as below:

The complete role model of submission to God is Abraham. He did not spare even his most beloved and direly essential asset, i.e. his only son, from God. Whosoever among *all the nations of the earth* completely obeys the Lord, shall *be blessed*, because 'submission to God' brings harmony among the faiths and peace among all the people of God.

Transliteration Table

ع medial	:	'	ع	:	'		
ع final	:	'	غ	:	gh		
ع initial	:	not expressed	ف	:	f		
ا	:	a	ق	:	q		
ب	:	b	ک	:	k		
پ	:	p	گ	:	g		
ت	:	t	ل	:	l		
ٹ	:	t̲	م	:	m		
ث	:	th	ن	:	n		
ج	:	j	ں	:	ṇ		
چ	:	ch	و	:	w		
ح	:	ḥ	ه	:	h		
خ	:	kh	ۃ	:	ah (e. g. sunnah)		
د	:	d	ـة	:	at (in construct form e. g. sunnat al-Rasūl)		
ڈ	:	d̲	ی	:	y		
ذ	:	dh	ال	:	al- ('l in construct form e. g. Abū'l)		
ر	:	r					
ڑ	:	ṛ					
ز	:	z					
ژ	:	z̲					
س	:	s					
ش	:	sh					
ص	:	ṣ					
ض	:	ḍ					
ط	:	ṭ					
ظ	:	ẓ					

بھ	:	bh
پھ	:	ph
تھ	:	t̲h̲
ٹھ	:	t̲h̲
جھ	:	jh
چھ	:	c̲h̲
دھ	:	d̲h̲
ڈھ	:	d̲h̲
کھ	:	k̲h̲
گھ	:	g̲h̲

VOWELS			DIPTHONGS		
Short ـَ	:	a	ـَو	:	aw
ـِ	:	i	ـَي	:	ay
ـُ	:	u	ـَے	:	ae
Long ـَا	:	ā	Double		
ـِی	:	ī	ـُوّ	:	uwwa
ـُو	:	ū	ـِيّ	:	iyya
و	:	ō	ـَنّ	:	anna
اے	:	ē			
عطف	:	-o- (اردو/فارسی)			
اضافت	:	-i- (اردو/فارسی)			

PREFACE

To the First (2004) Edition

Originally the present work was intended to be written as an 'Appendix' to this writer's book *Pārān Prophecy of the Bible regarding the Prophet of Islām*. When, in the form of an article (appendix), it was presented by the writer to Mr. Javed Aḥmad Ghāmidī, President, Al-Mawrid, Institute of Islāmic Sciences, he agreed to the idea of further research on the theme, and, if it genuinely becomes of size, it might be put forth in the form of an independent book. Inspired by the idea, a thorough probe into the theme was undertaken. A number of times he was resorted to for his guidance mostly during our way to the Mosque for our 'Aṣr prayer. He always solved the problem in a few sentences. He had been a constant source of guidance and consolation throughout this huge undertaking. The writer is earnestly thankful to him.

The present work is neither of a polemic nature nor simply a general informative paper. It is an attempt to address a long discussed problem on the principles of objective research. It has been tried not to make any assertion or set forth an explanation to some word or theme without affording a referential authority. It has also been tried to provide sufficient evidence to establish the themes that it may not be blamed to be based on scanty or one-sided evidence. It has further been tried to present the evidence faithfully and without any manipulations. As regards the 'aggressive referencing', as has been observed by a worthy friend, the writer may be excused for it. The nature of the article required it and it was unavoidable. The reader may occasionally feel a sort of repetition of some data. Besides being useful towards sound appreciation, it was the requisite of the spot and it would spare the reader from turning over the pages, which may mar the effect and interest of the situation. It is hoped that its objective study would be useful. Suggestions towards the improvement of the theme would be appreciated. It would be tried to answer queries. In fact the incident of 'offering' is not a merit for the 'only son' to be offered, if he be not given to know it; and Isaac did not know what was going to be done of him unless he was allegedly put to 'Akedah'[1]. According to the Muslims, the 'only son' offered for sacrifice was taken into full confidence and he wholeheartedly accepted it. No doubt it reveals his duteousness and complete surrender to the will of God and the duty to his father, which, of course, is quite commendable. Yet the Muslims do not claim it as a cause of superiority for him. They take it as godliness and dutifulness of Abraham in response to the 'temptation' (test and trial) by the Lord and a positively desirable cooperation of a son and his duteous compliance with his father's desire to carry out the will of God.

Some of the Muslim scholars misapprehend that it was Isaac who was offered for sacrifice. They depended solely on the Biblical sources. The matter has been settled once for ever by the renowned South Asian Muslim scholar Imām Ḥamīd al-Dīn Farāhī[2] in his scholarly Arabic treatise '*al-Ra'y al-Ṣaḥīḥ fī man huwa al-dhabīḥ*'[3]. It is impossible for this humble writer to address the theme at that level, so he has not touched the Muslim authorities and their stance. Farāhī's esteemed work 'al-Ra'y al-Ṣaḥīḥ fī man Huwa al-Dhabīḥ' is recommended to be consulted for the purpose. The article on 'Beersheba' has been appended to this book, which is to be taken as a part of it. The main theme of the book required it to be explored in detail. When a detailed study of the theme was undertaken, it developed as an independent article. It has thus been attached as an 'Appendix' to the book.

The problem of the 'Corruption in the Text of the Bible' had frequently to be addressed during the development of the theme. It was considered proper to undertake a fairly detailed study of the theme as well. It has also been appended to the book. It should be used only as an instrument to ascertain the status of certain statement of the Bible; but it should not be considered that the whole of the Bible is incredible or unreliable.

During the course of the present assignment a number of themes emerged to be addressed to accomplish the main theme. It has broadened the scope of the book to a great extent, but every point is quite relevant and pertinent at its place. It has made the book even more valuable and exclusive. It has covered the relevant themes of the site of Makkah according to the Bible; Pilgrimage of Makkah in the B; Site of Al-Marwah in the B; Visit and Pilgrimage of Makkah by King David and his later longing for it; Offering of Sacrifices at Makkah in the book of Isaiah of the B; the Well of Zamzam (Beersheba); Hagar's being a princess and not a slave girl (footnote 298); and a brief sketch of the history of the Solomon's Temple at Jerusalem. It has contributed a lot to the worth of the present work.

In the footnotes the name of the book is generally italicized and the publisher's address and the year of publication have been placed in parentheses.

Abdus Sattar Ghawri

February 1, 2004
Al-Mawrid, Institute of Islāmic Sciences, 51-K, Model Town, Lahore.
Ph (92-42) 5834306, 5865145; Fax: (042) 5864856, e-mail <asghawri@hotmail.com>
<asghawri@gmail.com>

References

1. Dr. Cecil Roth, ed., *The Standard Jewish Encyclopedia*, (London: W. H. Allen, 1959, p. 61), explains 'Akedah' as:

   (Heb. 'binding'): Traditional designation of Abraham'ș intended offering of [Isaac] (Gen. 22), the consummation of which was prevented at the last minute by Divine intervention.

   It is of the same triliteral root as the Arabic 'Aqada, y'qidu, 'aqdan, 'uqdah; which means 'to tie, knot,' (Ma'an Z. Madina, *Arabic-English Dictionary*, NY: Pocket Books, 1973). It alludes to the alleged 'binding' of Isaac by his father Abraham for the 'burnt offering'.

2. Imām Ḥamīd al-Dīn Farāhī (1862-1930) was born in Pharīha (hence the name Farāhī), a village in district A'ẓam Gaṛh (Uttar Paradesh, India). While studying in the M.A.O. College, Alī Gaṛh, he translated Ibn Sa'd (AD 784-845)'s classic on Islāmic History *'al-Ṭabaqāt al-Kubrā'* into Persian. His translation was so fine that Sir Sayyid Aḥmad Khān, the Founder Patron of the College, included it in the College curricula. Farāhī did his graduation from Allāhbād

University. While teaching Arabic at the M.A.O. College, Alī Gaṛh, he learnt Hebrew from the German Orientalist, Joseph Horovitz (1874-1931 AD), who was his colleague and the professor of Arabic there. In 1925, he took over the charge of the Madrasah al-Iṣlāḥ (Institute of Reformation). There he trained some of his students as great scholars of the Arabic language and literature, Islāmic studies, and History. Among them was Amīn Aḥsan Iṣlāḥī, who, consequently, became the greatest exponent of his thought. Farāhī spent almost fifty years of his life in the research study of the Qur'ān. His most conspicuous contribution towards the Qur'ānic exegesis is the systematic presentation of the 'COHERENCE' in the Qur'ān that no Qur'ānic scholar could have uncovered and presented in so masterly a manner prior to him. He proved that a single interpretation of the Qur'ānic themes was possible through the in depth study of the three constituents of the NAẒM of the Qur'ān, i.e., (i) ORDER, (ii) PROPORTION, and (iii) UNITY. He restructured many of the disciplines of the Arabic language which are prerequisite towards undertaking the research study of the Qur'ān. Most of Farāhī's works are in Arabic, which include: '*Majmū'ah Tafāsīr Farāhī*' (Exposition of 14 Surahs of the Qurān, translated into Urdu By Amīn Aḥsan Iṣlāḥī); 'Mufradāt al-Qur'ān' (explanation of some difficult single words of the Qur'ān in the light of the pre-Islāmic structural and literary tradition of the Arabic language); '*Aqsām al-Qur'ān*' (Oaths of the Qur'ān); '*al-Ra'y al-Ṣaḥīḥ fī man Huwa al-Dhabīḥ*' (Who was Offered for Sacri-fice); '*Jamharah al-Balāghah*'; '*Asālīb al-Qur'ān*'; '*Dalā'il al-Niẓām*' '*Asbāq al-Naḥv*'; '*Ūṣūl al- Ta'wīl*'; '*Fī Malakūt Allāh*'; '*Al-Qā'id ilā 'Ūyūn al-'Aqā'id*'; '*Ḥijaj al-Qur'ān*'; '*Kitāb al-Ḥikmah*'. Some of his books, including this '*al-Ra'y al-Ṣaḥīḥ fī man Huwa al-Dhabīh*', have also been translated into Urdu and English. The English translation of '*al-Ra'y al-Ṣaḥīḥ fī man Huwa al-Dhabīh*' has recently been accomplished by Mr. Nādir 'Aqeel Anṣārī, while its Urdu translation had been accomplished by Amīn Aḥsan Iṣlāḥī and published in 1975.

3. An Arabic book containing 164 pages of 8.5" x 5.5" size, published by Dār al-Qalam, Damascus, 1999.

Introduction

According to the Jews and the Christians the 'Only Son' whom God had asked Abraham to offer for sacrifice, was 'Isaac' and not 'Ishmā'el'. The Bible has recorded the story in a fairly detailed narrative. It is only once in the actual words of the Lord in the whole of the narrative that the name of the 'Only Son' has been mentioned as 'Isaac' which is quite misfit in, rather contrary to, the context.[1] There are contradictions in the narrative that render the stance of the Jews and the Christians quite incredible. On the other hand a majority of the Muslim scholars claims that it was Ishmā'el, and not Isaac, whom God had asked Abraham to offer for sacrifice. But it does not mean that the Muslims claim any superiority for Ishmā'el over Isaac. According to the Muslims all the prophets are equal in status being the apostles of Allah.

It is also to be made clear that at some places the writer of this book had to reproduce some Biblical authorities, which imply comparison between the prophets. The Biblical scholars have taken much liberties with the interpretations of Biblical themes while depicting the characters of Abraham, Ishmā'el, and Isaac. Similarly, noble Sarah has been depicted as a very cruel, jealous, and revengeful woman while dealing with noble Hagar and her son, Ishmā'el. It is only the viewpoint of the Biblical scholars. The writer of the present book holds all of these great personalities equally respectable, honourable and innocent.

An objective study has been undertaken to thrash out the theme of the book. It may be noted at the very outset that this event of the offering for sacrifice was committed to writing in the Bible more than a thousand years after its happening. It is quite unknown who its writer had been and what his credentials might be, but, of certain, he was not the eyewitness of the event. The writer being himself obscure, how can it be ascertained from whom he had taken it and what the status of the credibility of that reporter had been. It can also be appreciated what 'corrections' and 'adjustments' might have been exercised within this narrative[2] by the chain of reporters of the oral tradition who had been admittedly jealous rivals to the progeny of Ishmā'el and who were the claimants of the 'privilege' of the 'chosen people'. It means that the narrative is to be analyzed rationally and critically and any of its statements can only be accepted on its own merit.

It may also be noted here that the original Arabic word of the Qurā'n for this 'test' or the Biblical 'tempt' does not necessarily connote the actual slaughter of the 'Only Son'. It signifies only to verify and testify the absolute preparedness of Abraham to surrender to the will of God, which was accomplished by laying the 'Only Son' to be offered for sacrifice. Similarly in Sūrah Ṣāffāt 37:102 the words of the Qurā'n 'I see in the dream that I slaughter you' denote that it was a mere dream and not an actual reality. Then he does not use the words 'I have slaughtered you' or 'I slaughtered you'. He rather says, 'I [intend to] slaughter you', which shows that ultimately the the actual slaughter might not have been required.

References

1. It may be noted here that the name of the son, required to be offered for sacrifice, has been recorded five times in the narrative. But it is only once in the whole of the narrative that it has been made to be uttered by the 'Lord' Himself. At the remaining four places (vv. 3,6,7,9) it has been uttered by the redactor of the book. The son has been mentioned three times by Abraham (vv 5,7,9); but at all these three places he has not mentioned the name of the son as 'Isaac'. In verse 5 he used the words 'I and the lad' for him and in vv 7 and 8 he has used for him the words of 'my son'. Even the angel of the Lord did not mention him by the name 'Isaac' at any place.
2. An appendix 'SOME TYPES OF CORRUPTION IN THE TEXT OF THE BIBLE' has been given at the end of this book to elaborate the theme.

1

The Story of the Offering
in the Bible

It is recorded in the Bible that the Lord asked Abraham to offer his 'only son' as a burnt offering. It is quite clear that it was only Ishmā'el who could have been called the 'only son', because it was only he who remained the 'only son' of Abraham for fourteen years, until Isaac was born. The Jewish scholars thought it an honour to be offered before the Lord; and they did not like it to be attributed to the actual 'only son', Ishmā'el, who was not their 'real ancestor', but was their 'uncle ancestor'. So they managed to manipulate it in favour of their 'real ancestor', Isaac.

According to the narrative of the Bible the objective of the sacrifice was to 'tempt' (test/try) Abraham which has been explained in the very first sentence. In the holy Qur'ān, as well, there is the mention of 'tempting' Abraham:

وَإِذِ ابْتَلَىٰ إِبْرَاهِيمَ رَبُّهُ بِكَلِمَاتٍ فَأَتَمَّهُنَّ قَالَ إِنِّي جَاعِلُكَ لِلنَّاسِ إِمَامًا قَالَ وَمِن ذُرِّيَّتِي قَالَ لَا يَنَالُ عَهْدِي الظَّالِمِينَ [1]

And recall to mind when his Lord put Abraham to test with certain commands, all of which he fulfilled. He said: 'I am going to make you the leader of the humankind.' He asked: 'Does this promise apply to my offspring!' He answered: 'My Promise does not apply to the transgressors.'

It is to be noted that it was merely a test and was not meant to be carried out *verbatim*, which is evident from the story.

THE BIBLE STORY

The story of the 'Offering of Abraham his "only son" for Sacrifice' goes in the Bible as follows:

> And it came to pass after these things, that God did tempt [see last paragraph of 'Introduction', page 6] Abraham, and said unto him, Abraham: and he said, Behold, *here* I *am*. (2) And he said, Take now thy son, thine only *son* Isaac, whom thou lovest, and get thee into the land of Moriah; and offer him there for a burnt offering upon one of the mountains which I will tell thee of. (3) And Abraham rose up early in the morning, and saddled his ass, and took two of his young men with him, and Isaac his son, and clave the wood for the burnt offering, and rose up, and went unto the place of which God had told him. (4) Then on the third day Abraham lifted up his eyes, and saw the place afar off. (5) And Abraham said unto his young men, Abide ye here with the ass and I and the lad will go yonder and worship, and come again to you.[2] (6) And Abraham took the wood of the burnt offering, and laid *it* upon Isaac his son; and he took the fire in his hand, and a knife[3]; and they went both of them together. (7) And Isaac spake unto Abraham his father, and said, My father: and he said, Here *am* I, my son. And he said, Behold the fire and the wood: but where *is* the lamb for a burnt offering? (8) And Abraham said, My son, God will provide himself a lamb for a burnt offering:[4] so they went both of them together. (9) And they came to the place which God had told him of; and Abraham built an altar there, and laid the wood in order, and bound Isaac his son, and laid him on the altar upon the wood. (10) And Abraham stretched forth his hand, and took the knife to slay his son. (11) And the angel of the Lord called unto him out of heaven, and said, Abraham, Abraham: and he said, Here *am* I. (12) And he said, Lay not thine hand upon the lad, neither do thou any thing upon him: for now I know that thou fearest God, seeing thou hast not withheld thy son, thine *only son*[5] from me. (13) And Abraham lifted up his eyes, and looked, and behold behind *him* a ram caught in a thicket by his horns: and Abraham went and took the ram, and offered him up for a burnt offering

in the stead of his son. (14) And Abraham called the name of that place Jehovah-jireh: as it is said *to* this day[6], In the mount of the Lord it shall be seen. (15) And the angel of the Lord called unto Abraham out of heaven the second time, (16) And said, By myself have I sworn, saith the Lord, for because thou hast done this thing, and hast not withheld thy son, thine ***only*** *son*: (17) That in blessing I will bless thee, and in multiplying I will multiply thy seed[7] as the stars of the heaven, and as the sand which *is* upon the sea shore; and thy seed[8] shall possess the gate of his enemies[9]; (18) And in thy seed shall all the nations of the earth be blessed[10]; because thou hast obeyed my voice.[11]

THE STATUS OF THE STORY OF THE BIBLE.

The above story regarding Abraham's offering of his 'only son' for sacrifice had been subjected 'considerably' to a number of 'alterations' for so many times, as is evident from the following quotation from the Encyclopaedia Biblica, which is admittedly one of the most reliable authorities on the subject:

It has become certain that the story has been considerably altered since E wrote it. The editor or compiler of JE not only appended vv. 14b-18 (an unoriginal passage, full of reminiscences), but also introduced several alterations into vv. 1-14[a]. (2175...). So far, however, as an opinion is possible, the form of the Elohist's story is, apart from the detail about the ram, all his own. It was suggested, indeed, by circumstances already related in the traditional narratives; but it was moulded by himself, and it is bathed throughout in an ideal light. Evidently this pious writer felt that for the higher religious conceptions no traditional story would be an adequate vehicle. The course which he adopted shows the writer to have been a great teacher. He admits the religious feeling which prompted the sacrifice of a firstborn son.[12]

The quotation calls for a conscientious perusal. Putting it forward under separate and specific clauses, it can be categorized as below:

(a) 'Alterations' and 'additions' have been freely exercised in the story.

(b) The act of 'alterations' is not merely a supposition; 'It has,' rather, 'become certain'.

(c) The 'alteration' is in a 'considerable' amount.

(d) The main theme of the story relates to the 'Elohist' narrative.

(e) The editor (or, properly saying, 'the redactor'), who compiled the story from the 'Elohist' and 'Yahwist' narratives etc, (a) 'not only appended [added] *vv* 14b-18,' (b) 'but also introduced several alterations into vv. 1-14a.' It shows that (a) vv. 14b-18 are the addition from some redactor and they did not exist in the original story. (b) The redactor 'introduced several alterations into vv. 1-14a' as well. It can thus be concluded that although the story relates the famous event of Abraham's offering his only son for sacrifice, the credibility of none of its details is beyond doubt. Therefore one is to consider any of the events of the story on its own merit after a careful and critical analysis.

(f) The editor, being a 'pious writer' and 'a great teacher', seeing that 'no traditional story would be an adequate vehicle' exercised full liberty and 'moulded [it] by himself' as he deemed fit 'for the higher religious conceptions' of his own.

(g) 'Sacrifice of a firstborn son' was considered 'religious'.

References

1. Al-Qurān, al-Baqarah 2:124.
2. Abraham was taking his son to offer him as a burnt offering; and it is not the whole truth that they were going there for worship. However, if the worship be taken here to mean sacrifice, it is clearly false to say that he and the lad will 'come again' to them. He was taking his 'only son' to offer as a sacrifice; and as such he and the lad, both of them together, could not have 'come again' to them. Having Isaac sacrificed, it could have been only Abraham to 'come again'. Anyhow, if it be claimed that Abraham was not telling a lie, and he before hand knew that a lamb was to be provided for offering in lieu of the lad, then the whole drama of the so called offering becomes quite insignificant and the plea of 'tempting' becomes quite vague and meaningless. It shows that this part of the story is a

concocted one, because it depicts Abraham as a false and deceiving person. It is quite contrary to the status of a Prophet. A person who is not sincere and dependably veracious and honest cannot be taken as a Prophet.

3. It again looks unbecoming of the patriarch and Prophet Abraham to put the heavy load of the wood on the shoulders of his son who is supposed to be just going to be offered for a sacrifice and keep the lighter one for himself. It is simply an indifferent ruthlessness, hence unbelievable regarding the patriarch and Prophet Abraham. As such this episode of the story loses its credibility.

4. Here again it is not true on Abraham's part to say 'God will provide himself a lamb for a burnt offering.' He was asked by the Lord to sacrifice his son and he was going to do so. He did not know before hand that a lamb would be provided to be sacrificed in his son's stead; otherwise the '*temptation*' would have been a mere drama and should have lost all significance. The clause 'God will provide himself a lamb for a burnt offering.' was obviously a false statement if claimed to be uttered by the patriarch Abraham and as such it can be taken as if appended by some redactor. It is inconceivable of the patriarch and Prophet Abraham that he would try to appease his son through such mis-statements. It means that this part of the story is not true.

5. The phrase 'thine only son' indicates the stress and significance of the event of the 'offering' the only son by an old man of about a hundred years, who direly needed the assistance of his young son at this advanced stage of his life; and who had no other son so far. It reveals the gravity of the situation and makes the 'temptation' perfect.

6. 'as it is said *to* this day' is obviously a later interpolation inserted, may be, centuries after the occurrence of the incident by some simple redactor. Some commentators attribute it to Moses, e.g.

   This name, Moses adds, gave birth to the proverb, 'In the Mount of Jehovah it shall be seen.' [*7th Day Adventist BC*, ed. Francis D. Nichol et al. (Hagerstown: Review & Herald Publishing Association, 1978), 1:353].

   But now no credible scholar assigns the Pentateuch to Moses, as it was not written until the lapse of almost half a millennium after him (See Appenix-II at the end of this book).

7. The context dictates that this promise be considered to relate to the son who is being discussed here and who had just been offered to be sacrificed by Abraham. However, when 'thy seed' be spoken in such an indefinite, unqualified, and absolute manner, it can also be applied to the others of 'his seed' as well. But it would by all means include Ishmā'el and his descendants in the first place. So the progeny of Ishmā'el is definitely included in the promise of 'Blessing' and 'multiplying'.

8. Here again 'thy seed' can genuinely be applied only to the progeny of Ishmā'el among whom 'a Prophet' was to be raised for all the peoples of earth, whereas the Jews do not extend the blessings of revelation and faith to the whole of humamnity. They rather keep it restricted unto the children of Israel exclusively.

9. It obviously relates to the progeny of Ishmā'el, which captured almost all of the Arabia and perpetually dominated there. They never went under the captivity of any of their enemies, whereas the Jews had to suffer the captivity at the hands of Egyptian Pharaohs. The progeny of Ishmā'el never suffered any exile, whereas the Jews had to suffer ethnic cleansing and exile at the hands of the Assyrians (in 722 BC) and Babylonians (in 586 BC). As such the clause of the verse cannot be applied to the seed of Isaac. Not to speak of possessing 'the gate of their enemies', they could not retain and protect their own gates–and even the gates of their Temple–from their enemies throughout their history excepting an ignorably short period during the united kingdom.

10. As far as the Jews are concerned, they consider '*only*' themselves as the 'Chosen People', as can be appreciated from the following excerpts:

    [i] 'You only have I singled out of all the families of the earth' (Amos 3:2);

    [ii] 'Thou art an holy people unto the Lord thy God, and the Lord hath chosen thee to be a peculiar people unto himself, above all peoples that are upon the face of the earth.' (Deut. 14:2);

    [iii] 'And when the Lord thy God shall deliver them before thee; thou shalt smite them, and utterly destroy them; thou shalt make no covenant with them, nor shew mercy unto them: Neither shalt thou make marriages with them; thy daughter thou shalt not give unto his son, nor his daughter shalt thou take unto thy

son. For they will turn away thy son from following me, that they may serve other gods: (...). For thou art an holy people unto the Lord thy God: the Lord thy God hath chosen thee to be a special people unto himself, above all people that are upon the face of the earth. The Lord did not set his love upon you, nor choose you, because ye were more in number than any people; for ye were the fewest of all people: But because the Lord loved you, and because he would keep the oath which he hath sworn unto your fathers, hath the Lord brought you out with a mighty hand, and redeemed you out of the house of bondmen, from the hand of Pharaoh king of Egypt. Know therefore that the Lord thy God, he is God, the faithful God, which keepeth covenant and mercy with them that love him and keep his commandments to a thousand generations; (...). And he will love thee, and bless thee, and multiply thee: he will also bless the fruit of thy womb, and the fruit of thy hand, thy corn, and thy wine, and thine oil, *the increase of thy kine, and the flocks of thy sheep* [NIV translates it as: '*the calves of your herds and the lambs of your flocks*'], in the land which he sware unto thy fathers to give thee. Thou shalt be blessed above all people: there shall not be male or female barren among you, or among your cattle [This promise looks to be against the fact, as there may be thousands of the Jews and their cattle 'barren']. And the Lord will take away from thee all sickness, and will put none of the evil diseases of Egypt, which thou knowest, upon thee; but will lay them upon all them that hate thee [This again seems to be a credulously wishful statement and is against the ground reality. It also depicts the base mentality of the so-called 'People of God']. And thou shalt consume all the people which the Lord thy God shall deliver thee; thine eye shall have no pity upon them [What a pity for those unfortunate peoples who fall victim to this God's 'Chosen People'!]: (...). And the Lord thy God will put out those nations before thee by little and little: thou mayest not consume them at once, lest the beasts of the field increase upon thee. But the Lord thy God shall deliver them unto thee, and shall destroy them with a mighty destruction, until they be destroyed. And he shall deliver their kings into thine hand, and thou shalt destroy their name from under heaven: there shall no man be able to stand before thee, until thou have destroyed them.' (Deu. 7: 2, 3, 4a, 6-10, 13-16, 22-24).

The Jewish Enc. 4:45, as well, has recorded the following lines:

Thou art an holy people unto the Lord thy God, and the Lord hath choseen thee to be a particular people unto himself, above all peoples that are upon the face of the earth. (Deu. 14:2 RV)

It has further quoted from 'Mek. Yitro, Pes. R. K. 103b, 186a, 200a':

The Lord offered the Law to all nations; but all refused to accept it except Israel. (*The Jewish Enc.* 4:45)

The Jewish people virtually take it to be their special privilege. The perpetually prevailing practice among them also endorses it. As such 'And in thy seed shall all the nations of the earth be blessed;' in no way befits the Jewish people; and has nothing to do with the entire history of this people. It can thus be appreciated that 'all the nations of the earth' can by no means 'be blessed' through the seed of Isaac. The Jews are rather like a curse for 'all the nations of the earth'. It is only Ishmā'el who was offered for sacrifice, and it is only he, in whose seed all the nations of the earth have genuinely been blessed.

11. Gen. 22:1-18 KJV.
12. *Encyclopaedia Biblica*, ed. Rev. T. K. Cheyne, (London: Watts and Co., n.d.), 2:2175,77.

2

Abraham was Required to Offer His 'Only Son' for Sacrifice

The Bible categorically states that the son, who was required to be offered for sacrifice, was Abraham's 'only son'. It is a very conspicuous, pivotal, and decisive point and is not to be ignored, overlooked or taken lightly. The firstborn and the 'Eldest son of Abraham'[1] was Ishmā'el. 'And Abram was eighty-six years old when Hagar bore Ishmā'el to him.' The Bible says:

Now Sarai, Abram's wife had borne him no *children*, (...). (3) And after Abram had lived ten years in the land of Canaan, Abram's wife Sarai took Hagar the Egyptian, her maid[2], and gave her to her husband Abram as his wife. (...). (15) So Hagar bore Abram a son; and Abram called the name of his son, whom Hagar bore, Ishma'el. (16) And Abram was eighty-six years old when Hagar bore Ishma'el to him.[3]

But when Isaac was born to Abraham, he was one hundred years old, which means that Ishmā'el was already fourteen years old when Isaac was born. The Bible states:

> (15) Then God said to Abraham, 'As for Sarai your wife, you shall not call her name Sarai, but Sarah *shall be* her name. (16) And I will bless her, and indeed I will give you a son by her. Then I will bless her, and she shall be *a mother of* nations; kings of peoples shall come from her.' (17) Then Abraham fell on his face and laughed, and said in his heart, 'Will a child be born to a man one hundred years old? And will Sarah, who is ninety

years old, bear *a child*?' (18) And Abraham said to God, 'Oh that Ishma'el might live before thee!'[4]

Abraham was one hundred years old when his son Isaac was born to him.[5]

And as such Ishmā'el retained the status of the 'only son of Abraham' until the age of fourteen years.

If the relevant passage of the Bible, given in the beginning of this book, be studied again, it will be noted that God has used in it the words 'thy son, thine only son' *three times*, qualifying the 'lad' to be offered for sacrifice; but He has used this son's name as 'Isaac' only once in all His speech. Setting aside the words that have been added by the storywriter and the redactor to complete this narrative, the words ascribed to God in the said passage are as follows:

> Abraham: ...Take now thy son, thine only *son* Isaac [stress added], whom thou lovest, and get thee into the land of Moriah; and offer him there for a burnt offering upon one of the mountains which I will tell thee of. ... Abraham, Abraham: Lay not thine hand upon the lad, neither do thou any thing upon him: for now I know that thou fearest God, seeing thou hast not withheld thy son, thine *only son* [stress added] from me. ... By myself have I sworn, ..., for because thou hast done this thing, and hast not withheld thy son, thine *only son* [stress added]: That in blessing I will bless thee, and in multiplying I will multiply thy seed as the stars of the heaven, and as the sand which *is* upon the sea shore; and thy seed shall possess the gate of his enemies; And in thy seed shall all the nations of the earth be blessed; because thou hast obeyed my voice.

The son to be offered for sacrifice has been mentioned here:

(*a*) For three times with the pronouns: 'whom, him' (if the interpolation of the word Isaac be ignored, it cannot be determined by means of these pronouns which of the sons is here meant);

(*b*) Once with the word 'lad' (which also does not indicate which of the two sons the 'lad' was); and (*c*) Three times with the words 'thy son, thine only son' (Obviously, it can be none other than Ishma#'el, because Isaac could not have been called 'thine only son' at any stage of his life).

It is only once that the word Isaac has been used in it; and this is when the words 'thy son, thine only son' have been used for the first time. Any reader, having a little bit of literary taste together with objective, unprejudiced and independent thinking, can appreciate that the word 'Isaac' is quite superfluous, irrelevant, and out of place here. Had it been Isaac, who was required to be sacrificed, it had been sufficient to say: 'Take now your son Isaac'. God would not have used the phrase 'thine only son', because it was, by all means, a false statement in favor of Isaac and it is unbecoming that God may have made a false statement. 'Thine only son' and 'Isaac' cannot stand together for a single entity, and could in no case have been used simultaneously, because, circumstantially, they are quite contradictory to each other. The structure and use of the words make it quite clear that originally it was the 'only son' who was required for offering; and it was the distinctive trait of 'singularity', which was conspicuously a prerequisite for the son to be offered. That's why 'Thine only son', which has been used for three times in the passage, has been used twice without 'Isaac' independently and only once with 'Isaac.' The structure of the phrase 'thy son, thine only son' indubiously declares that the stress is: (i) on the 'singularity of the son', which shows the intention of the speaker that the son required is the 'only' one; and (ii) on the qualifying pronouns 'thy, thine', which shows that the son required to be offered is 'your son, O Abraham, and your own one only (and not your wife's only)'. Had God meant 'Isaac' to be offered for sacrifice, He would have categorically asserted: 'Sarah's only son' or 'your only son from Sarah'; and would, in no case, have said 'thy son, thine only son', to confuse him, and subsequently the whole of the religious world for all times to come. The use of the name 'Isaac' in such an ugly and self-contradictory way shows that an interpolation has been exercised by some unwitty redactor quite unbecomingly.

It would be very useful if, at this juncture, the reader once again goes through the relevant passage (Gen. 22:1-18) attentively, and without any reservations. The flow of the passage reveals the intent and purpose of the speaker quite clearly. The speaker (the Lord) uses the words 'thy son, thine only son' for the boy, required to be sacrificed, in the passage. The Lord does not use anywhere in the passage the words of merely 'thy son' without attaching 'thine only son' to them, so that any possibility of misunderstanding be completely ruled out. Obviously the words 'thine only son' and 'Isaac' are mutually opposed and contrary words and cannot be used together, as Isaac had never been an 'only son' at any stage of his life. That's why Abraham did never use the words 'only son' for Isaac. It has been pointed out that the Jews added deleted, altered, and interpolated freely in the text of the Bible for 'theological' or 'religious' purposes. They saw no harm in it. It may also be borne in mind that it was the 'religious' necessity of the Israelites to present the offspring of Isaac as a chosen and superior people. It is, therefore, easy to understand that when some 'pious' rabbi would have seen the words 'thy son, thine only son' for the first time, he must have inserted the word 'Isaac' as an explanation under his 'wishful preconception'. Finding it useful for their purpose, the later scribes would have included it in the text.

It is strange that the Bible claims 'Isaac' to be the 'only' son of Abraham. Obviously, it is one of the interpolations, or, as the *Encyclopaedia Biblica* puts it, 'alterations', as quoted above.[6] The scholars and commentators of the Bible might have discerned that it was a discrepancy (which, they, of course, discerned)[7] and they ought to have been bold enough to rectify it (but, alas, they have not been bold enough to rectify it). In spite of understanding that it was clearly an addition and adulteration of the redactor of the Bible, they willfully clung to it. Matthew Henry's Bible Commentary suggested a revised and improved rendering of the Hebrew Bible by adding 'one' to the 'only':

That son *whom thou lovest*. It was a trial of Abraham's love to God, and therefore it must be in a beloved son[8], and that string must be touched most upon: in the Hebrew it is expressed more emphatically, and, I think, might very well be read thus, *Take now that son of thine, that only one of thine, whom thou lovest, that Isaac.*[9]

It suggests that the correct translation required the qualifying words '*only one*' and not mere '*only*'. Even if the translation suggested by Matthew Henry be adopted, the sense remains the same. Even the suggested translation, 'that only one of thine', implies that Abraham had got only one son at that time and no other son had yet been born. Naturally, it could have been none other than Ishmā'el, who was really the *only one* son of Abraham until the second son, Isaac, was born; and by that time Ishmā'el was already fourteen years of age.

The Biblical scholars have fruitlessly and futilely tried to evade the real sense of the word. It is, therefore, imperative that a study of the word 'only' be undertaken. In the Hebrew Bible the word 'yaḥeed' (**éçéã**) has been used for 'only'. The meanings of the word 'yaḥeed' are: 'sole; lonely; only (child, son), solitary' (*Strong's Dic.* p.49:3173, *Heb. & Aramaic Dic. of OT*, Brill, 2001, 406). In the whole of the OT of the Bible it has been used at the following four places else:

When I was my father's son, tender and the only one (Pr 4:3).

Make mourning *as for* an only son (Jer 6:26).

I will make it like mourning for an only *son* (Amos 8:10).

(...) as one mourns for his only son (Zec 12:10).

At all these places it can only be translated with the word 'only' and no other meanings go well with the context. It can thus be appreciated that the Bible uses 'yaḥeed' only in the sense of 'only'; and no other meanings can be given to this word according to the usage and context of the Bible.

Some of the commentators of the Bible have afforded ridiculous expositions to justify this adulteration. One of the renowned Jewish Rabbis, the French-born Shelomoh Yitschaki, Solomon ben Isaac, commonly known as Rashi (1040-1105 AD), has recorded some interesting observations on this passage of the Bible in his commentary on the Pentateuch. He has given it the shape of an imaginative conversation and has thus exhibited a wonderful skill of subjectively interpreting or twisting a simple statement according to his presumptions in his following exposition. No comments on this quotation have been recorded in the body text of the book. On the spot comments, however fairly lengthy they be, have been afforded in the footnotes.

Rashi's comments (with their rejoinders in footnotes):

thy son. 'But I have two sons,'[10] Abraham said. '*Thine only son*,'[11] was the reply. 'But each is the *only one* of his mother!'[12] '*Whom thou lovest*,'[13] he was told. 'But I love both!'[14] and the answer came '*Even Isaac*.'[15] Why did not God name Isaac at once?[16] Lest Abraham's mind reeled under the sudden shock.[17] Further, to make His command more precious to him.[18] And finally, that he might receive a reward for every word spoken.[19]

It may also be noted in this connection that the words 'thine only son' signify that no other son (even Isaac) had been born by that time. It means that Abraham might have offered Ishmā'el for sacrifice when he was about thirteen; because when Ishmā'el was fourteen, Isaac had already been born; and the status of Ishmā'el being the 'only son' of Abraham had come to an end.

To recapitulate the theme of the second point, here are some salient features of it:

(1) God had asked Abraham to offer 'thy son, thine *only son'* for sacrifice categorically and not one/any of his sons.

(2) Abraham's first-born son was 'Ishmā'el' and was born when Abraham was 86.

(3) Isaac was Abraham's second-born son and was born when Abraham was 100.

(4) As such, 'Ishmā'el' remained Abraham's only son unto the age of about 14 years, during which period Abraham had no other son: as Isaac was born when Ishmā'el was already of about 14 years. It also signifies that when Abraham offered his 'only son' for sacrifice, Isaac should not have been born by that time.

(5) God had asked Abraham to offer his own 'only' son for sacrifice. In the whole of the Bible, God had no where asked Abraham to offer Sarah's 'only' son for sacrifice, as the learned commentators of the Bible have tried to make God purport. So

the son required to be offered for sacrifice could have been none other than 'Ishmā'el'.

(6) As recorded above, the *Encyclopaedia Biblica* has asserted that the story of the offering of Abraham's only son for sacrifice had been subjected 'considerably' to a number of 'alterations' for so many times. The addition of 'even Isaac' to 'thy son, thine *only son*' looks obviously an 'addition' by the redactor of the Book.

(7) The 'only son' required to be offered for sacrifice, was, and should naturally have been, the beloved son of Abraham, to make the 'test' perfect; or, as the commentator *Rashi,* puts it, 'to make His command more precious to him'. And it has been discussed in detail elsewhere in this book that Abraham's beloved son was 'Ishmā'el' and not 'Isaac' (see chapter IV).

(8) The son required to be offered was a 'lad', i.e., in his early teens; whereas according to the commentators of the Bible Isaac was either a child of approximately 3 years (just weaned) or a young man of 20-37 when he was allegedly to be offered for sacrifice. It means that Isaac was not a 'lad' when he was allegedly required to be sacrificed, whereas the Bible uses the word 'lad' or 'boy' for the son required to be offered. Besides it being a discrepancy, at no stage of his life Isaac could have been an 'only lad' of his father.

References

1. *The Jewish Enc.*, ed. Isidore Singer (USA: KTAV Publishing House, Inc.), 6:647.

2. It is not true that Hagar was a maid, or a slave-girl, or a bond-woman of Sarah. She was a princess, being the daughter of the Egyptian king, who offered her to Abraham to serve him and his wife Sarah, and to be brought and reared up in a pious atmosphere. She had been purposely described by the redactors of the Bible as a slave girl, as can be appreciated from the following excerpts:

   That Hagar appears as a slave-woman is a necessary consequence of the theory on which the Hebrew myth is based, the notion being that Ishma'el was of inferior origin. (*Enc. Biblica*, p. 1933).

It purports that slavery was attributed to Hagar to prove Ishmā'el inferior to Isaac. Whereas the fact is that she was an Egyptian princess; as is clear from the following quotation of *the Jewish Encyclopedia*:

According to the Midrash (Gen. R. xiv.), Hagar was the daughter of Pharaoh, who, seeing what great miracles God had done for Sarah's sake (Gen. xii, 17), said: 'It is better for Hagar to be a slave in Sarah's house than mistress in her own.' In this sense Hagar's name is interpreted as 'reward' ('Ha-Agar' = 'this is reward'). (...). Hagar is held up as an example of the high degree of godliness prevalent in Abraham's time, (...). Her fidelity is praised, for even after Abraham sent her away she kept her marriage vow, (...). Another explanation of the same name is 'to adorn,' because she was adorned with piety and good deeds (l.c.). (*Jewish Enc.*, 6:138).

For further information on this theme please see footnote 302 (App. I).

3. Gen. 16:1,3,15,16 NASB.
4. Gen. 17:15-18 NASB. It reveals the great degree of Abraham's love for Ishmā'el .
5. Gen. 21:5 NASB.
6. Please see Chapter I section 'The Status of the Story of the Bible'.
7. Of course, some of them, in one way or the other, have noted this discrepancy, e.g., William Whiston, translator of *The Works of Flavius Josephus*, in his footnote on the phrase 'Isaac, as being his only-begotten', observes:

   Note, that both here and Heb. xi. and 17. Isaac is called Abraham's only-begotten son, though he at the same time had another son, Ishmael. The Septuagint expresses the true meaning, by rendering the text the beloved son. (*The Works of Flavius Josephus*, tr. W. Whiston, Boston: D Lothrop & Co., nd., footnote 1 on ch. XIII, paragraph 1, p. 42).

   In fact 'rendering the text the beloved son.' is quite arbitrary and without any lexical ground. It is rather a sort of adulteration to translate a word in this manner to satisfy one's whims or to get rid of some awkward situation. The original Hebrew word for this 'only' is 'Yacheed', which, in Arabic, is 'Waheed'; and literally means 'only'. *New Jerome Bible Com.*, (Bangalore, India: T.P.I., 1994, p. 25) has also made the same arbitrary claim that the use of the 'thine only son' for Isaac is wrong when he observes:

'Only son' is inaccurate, since Abraham will have other sons; already the LXX *ton agapeton* correctly interpreted the Hebrew word as 'favored' by God.

It is remarkable to note here that almost all the translations of the Bible rendered the word 'éçéã' (yacheed) as 'only' (which is imperatively required in view of its primary root 'éçã', i.e. 'yachad', that means 'to be one' exclusively), except a few brave Jews, who purposefully corrupted the translation.

8. Who was none other than Ishmā'el, as has been explained in an independent chapter of this book in detail.
9. *Matthew Henry's Bible Com.*, 1:80.
10. The sentence 'But I have two sons,' implies that God was mistaken. He did not know that Sarah had already given birth to a second son for Abraham. It means as if Abraham brings to the notice of the mistaken and ignorant God [May God forgive the writer who used these words to show the implications of the wording of the sentence.] and declares: 'But I have two sons,'. It does not matter to the worthy commentator if God be depicted as being ignorant; but he is satisfied that he has succeeded in depriving Ishmā'el of his genuinely deserved credit of being offered for sacrifice as the 'only son' and has tried to establish the honour of being offered for sacrifice in favour of Isaac.
11. The original Hebrew word for this 'only' is 'éçéã', i.e. 'Yawkheed'. *Strong's Dic. of Heb. Bible*, entry 3173, p. 49 has recorded its meanings as: from 3161; *sole*; also *lonely*; only (child, son), solitary.

    Entry 3161 is 'éçã' (yachad), which is a 'primary root' of 'éçéã' (yacheed); and exclusively means: 'to be (or become) one'. It is the same word which, in Arabic, is 'wahada' with the same meanings. *Heb. and Aramaic Dic. of the OT* (Leiden: Brill, 2001), p. 406 has also recorded its meanings as: only, single, alone, the only son, the only one.

    It is quite inconceivable that a scholar of Rashi's calibre may not have discerned the significance of the word. Simply, if a man has, at a time, two sons, none of them can be called his 'only son'. Each of them can be called 'one of his two sons'. Calling one of them 'his only son' is as confusing and irrational as to ascribe the word 'one' for 'three'. Even some commentators of the Bible have noted the absurdity of the statement. Richard J. Clifford and R. E. Murphy, in their Commentary to the Book of Gen. in the *New Jerome Bible Com.* (p.25) assert:

Only son is inaccurate, since Abraham will have other sons.

From the above discussion it can be safely concluded that by the time Abraham offered the sacrifice, he had only one son; and it could naturally have been 'Ishmā'el' and by no means 'Isaac'.

It is also to be noted that a few of the Jewish translations (e.g. *The Torah According to the Masoretic Text*, Philadelphia: Jewish Publn. Society of America, 1967, pp. 35f; and *The Torah A Modern Com.*, NY: Union of American Hebrew Congregations,1981, pp. 146f. The latter contains the Hebrew text as well and it has used the same word yacheed 'éçéã' in it.) have rendered this word 'only' as 'favored one', ignoring the primary root. It is obviously a *mala fide* act.

There is another word in the story that makes the point more clear and definite; and it is 'lad'. It has been used twice in the relevant narrative of the Bible (Gen. 21:5,12: the former by Abraham himself and the latter by the angel of the Lord). The original Hebrew word for 'lad' is 'ðòø' (na'ar) which means: 'a *boy*, from the age of infancy to adolescence; by impl. a *servant*; also (by interch. of sex), a *girl* (of similar latitude ın age):—babe, boy, child, damsel, lad' (*Heb. Dic. in Strong's Exh. Concordance*, entry 5288, p. 79.).

It dictates that the son to be offered for sacrifice should both be a *boy of early teens* and *the only son of his father* . Both these pre-requisites are promptly met in the person of Ishmā'el, whereas Isaac meets none of these pre-requisites, to being offered for sacrifice, as spelled out by the Lord while commanding for the offering. As to the age of Isaac when he was allegedly made to be offered for sacrifice, it has amazingly been attributed either earlier than the status of boyhood or after his teens.

The Jewish commentators of the Bible have different opinions as to the age of Isaac when he was allegedly offered by Abraham for sacrifice. W. Gunther Plaut, in his '*The Torah: A Modern Commentary*' (NY: Union of American Hebrew Congregations, 1981), p. 146 asserts:

According to the Rabbis, Isaac was thirty-seven years old. However, the story should be read not in chronological order but rather as an unrelated unit; here Isaac is a mere boy. The Rabbis took the death of Sarah to be immediately related to the Akedah [sacrifice]; therefore, with Sarah dying at 127 years of age, Isaac would be 37, having been born when his mother was 90.

He further records on page 159:

Abraham returned alone from Moriah, and Sarah, believing Isaac to have been sacrificed, died of grief. — Midrash.

Josephus asserts in his *Antiquities*, Book I, Chap. XIII, para. 2, p. 42:

Now Isaac was twenty-five years old. And as he was building the altar, he asked his father what he was about to offer, since there was no animal there for the oblation:

The Jewish Enc. (6:617) records:

In Jose ben Zimra's opinion, the akedah took place immediately after Isaac's weaning [at the age of 2 or 3 years].

The Bible asserts:

And Abraham took the wood of the burnt offering and laid it on Isaac his son.

How is it possible that a child who had just been weaned, be made to carry such a load of wood? Ellen G. White, in *Seventh Day Adventist Bible Com.*, 1:349, asserts: 'Isaac was now a young man of 20.'

Whether Isaac be made to be allegedly offered for sacrifice when he had been 'just weaned' or of the age of thirty seven, or twenty five, or twenty years or whatsoever, in any case, he cannot be called a 'lad'. Then whatever the age of Isaac be, he cannot be called 'Thine only son' at any stage of his life, whereas Ishmā'el retains the status of 'Thine only son' and a 'lad' until the age of fourteen years. And as such, the statement 'Thine only son' becomes quite absurd, if Isaac be considered as required to be offered for sacrifice.

12. Where has the phrase 'his mother' stepped in from? It is simply unbelievable that such an erudite scholar can pass so absurd a comment, on such a simple statement: 'thine only son'. It is to be noted that the dialogue is only between God and Abraham. No third person is involved in this dialogue. In this phrase, God is the first person, because He is addressing Abraham, and Abraham is naturally the addressee, for whom a second person pronoun is required. That's why God has used the II person pronoun 'thine' for Abraham, which by no stretch of sense can be attributed to Sarah, who is a III Person here. God had not left the 'only son' unqualified, so as to leave room for some speculations or self-assessments. The 'only son' is

categorically preceded by a specific qualifying word 'thine': which unequivocally means 'O Abraham, it is "your" only son, who is required; and not any mother's only son.' As regards Abraham, it is quite unconceivable about a discreet person of his calibre that he would retort so indiscreetly as this 'But each is the *only one* of his mother!', to such a self-explanatory phrase as this 'thine only son.' What has this 'of his mother' got to do with this 'thine only son!'.

13. It has been explained in detail in chapter IV of this book.

14. The learned speculative and imaginative commentator has made Abraham speak these words. He put the words 'But I love both' into Abraham's mouth. The word 'both' here obviously means both Ishmā'el and Isaac. If a man has two sons, none of them can be called 'only'. It is queer that on the one hand Abraham is asked by his Lord to offer his 'only son' for sacrifice; and on the other hand the worthy commentator puts the words 'But I love both' into Abraham's mouth. These statements are self-contradictory. As such the words 'But I love both' are absurd, arbitrary, and quite baseless.

15. As far as the words 'even Isaac' are concerned, they are obviously superfluous to and inconsistent with the flow of the sentence. Had it been Isaac, who was required to be offered for sacrifice, God should have been discreet enough to say 'your son, Isaac'. But when He says 'thy son, thine only son', only 'Ishmā'el' can be meant. 'Isaac' is an unjustifiable interpolation by some crafty but indiscreet redactor.

16. It should be noted here that all these imaginative questions and their sequence are the contrivance of the commentator. There is no hint or mention of them in the Bible. Had some clumsy redactor not interpolated '*Isaac*' here, how could the learned commentator exercise his imaginative creativity to give his desired meaning to an absurd statement.

17. 'Lest Abraham's mind reeled under the sudden shock.' What a rare skill of psycho-analysis!

18. 'Further to make His command more precious to him.' The readers should note the technique of making their command more precious to someone! 'And finally that he might receive a reward for every word spoken.' What a justification of distorting the statement and disturbing the proper order and structure of the sentence!

19. As quoted by Dr. A. Cohen in *The Soncino Chumash*, (Hindhead, Surrey: The Soncino Press, 1947), 108.

3

The Tradition of Offering The First-Fruit or the First-Born Son

When a human sacrifice was required to be offered, it was desired to be the 'first-born' one. Even if the sacrifice required to be offered was not a human one, but was of an animal or a fruit, it had to be first-born animal or the first-fruit. Some of the authorities are being quoted here to elaborate the point. *A New Commentary on Holy Scripture* asserts:

> At the time of Abraham human sacrifice was customary and frequent among his Canaanite neighbors, and the early legislation of Ex 22[29], which states without modification that first-born sons are to be given to God[1], seems clearly to imply a stage in Israel's thought which regarded such sacrifices as a religious duty.[2]

The Rev. T.K. Cheyne, while discussing the sacrifice of Isaac in the entry 'Isaac', states:

> The course that he adopted shows the writer to have been a great teacher. He admits the religious feeling which prompted the sacrifice of a firstborn son.[3]

Marcus Dods records the prevailing tradition of the time that the most exalted form of religious worship was the sacrifice of the first-born, because it was unbecoming to offer to God something which was not truly valuable. (Which of the two sons was truly valuable to Abraham, has been discussed elsewhere in this book in detail):

> Abraham was familiar with the idea that the most exalted form of religious worship was the sacrifice of the first-born. He felt, in common with godly men in every age, that to offer to God cheap sacrifices while we retain for ourselves what is truly precious, is a kind of worship that betrays our low estimate of God rather than expresses true devotion.[4]

Stanley A. Cook observes that the offering of the firstborn to Yahweh was at one time considered strictly to be as binding as the offering of firstlings and first-fruits:

> The firstborn male enjoyed the privileges of which he was not to be deprived (...). Not only were the first-fruits as acceptable an offering as the firstlings, but when (in exceptional cases) a human victim was required it was a firstborn that was preferred (2K. 3:27). (...). No doubt, strictly, the offering of the firstborn to Yahweh was at one time considered to be as binding as the offering of firstlings and first-fruits, and, indeed, the evidence goes to show that in exceptional cases the offering was actually made. However, just as the first-fruits were offered as a part of the whole, it is conceivable that originally the rite of circumcision was instituted upon the same principle to typify the offering of the firstborn.[5]

The very first sentence of the above passage asserts that 'The firstborn male enjoyed the privileges of which he was not to be deprived'. The Bible itself has also laid it down categorically in the following terms:

> If a man have two wives, one beloved, and another hated, and they have born children, *both* the beloved and hated; and *if* the firstborn son be her's that was hated: then it shall be, when he maketh his sons to inherit *that* which he hath, *that* he may not make the son of the beloved firstborn before the son of the hated, *which is indeed* the firstborn: But he shall acknowledge the son of the hated *for* the firstborn, by giving him a double portion of all that he hath: for he *is* the beginning of his strength; the right of the firstborn *is* his.[6]

It shows that, according to the Bible itself, the privilege of the firstborn son is irrevocable. Even if some father, on account of his inclination towards one of his wives, wishes to deprive the son of the other wife of his due and legitimate right of the firstborn son, he is not allowed to do so. And the exalted form of sacrifice was to offer the firstborn son. Therefore the privilege of being offered to God was Ishmā'el's irrevocable and irreversible right, which, in no case, could have been transferred to Isaac.

The Book of Jubilees, of course, is not a canonical book; but it is not an outright rejected book either. Scholars of the Bible liberally quote from it to establish their point of view without much reservation. S. Tedesche has dilated upon it in his article on *Jubilees, Book of* in the *Interpreter's Dic. of Bible* Some of the excerpts are afforded below to acquaint the reader with its real significance:

> One of the most important books of the Pseudepigrapha. It gives a graphic picture of Judaism in the two pre-Christian centuries. Its purpose was to show that Judaism, as it then was, had been the same from the very beginning of known history. (...). Emphasis is also placed on Jewish tenets and customs, and the importance of preserving the difference between Jews and Gentiles is stressed. (...). The purpose of the author was to do for Genesis what the Chronicler did for Samuel and Kings—to rewrite the facts in such a way that it would appear that the law was rigorously observed by the patriarchs. (...). His desire was to save Judaism from the demoralizing effects of Hellenism by [i] glorifying the law and [ii] picturing the patriarchs as irreproachable; by [iii] glorifying Israel [iv] urging her to preserve the separateness from the Gentiles; and by [v] denouncing the Gentiles and also Israel's national enemies. The 'Angel of the Presence' reveals to Moses on Sinai the history and religious laws of Gen. 1-Exod. 3 in the form of sermonized translations, or Midrashic Targums, which show only favorable practices and omit anything derogatory. (...). The contrast between Jews and Gentiles is sharply drawn, and Israel is warned to keep separate. (...), and anything is omitted that would put the patriarchs in an unfavorable light.[7]

It shows about the *Book of Jubilees* that:

(1) It is One of the most important books of the Pseudepigrapha.

(2) Emphasis is placed on the difference between Jews and Gentiles and

(3) Every effort has been made to depict the superiority of the Jews and the inferiority of the Gentiles. (…), and

(4) 'The purpose of the author was to do for Genesis what the Chronicler did for Samuel and Kings' which means that, as far as the themes of Genesis are concerned, the *Book of Jubilees* is not less reliable than the 'Chronicles' is with regards to the 'Samuel' and the 'Kings'.

(5) The desire of its author 'was to save Judaism from the demoralizing effects of Hellenism by glorifying the law and picturing the patriarchs as irreproachable; by glorifying Israel and urging her to preserve the separateness from the Gentiles; and by denouncing the Gentiles and also Israel's national enemies.' It means that he could not have afforded therein anything, which might have been damaging to the pride and interest of the Jews.

(6) As to the patriarchs, he has tried his best to extend every favour and respect to them,

(7) 'and anything is omitted that would put the patriarchs in an unfavourable light'.

It can thus be appreciated that the *Book of Jubilees* is not an unimportant book and it could not include anything in it which be against the interest of the Jews and the patriarchs; and that's why the scholars of the Bible liberally quote from it to strengthen their themes. This *Book of Jubilees* asserts:

> And he drew near to the place of the mount of God. (…). And I called to him from heaven, and said unto him: 'Abraham, Abraham;' and he was terrified and said: 'Behold, (here) am I.' And I said unto him: 'Lay not thy hand upon the lad, neither do you anything to him; for now I have shown that thou fearest the

Lord, and hast not withheld thy son, thy first-born son, from me.'[8]

Then again, in 18:15 of the same book, it is stated:

And the Lord called Abraham by his name a second time from heaven, (...). And he said: 'By Myself have I sworn, saith the Lord, Because thou hast done this thing, And hast not withheld thy son, thy beloved son, from Me, That in blessing I will Bless thee,[9]

The editor has afforded a footnote to 'thy beloved son'. He asserts in it:

But here *c d* have 'thy first-born son'.

The '*c'* and '*d'* have been explained in the introduction of this version of the Book of Jubilees on p.2. According to it the '*c'* signifies the Ethiopic MS (Manuscript) of this book which belongs to the University Library at Tubingen, and the '*d*' signifies the Ethiopic MS of this book which belongs to the National Library in Paris. It makes quite clear that according to vv 11 and 15 of chapter 18 of the Book of the Jubilees, Abraham was asked to offer 'thy [Abraham is the addressee of this phrase] first-born son' for sacrifice.

The authorities have thus explained that if, at all, a physical offering was required under some special circumstances, it should have been only the first-born son of his father or the first-born animal. Otherwise, as a general rule, it was required that the first-born son of a father or a first-born animal should be ransomed and redeemed. A number of other scholars also maintain the same theme. Some of them are: Peake's BC.[10], NJB.[11], Christian Community B.[12]

As to the fact that Ishmā'el is Abraham's universally acknowledged firstborn son, it has so explicitly been stated in unequivocal terms in the Bible and other relevant record that one feels embarrassed in putting forward some argu-mentation with regard to it. But it is a matter of grave concern that some scholars of the Bible have felt no hesitation in defying and defiling this plain fact. So the theme is being undertaken below quite briefly:

Isaac as Abraham's Son

Sarah thy wife shall bear thee a son indeed; and thou shalt call his name Isaac:[13]

And Abraham was an hundred years old, when his son Isaac was born unto him.[14]

Ishmā'el as Abraham's Son

And Hagar bare *Abram* [stress added] a son: and Abram called *his son's* [stress added] name, which Hagar bare, Ishma'el. And Abraham was fourscore and six years old, when *Hagar bare Ishma'el to Abram* [stress added].[15]

And *Abram took Ishma'el his son* [stress added], and all that were born in his house, and all that were bought with his money, every male among the men of Abraham's house; and circumcised the flesh of their foreskin in the selfsame day, as God had said unto him. [16]

But *the son of the slave woman is also your son* [stress added], and I will make his descendants into a great nation.[17]

I will also give many children to the son of the slave-girl, so that they will become a nation. He too is your son [stress added].[18]

Stress has been added to some words and phrases of the above sub-heading '*Ishmā'el as Abraham's Son*', which shows that Ishmā'el is as genuinely and legitimately Abraham's own real son as Isaac. It thus abundantly makes clear that according to the Bible, Ishmā'el and Isaac, both of them, were Abraham's equally real, legitimate, and genuine sons. If somebody arbitrarily claims that Ishmā'el was not Abraham's son, or had ceased to be his son after being cast away, it is quite against the facts and without any justification. God told Abraham that Ishmā'el would remain his son even after being settled elsewhere. Ishmā'el was born when Abraham was eighty-six years old; and Isaac was born when Abraham was a hundred years old. As such, it was Ishmā'el who was the 'First Born Son of Abraham'. *The privilege of being his father (Abraham)'s first-born son was Ishmā'el's irrevocable and irreversible right and nobody could have deprived him of it. Isaac was Abraham's second-born son and could not have been called the first-born son of his father at any stage of his life by any stretch of meanings.* Then *it was Ishmā'el who retained the status of the only son of Abraham for nearly fourteen years; whereas Isaac could not enjoy the status of an only son of Abraham for even a single day of his life.* The son, asked to be offered for sacrifice had to be Abraham's 'only son' (as categorically and repeatedly directed in the Bible) as well as his 'first-born son' (as required by the prevalent tradition of offering to make the offering precious). Had God meant to require some 'only heir' or 'Sarah's only son', as some scholars have tried to put these words in God's mouth, He could plainly have used these words. He should not have puzzled Abraham by asking him to offer 'thy son, thine only son'. How can a man on earth say that it could, in any way, or by any stretch of meaning, be Isaac who was required to be offered for sacrifice! Isaac was neither Abraham's 'only son' nor his 'first-born' one at the time of his birth, or at any stage of his life. He was not the 'only son of Abraham' as long as Abraham was alive, because Ishmā'el had throughout been very much alive together with him until Abraham breathed his last. Now it is unto the reader to appreciate the truth.

It can thus safely be concluded from the fairly detailed above data regarding the privilege of the first-born son that:

1. Human sacrifice was customary and frequent among Abraham's Canaanite neighbours, and the early legislation of Ex 22:29 also states that first-born sons are to be given to God.
2. Not only were the first-fruits as acceptable an offering as the firstlings, but when (in exceptional cases) a human victim was required it was a first-born that was preferred (2K. 3:27).
3. The first-born male enjoyed the privileges of which he was not to be deprived.
4. One of the most important books of the Pseudepigrapha, the '*Book of Jubilees*', reports God as saying: 'for now I have shown that thou fearest the Lord, and hast not withheld thy son, thy first-born son, from me.' It means that the son who was offered for sacrifice was the 'First-born son of

Abraham'; not only according to the Bible, but also according to all the available record.

5. It is a universally acknowledged fact that, inter alia, both Ishmā'el and Isaac are Abraham's real and legitimate sons.
6. Only one son of a person can be called his 'first-born son'; and it was Ishmā'el who was Abraham's 'first-born son'; and was born nearly fourteen years prior to Isaac's birth.
7. In addition to being Abraham's 'first-born son', Ishmā'el retained the status of being Abraham's 'only son' for nearly fourteen years, whereas Isaac had not enjoyed this privilege at any time of his life. It means that Isaac could neither have been called 'the only son of Abraham' nor his 'firstborn son' at any stage of his life.
8. God had asked Abraham to offer his 'only son' for sacrifice. Moreover, it should have been the 'first-born son' who was customary to be offered. These prerequisites naturally nominate Ishmā'el to be offered for sacrifice. Isaac does not fulfil any of these conditions. So it could have been only Ishmā'el who was required to be offered for sacrifice; and it could, by no means, have been Isaac.
9. The above discussion further suggests that to make the sacrifice more significant, precious, and for attesting the fidelity of Abraham in true sense of the word, it could have been his 'first-born and the only son' whom God might have asked Abraham to offer for sacrifice. He was very old. His wife Sarah was also very old, past menopause, and barren. He did not expect any further offspring. He had only one son who had now become of a reasonable age to extend him a helping hand that he extremely needed at such a stage of his life. He had no ray of future hope if he be deprived of his youthful son Ishmā'el. Had it been one of his two sons who was required to be offered for sacrifice, and that too his younger son Isaac, who was less useful, less vigorous, less versatile, and less helpful to him; the test could not have been so grave, meaningful, and perfect; as it could have been

in case of the 'only and the first-born son' to be required for sacrifice.

10. In a situation like this: where God is going to 'tempt' Abraham through asking him to offer his firstborn and the only son for sacrifice; and that too, at such a stage of his life: it would be redundant if God adds the name of Abraham's son to 'your son, [your firstborn son, who is] your only son'. Making the expression grim-grimmer-grimmest with the words 'your son, [your firstborn son, who is] your only son' the command has been taken to its climax. It would rather mar the effectiveness and significance of the command if 'even Isaac' be inserted into it. The mention of the name of the only son is a useless addition, and cannot be expected by some eloquent, impressive and intelligent communicator. This is an ugly instance of interpolation incorporated by some committed but naive redactor that exposes his guilty conscience and ulterior '*holy and pious*' motives.

References

1. Ex. 22:29-30 (NKJV) reads as:

(29) You shall not delay to *offer* the first of your ripe produce and your juices. The firstborn of your sons you shall give to Me. (30) *Likewise you shall do with your oxen* (stress added) *and* your sheep. It shall be with its mother seven days; on the eighth day you shall give it to Me.

Peake's Commentary on the Bible (p. 221) explains it as:

Every first-born is the property of Yahweh. (...). It [set apart] is the word used also for sacrificing children to Molech. Since the Canaanite practice, resorted to on occasion certainly, was abhorent to Israel, it is unlikely that the term was borrowed from them. (...). Though in Israel the first-born were to be set apart to Yahweh as his, they were not to be given to him by sarifice, but they were to be 'ransomed' from him, a term which could suggest that they were sacrificed in theory, though not in actual fact. (...). The price of the redemption of the first-born of human beings, which is not stated here, was later fixed at 5 shekels, Num. 18:15f.

Num. 18:15,16 (NKJV) reads as:

(15) Everything that first opens the womb of all flesh, which they bring to the Lord, whether man or beast, shall be yours (Levite's); nevertheless the firstborn of man you shall surely redeem, and the firstborn of unclean animals you shall redeem. (16) And those redeemed of the devoted things you shall redeem when one month old, according to your valuation, for five shekels of silver, according to the shekel of the sanctuary, which is twenty gerahs.

The Jewish Encyclopedia (5:396) explains it as follows:

According to Talmudic tradition, the first-born acted as officiating priests in the wilderness, until the erection of the Tabernacle, when the office was given to the tribe of Levi. In consequence of the deliverance from the tenth plague, when 'the Lord slew all the first-born in the land of Egypt' but spared the first-born of the Israelites, the following commandment was given: 'Sanctify unto me all the first-born whatsoever openeth the womb among the children of Israel, both of man and of beast: it is mine'. The first-born of clean beasts were thus made holy and were unredeemable, while the first-born of unclean beasts and of man had to be redeemed from the priests. (….).

Every Israelite is obliged to redeem his son thirty days after the latter's birth. The mother is exempt from this obligation. The son, if the father fails to redeem him, has to redeem himself when he grows up. The sum of redemption as given in the Bible (Num. 18:16) is five shekels, which should be given to the priest.

It may be noted here that this legislation regarding the redemption of the first-born son relates to the Israelites of the post-Exodus period. It cannot be made applicable to the patriarchs Abraham and his first-born son.

2. Charles Gore, Goudge, Alfred Guillaume, *A New Commentary on Holy Scripture*, (London: 1928), 53.
3. *Enc. Biblica*, 3:2177.
4. Marcus Dods, *The Expositor's Bible*, (NY: 1903), 1:199,200.
5. *Enc. Biblica*, 2:1525,26.
6. Deu. 21:15-17 KJV.
7. *The Interpreter's Dictionary of Bible* (1962), s.v. 'Jubilees, Book of', 2:1002-3.

8. *The Book of the Jubilees*, 18:11, in *The Apocrypha and Pseudepigrapha of the OT in Eng.*, ed. R. H. Charles, (Oxford: The Clarendon Press, 1968), 2:40.
9. *The Book of the Jubilees*, 18:15; 2:40.
10. *Peake's Com. On Bible*, ed. H. H. Rowley, (London: Thomas Nelson & Sons Ltd., 1967), 193 states:

    The story may also have been intended to explain the early Hebrew custom of ransoming the firstborn of male children (cf. Exod. 34:20).
11. *The New Jerusalem Bible*, Henry Wansbrough, gen. ed. (London: Darton, Longman & Todd Ltd., 1993), 41 explains:

    The story as it stands justifies the ritual prescription for the redemption of the first-born of Israel: like all 'first-fruits' these belong to God;
12. *Christian Community Bible*, ed. Patricia Grogan, (Catholic Bishops' Conference of the Philippines, 1995), 73 says:

    In a first reading the text also justifies the ransom of the firstborn children. As for all first-fruits they belong to God; but unlike the firstborn of animals which are immolated, children are redeemed (Ex 13:13).
13. Gen. 17:19 KJV.
14. Gen. 21:5 KJV.
15. Gen. 16:15-16 KJV.
16. Gen. 17:23 KJV.
17. Gen. 21:13 CEV.
18. Gen. 21:13 GNB.

4

Abraham was Required to Offer his Beloved Son[1] for Sacrifice

The Bible states that the son, who was to be offered for sacrifice, was the *only son* whom Abraham loved. It is a conspicuous point and is to be taken properly.

'Whom did Abraham love?' is to be keenly explored before passing some judgement on it. The first thing to be noted is that '*Whom thou lovest,*' is not a simple remark about the relevant son; it is rather a distinguishing attribute. It should not be loosely applied to any of the sons of Abraham. It should be applied very conscientiously to the pertinent son of Abraham after thrashing out his relevance carefully.

As far as Isaac is concerned, the phrase '*Whom thou lovest,*' cannot positively be applied to him. No doubt Abraham might have been showing due paternal affection towards Isaac—which he ought to have shown—but he did not have any extra-ordinary love and attachment for him. When Abraham was told about the birth of Isaac:

> As for Sarai your wife, you shall not call her name Sarai, but Sarah shall be her name. And I will bless her, and indeed I will give you a son by her. Then I will bless her, and she shall be *a mother of* nations; kings of peoples shall be from her[2];

he was not pleased with it. He rather showed indifference towards the forthcoming son—his sole desire and topmost priority being Ishmā'el —as has been reported in the Bible:

> And Abraham said to God, 'Oh that Ishmael might live before you! [Abraham's deep concern for Ishma'el and his indifference towards Isaac is particularly to be noticed]' (...). And as for Ishma'el, I have heard you. Behold, I have blessed him, and will make him fruitful, and will multiply him exceedingly. He shall beget twelve princes, and I will make him a great nation.[3]

Commentators of the Bible have genuinely taken it as a love token by Abraham in favor of Ishmā'el. The *Nelson Study Bible* has observed:

> What is more, he still loved his son Ishmā'el (16:15; 17:18).[4]

The *Wycliffe Bible Com.* has noted it as:

> Sarah may have feared that Abraham, out of love for Ishmael, would give the older lad the prominent place in the inheritance. (...). To drive them out must have been exceedingly grievous to Abraham, for he loved the boy.[5]

It shows that Abraham's love for Ishmā'el was so obvious that even Sarah was fully aware of it. J. Fawsett puts it as:

> He [Abraham] bears Ishma'el upon his heart, and expresses a laudable concern for him.[6]

Marcus Dods has recorded beautiful comments to show that Ishmā'el was the son whom Abraham loved very much. He has also recorded the justifications for this immense love. He comments:

> Abram's state of mind is disclosed in the exclamation: 'Oh, that Ishmael might live before Thee!' He had learned to love the bold, brilliant, domineering boy. (...). But there he was, in actual flesh and blood, full of life and interest in everything, daily getting deeper into the affections of Abram, who allowed and could not but allow his own life to revolve very much around the dashing, attractive lad [It may be noted that when Ishmā'el was still a 'lad', Isaac had either not been born, or would have been still a suckling baby]. (...). 'Oh, that Ishmael might serve Thy turn!' Why call me again off from this actual attainment to the vague, shadowy, non-existent heir of promise, who surely can never have the brightness of eye and force of limb and lordly ways of this

> Ishmael? Would that what already exists in actual substance before the eye might satisfy Thee and fulfil Thine intention and supersede the necessity of further waiting! Must I again loosen my hold, and part with my chief attainment?[7]

It may be appreciated that Abraham shows profound love for Ishmā'el on account of his being full of promise, potentate and talent, as has been recorded above. Seventh Day Adventist BD asserts:

> When 13 years later, God announced the imminent birth of Isaac (ch 17:1-8, 15-17), Abraham interceded on behalf of Ishma'el, whom he dearly loved.[8]

Dr. Cohn asserts:

> I (...) would be satisfied if only Ishma'el lived before Thee.[9]

As for Isaac, Abraham showed an indifference towards him due to lack of these traits in him. Scholars have plainly acknowledged the weaknesses of Isaac. J. Hastings states in his *DB*:

> Isaac is a less striking personality than his father is. Deficient in the heroic qualities, he suffered indisposition from an excess of mildness, and the love of quiet (...). He was rather shifty and timid in his relations with Abimelech (26:1-22), too easily imposed upon, and not a good ruler of his household–a gracious and kindly but not a strong man.[10]

Similar views have been expressed by William Neil about Isaac:

> Isaac is generally referred to in the commentaries as a colourless personality. Certainly when we compare him with Abraham and Jacob it is impossible to form a clear picture of him. Few stories are recorded about him, presumably because there was little known of him that was worth recording, and in those stories in which he does feature he is generally a minor participant in the narratives dealing with his more notable father or son.[11]

It shows that according to the scholars of the Bible Isaac had a less attractive and impressive personality than Ishmā'el, although, according to the Islāmic tradition one cannot endorse it. According to Islām both of them were the prophets of equal status and it is not proper to prefer one on the other. It may only be due to physical strength and practical support that Abraham felt more love and attachment towards him.

There is another evidence that confirms the love of Abraham for Ishmā'el . When Sarah asked Abraham to expel Ishmā'el and his mother Hagar, Abraham was very much disturbed at it, which showed his grave concern for his son Ishmā'el. The event has been recorded in the Bible as follows:

> Therefore she said to Abraham, 'Drive out this maid and her son, for the son of this maid shall not be an heir with my son Isaac.' And the matter distressed Abraham greatly because of his son [The editor has recorded here a note: '*lit., was very grievous in Abraham's sight.*'].[12]

The love of Abraham for his son Ishmā'el is so evident here that even the Jewish commentators of the Bible did not fail to appreciate it. Dr. Cohen makes the following comment on it:

> Scripture points out that this grief was caused not by the prospect of loosing the woman but on account of Ishmael.[13]

It will be appreciated from the entire above discussion that '*Whom thou lovest*,' could have only been spoken of Ishmā'el and not of Isaac; and it was only Ishmā'el who was really offered for sacrifice by Abraham because it was Ishmā'el who was Abraham's 'beloved son'.

As far as the theme of Abraham's offering his 'only son' for sacrifice is concerned, fairly sufficient discussions have been undertaken in the above four chapters. Some relevant points will be studied in detail in the coming chapters. At the end of this part of the book it would be pertinent that a concluding note be recorded as an epilogue to this story of offering and as the last scene of the episode.

Abraham Returned Alone Without the 'Only Son'

The story concludes with the following last sentence:

> So Abraham returned unto his young men, and they rose up and went together to Beer-sheba; and Abraham dwelt at Beer-sheba. (Gen 22:19 KJV)

The reflective and conscientious consideration of the verse guides the heedful reader to these points:

(1) '*So Abraham returned unto his young men*' shows that during his return home, the 'only son', whosever the 'only son' had been, was not with him. W. Gunther Plaut observes:

The text says that Abraham returned from Moriah but omits a mention of Isaac. (…) Isaac did not come back with his father.[14]

Ignoring the word Isaac, as discussed in detail in this book at various places, the verse asserts that the 'only son' did not return with Abraham, because his abode was here near Moriah. Had it been Isaac who was to be offered for sacrifice, he must have returned with his father. It shows that the 'only son' was Ishmā'el, who dwelt near Moriah, and as such he had not to return with Abraham.

(2) It may be noted here that Abraham's family lived at Hebron; but he spent most of his time at Beer-sheba with his herds and flocks. He went back there leaving his only son, Ishmā'el, at his residence at Moriah.

(3) Had it been Isaac who was to be offered for sacrifice, it was not like him to show any displeasure or disregard towards his father by parting company with him.

References

1. The theme of the chapter is that Abraham was required to offer his 'Beloved Son' for sacrifice and his 'Beloved Son' was Ishma#'el and not Isaac. It by no means implies that Ishma#'el was superior to Isaac and Isaac was inferior to Ishma#'el. Both of the Prophets are equally honorable and innocent and the Muslims do not claim any superiority for one upon the other.
2. Gen. 17:15-16 NKJV in the *Nelson Study Bible*, ed. Earl D. Radmacher, (Nashville: Thomas Nelson Publishers, 1997), 36-37.
3. Gen. 17:18, 20 NKJV in the *Nelson Study Bible*, 37.
4. *The Nelson Study Bible*, footnote p. 43.
5. *The Wycliffe Bible Com.* (Chicago: Moody Press, 1987), 26.
6. John Fawsett, *The Devotional Family Bible*, (London: 1811), no paging has been recorded in this 2 centuries old book.

7. Marcus Dods, *The Expositor's Bible*, 1:160.
8. *Seventh Day Adventist Bible Dic.*, Rvd. 1979 edn., 526.
9. Dr. Cohen (the Jewish Commentary) *The Soncino Chumash*, 81.
10. Hastings' *Dic. of Bible*, Rvd. by Frederick Grant & H. H. Rowley (NY: Charles Scribner's Sons, 1963), 422.
11. William Neil, *Pocket Bible Com.* (HarperSanFrancisco, 1975), 50.
12. Gen. 21:10-11 NASB.
13. Dr. Cohen, *Soncino Chumash*, 102.
14. *The Torah A Modern Commmentary*, ed. Gunther Plaut, NY: Union of American Hebrew Congregations, 1981, 152.

5

The Sites Claimed to be Moriah As the Place of Offering

The Bible states that Abraham was asked to offer his only son for sacrifice 'upon one of the mountains' which was situated 'into the land of Moriah;'. It has been recorded in the Bible as follows:

> and go to the land of Moriah, and offer him there as a burnt offering on one of the mountains of which I shall tell you.[1]

It shows that the place of offering of the lad for sacrifice was some 'mountain into the land of Moriah'. The word 'Moriah' has been mentioned in the whole of the Bible at only two places: (i) Gen. 22:2, i.e.

> and get thee into the land of Moriah;

and (ii) II Chron. 3:1, i.e.

> Then Solomon began to build the house of the Lord at Jerusalem in mount Moriah, where the Lord appeared unto David his father, in the place that David had prepared in the threshingfloor of Ornan the Jebosite.

Scholars have different opinions as to whether the mention of Moriah at both the places of the Bible indicates one and the same place, or they denote different locations. Harper's BD has assigned two different places for 'Moriah' (p. 654). The Jewish Enc. asserts:

> Modern scholars who distinguish between these two places advance different theories as to the meaning of the word 'Moriah.'[2]

'Moriah' has been located at the following places by different scholars of the Bible and religious devotees:

(1) **A mountain near Hebron,** as *Hastings Revised Dic. of Bible* asserts: 'some scholars have proposed a location for Moriah on a mountain near Hebron.'.[3]

(2) **Mount Gerizim** near 'modern town of Nablus, 4 km NW of ancient Shechem,'[4] (Shechem is 'about 50 km N of Jerusalem and 9 km SE of Samaria'[5]) where 'Samaritan Temple' was built.

(3) **Mount Calvary**, where Christ was afterwards claimed to have been crucified as the *Devotional Family BC* Asserts: 'There is no improbability in the general opinion, that the very spot was mount Calvary[6] where Christ the great anti-type was afterwards crucified.'[7]

(4) **The threshingfloor of Araunah the Jebosite near Jerusalem**, which was bought from him by king David, and where subsequently the 'Temple' was built by Solomon.

The first three '*Moriahs*' are being discussed in this chapter. The 4th '*Moriah*' will be discussed in the next chapter.

(a) On a Mountain near Hebron

As regards *the 1st 'Moriah' located on a mountain near Hebron*, no discussion is required on it, because: (i) No notable scholar of the Bible considers it discussible, noteworthy, or mentionable either. (ii) It is contradictory to the Bible. Abraham had settled either at Hebron itself, or at Mamre[8], which is *4 km N of Hebron*[9]. The Bible says that Abraham had started his journey from his residence for 'Moriah' early in the morning and after three days' earnest journey he was 'afar off' from his destination. Is it conceivable that even after three days' earnest journey he could not cover so meager a distance!

(b) At Mount Calvary Where Christ Is Claimed to Have Been Crucified.

As regards *the 2nd Moriah, which is allegedly located at Mount Calvary where Christ is claimed to have been crucified*, no discussion is required on it too, because: (i) No notable scholar of the Bible considers it discussible, noteworthy, or mentionable either. (ii) It is also not agreeable with the contents of the Bible. It was either situated somewhere in the modern city of Jerusalem, but outside the walls of the ancient city; or quite close to it[10]. It is not more than twenty miles either from Jerusalem, Beersheba, Hebron or Mamre. It too could not have taken Abraham more than a few hours to reach here. How can it be conceived that even after three days' earnest journey he could not cover so meagre a distance!

(c) At Mount Gerizim

As regards *the 3rd 'Moriah', claimed to be situated at Mount Gerizim near the ancient city of Shechem*, the Samaritans attached it to the site of the Temple to establish the sanctity and importance of their sanctuary. The *Illustrated Bible Dic.* records: 'The Samaritan tradition identifies the site with Mt. Gerizim (as though Moriah = Moreh; cf. Gn. 12:6)'.[11] Dummelow's *Com. On Bible* has also noted the similar remarks about it.[12] *7th Day Adventist Bible Dic.* has afforded a fairly detailed account of the theme:

> The Samaritans, who consider Mount Gerizim the holy mountain of God, place the sacrifice of Isaac on that mountain, and believe that Moriah was Moreh near Shechem; and that it was the site of the first encampment of Abraham in the land of Canaan, where he built an altar to the true God (Gen 12:6,7). Such an identification, they believe, justifies their separation from Jerusalem, and their right to worship God on Mount Gerizim (see Jn 4:20, 21). It is, of course, entirely without support.[13]

Hastings Revised Single Volume Dic. of the Bible has also afforded a similar observation:

> There is some similarity between the names of Moriah and 'Moreh,' the latter located near Shechem (Gn 12:6, Dt 11:30) and Mount Gerizim. And it may have been owing to this that the Samaritans have claimed Gerizim as Abraham's mountain (cf Jn 4:20). Gn 22:4 has been often cited to suggest that Gerizim, a mountain visible for some distance, must be the Moriah of Abraham, because he 'lifted up his eyes and saw the place afar off.'[14]

The Samaritans were bitterly against the Southern kingdom of Judah. When the Chronicler attached the name of 'Moriah' to Solomon's Temple to establish the sanctity and importance of the Judean sanctuary, the Samaritans, in response to it, attached the name 'Moriah' to their sanctuary at Mount Gerizim or vice versa. S. R. Driver's observations in *J. Hastings' Dic. of Bible* conform to this opinion:

> In view of the rivalry which prevailed in later times between the Samaritans and the Jews, the preference of the former for Gerizim does not count for much; and with regard to the other arguments it may be doubted whether, in a narrative which cannot be by an eye-witness or contemporary of the facts recorded, the expressions used are not interpreted with undue strictness.[15]

The fertile brains of the Samaritans tried to explore the probabilities for their claim. It is a common phenomenon that every idea, howsoever absurd it be, attracts some curious 'scholars' and gains their support. By the passage of time even some unprejudiced scholars, unmindful of the ulterior motives of the innovators, consider the queer idea quite objectively and discover some logic in it. In the same way a few scholars do not outright reject the possibility of its carrying some logic; but most of the scholars do not find any difficulty in appreciating its absurdity. The name 'Moriah' has never been used for Mount Gerizim in the whole of the Bible. The annals of history and the realm of knowledge are totally void of any ground for this purposeful fabrication of the Samaritans.

From all the above discussion it would be appreciated that the Samaritans' claim about the location of Abraham's offering his only son for sacrifice at Mount Gerizim was forged due to some regional, sectarian, cultic and ethnic rivalries; and is without any real ground. It is to be noted that this Moreh was not a barren wilderness. It is a beautiful and fertile hilly area with thick forests and abundant greenery all around it (the Bible has also associated it with 'oaks'). Not very far in its W is the great sea (Mediterranean); at some distance in the E is the river Jordan; within the parameters of twenty to twenty five miles to its NNE and SSE are the Sea of Galilee and the Dead Sea. Abraham having lived here for a fairly considerable time, should have definitely been aware of it. It is sheer absurdity if he carries a load of fuel wood to Moreh for some so-called burnt offering. It is rather carrying coal to New Castle. Putting aside all the above discussion, only this single plea rules out every possibility of Abraham's taking his only son to this place to offer him for sacrifice.

After migrating from his homeland in Mesopotamia, Abraham traveled NW and reached Haran through Paddan-aram (i.e., the plain of Syria). After staying there for some time he again started his journey to SSW. Through Halab, Hamath, Damascus, etc. he entered the land of Canaan. Moreh was his first camping station in Canaan where he encamped his family for some time. He then proceeded further to Egypt[16] to explore some suitable base for his missionary activities. Seeing that Egypt was not a fertile field for his mission, he came back to Moreh and stayed there for some time to explore new horizons for his missionary activities. His nephew, Lot, remained with him throughout this missionary exploration. It was here at Moreh that they decided to extend their missionary activities in different lands. Lot chose to work in Edom and Abraham made his base camp for his mission about twenty miles south of (Jeru-) Salem[17] [the name of Jerusalem, in those days, was mere 'Salem'] and settled his family in the area of Mamre, Hebron, and Machpelah. Beersheba, about twenty-five miles SSW of Hebron, was the pasture of his herds and flocks. The family of Abraham had now permanently settled here and had left Moreh for good.

The above information about Moreh has been carefully collected from authentic sources such as atlases, commentaries, dictionaries, encyclopedias, and the proper text of the Bible. Only two brief excerpts are being provided hereunder. W. Smith 's *DB* states:

The oak of Moreh was the first recorded halting-place of Abram after his entrance into the land of Canaan. Gen. 12:6. It was at the 'place of Shechem,' ch. 12:6, close to the mountains of Ebal and Gerizim. Deut. 11:30.[18]

Rev. A. H. Gunner and F. F. Bruce explain in The *Illustrated BD*:

Dt. 11:30 makes reference to the 'oak of Moreh' in the district of Gilgal (i.e. the Shechemite Gilgal). It is recorded that Abraham pitched his camp there on arriving in Canaan from Harran, and it was there that God revealed himself to Abraham, promising to give the land of Canaan to his descendants.[19]

References

1. Gen. 22:2, NKJV.
2. *The Jewish Enc.*, 9:17.
3. *Hastings Dic. of Bible* 674-5.
4. *New Bible Dic.,* II edn., N. Hillyer Revision edn., (Leicestor: Inter-Varsity Press, Eng., 1986), 415.
5. *New Bible Dic.*, II ed., 1099.
6. Matt. 27:33, 4 *Christian Community Bible, Catholic Pastoral edn.*, 1995, p. 66-7 explains:

   When they reached the place called Golgotha (or Calvary) which means *the Skull*, they offered him wine mixed with gall. Jesus tasted it but would not take it.
7. John Fawcett, *The Devotional Family Bible Com.* (London: Suttaby, Evance & Co, 1811), Vol. I, no paging.
8. The place 'Mamre' should not be confused with 'Moriah'. Both the places have quite different significance and are located at different sites. F. F. Bruce writes in *The Illustrated Bible Dic.* on page 940:

   A place in the Hebron district, W from Machpelah (Gn. 23:17, 19; 49:30; 50:13), associated with Abraham (Gn. 13:18; 14:13; 18:1) and Isaac (Gn. 35:27). Abraham resided for considerable periods under the terebinth of Mamre; there he built an altar, there he learnt of the capture of Lot, there he received Yahweh's promise of a son and pleaded for Sodom, and from there he saw the smoke of Sodom and its neighbor cities ascend. The site has been identified at Rametel-Khalil, 4 km N of Hebron.

   The same scholar, F. F. Bruce, explains in his book '*Places Abraham Knew*' on pp. 41, 43, 46:

   In so far as Abraham had a place in Canaan which could be called his home, it was at Mamre. His family and household could stay here while he was leading caravans or taking part in pastoral activity elsewhere. (...). To Jews, Christians and Muslims, however, its fame is based on the fact that it was here that Abraham stayed and had those dealings with God which have won for him the name 'The Friend of God'.

It is also to be noted here that this Mamre is associated with some terebinth tree or 'oaks of Mamre'. It means that it was not an inarable or barren land, fuel wood was abundantly available there, and Abraham would not have needed to carry wood there for the burnt offering. It can, therefore, be safely concluded that this Mamre has nothing to do with Moriah, the place of Abraham's offering his only son for sacrifice, as some scholars have asserted.

9. *New Bible Dic.*, II edn., 1:730.

10. *Harper's Bible Dic.* has explained the word 'Calvary' (p. 150) as:

    the site of Jesus' crucifixion. Three gospels recorded both the Semitic name of this site, 'Golgotha,' and a translation, 'Place of the Skull' (Matt. 27:33; Mark 15:22; John 19:17). Luke 23:33 records only a shorter and more accurate translation, 'Skull.' The name 'Calvary' derives from the Vulgate's Latin translation of this word (calvaria). It is likely that the site was so named because of its habitual use for executions. Less likely is an explanation rooted in the physical appearance of the place. Apart from the name very little is confidently known about Calvary. John 19:20 and Jewish and Roman execution customs indicate that it was located outside Jerusalem's city walls. Roman crucifixion customs and the reference to passers-by (Matt. 27:39) also suggest it was near a thoroughfare, while the fact that the cross was visible from afar (Matt. 27:55) could indicate an elevated location. Nevertheless its precise location remains in dispute.

11. *The Illustrated Bible Dic.*, (Inter-Varsity Press, 1980), 2:1025.

12. J. R. Dummelow, *A Com. on The Holy Bible* (NY: The Macmillan Co, 1956), 30 says:

    The Samaritans assert that Mt. Gerizim was the scene of the event, regarding Moriah as Moreh in Shechem.

13. *7th Day Adventist Bible Dic.*, Revised edn., ed. Siegfried H. Horn (Hagerstown: Review & Herald Publishing. Association, 1979), 760.

14. *Hastings Dic. of Bible Rvd.*, 674-5.

15. *Hastings Dic. of Bible*, s.v. 'Moriah' by S. R. Driver, 3:437.

16. It may either be the North Eastern Egypt or the peninsula of Sinai.
17. (Gn 14:18), identified with Jerusalem in Ps 76:3 and in early Jewish tradition, which is accepted by modern interpreters. (J. L McKenzie's *Dic. of Bible*, 759).
18. W. Smith's *A Dic. of Bible*, 416.
19. *The Illustrated Bible Dic.*, 2:1025.

6

Jerusalem As the Site Claimed to be Moriah (The Place of Offering)

The claim of the Biblical Scholars regarding *the site of Moriah, at Jerusalem*, requires a fairly detailed discussion. It was given the name of 'Moriah' to attach importance and reverence to the house of the Lord, commonly known as the 'Temple'. McKenzie's *Dic. of Bible* explains:

> The hill on which Solomon's temple was built is called Moriah (2 Ch 3:1), the only other incidence of the name; but this is in all probability due to the theological invention, which identified the Temple, the place of Yahweh's dwelling and of Israel's worship, with the site of the sacrifice of Isaac.[1]

In fact the site of the Temple had previously been without any proper name. It was simply called 'the threshingfloor of Ornan the Jebosite.' The name 'Moriah' was ascribed to it usurpingly to attach reverence and importance to it. G.A. Barrois has expounded the point in the *Interpreter's DB* as below:

> Since the name Moriah appears nowhere else in the texts relative to the topography of Jerusalem, there is good reason to suspect that the author of Chronicles intended to ascribe an early origin to the royal sanctuary, by identifying the unnamed hilltop formerly used as a threshing floor with the mountain in the land of Moriah, where Abraham had made ready to sacrifice his son.[2]

The Chronicler himself, who has attributed the name of 'Moriah' to the place, does not use this name for the place anywhere else in his narratives, whereas he has referred to this place at a number of times. Had the place had its identification with the proper name 'Moriah', it must have been used by the Chronicler at other places as well. Moreover, it was claimed to be situated in the city of Jerusalem, which was the most important city for the Jewish people. Then it was claimed to be the site of Solomon's Temple, which had always remained the most important building to the Jewish community ever since its construction. How could it be that it had nowhere been mentioned with the nomenclature of 'Moriah' in the whole of the Bible except this forgery. Here is the fairly lengthy text of the narrative from the Bible to acquaint the reader with the background of the event:

> (15) And God sent an angel unto Jerusalem to destroy it: and as he was destroying, the Lord beheld, and he repented him of the evil, and said to the angel that destroyed, it is enough, stay now thine hand. And the angel of the Lord stood by the threshingfloor of Ornan the Jebusite. (...). (18) Then the angel of the Lord commanded Gad to say to David, that David should go up, and set up an altar unto the Lord in the threshingfloor of Ornan the Jebusite. (...). (21) And as David came to Ornan, Ornan looked and saw David, and went out of the threshingfloor, and bowed himself to David with *his* face on the ground. (22) Then David said to Ornan, Grant me the place of *this* threshing-floor, that I may build an altar therein unto the Lord: thou shalt grant it me for the full price: that the plague may be stayed from the people. (23) And Ornan said unto David, Take *it* to thee, and let my lord the king do *that which is* good in his eyes: lo, I give *thee* the oxen *also for* burnt offerings, and the threshing instruments for wood, and the wheat for the meat offering; I give it all. (24) And king David said to Ornan, Nay; but I will verily buy it for the full price: for I will not take *that* which *is* thine for the Lord, nor offer burnt offerings without cost. (25) So David gave to Ornan for the place six hundred shekels of gold by weight. (26) And David built there an altar unto the Lord, and

offered burnt offerings and peace offerings, and called upon the Lord; and he answered him from heaven by fire upon the altar of burnt offering. (27) And the Lord commanded the angel; and he put up his sword again into the sheath thereof. (28) At that time when David saw that the Lord had answered him in the threshingfloor of Ornan the Jebusite, then he sacrificed there.[3]

It may be observed in the above narrative that the alleged place of 'Moriah' has been mentioned in these few lines for eleven times with the names of (1) the threshingfloor of Ornan the Jebusite, or merely (2) the threshingfloor, or (3) the place of *this* threshingfloor, or simply (4) the place, or the pronouns (5) it, (6) there, and (7) therein. But the proper name 'Moriah' has not been attributed to it even for a single time in the whole of the narrative. It may further be observed that these different words for the place have been used by different persons as detailed below:

(a) The phrase 'the threshingfloor of Ornan the Jebusite': (1) once by the redactor of the book, (2) once by David, and (3) once by the angel of the Lord [which shows that even the angel of the Lord (and as he was speaking on behalf of God, that even the Lord Himself) did not know that the name of the site of the Temple was 'Moriah']. (Total: 3 times).

(b) The phrase 'the threshingfloor': only once, and that by the redactor of the book.

(c) The phrase 'the place of *this* threshingfloor': only once, and that by David.

(d) The word 'therein': only once, and that also by David.

(e) The word 'it': (1) twice by David, and (2) once by Ornan the Jebusite. (Total - 3 times).

(f) The word 'there': only once, and that by the redactor of the book.

(g) The Words 'the place': only once, and that also by the redactor of the book.

It means that neither the angel of the Lord (and as he was speaking on behalf of God, so it would mean that even the Lord

Himself) knew that the name of the place, where the Solomon's Temple was to be built later on, was 'Moriah', nor the redactor of the book, or King David, or Ornan the Jebusite knew it. It is simply unbelievable!

Had 'Moriah' been the name of the place, and that too, from the times of the Patriarch Abraham or even before that; and that too, in connection with such a conspicuous event as that of the offering of his only son for sacrifice at this place; how could it be possible that the angel of the Lord, and king David, and the redactor of the book, and the owner of the place, Ornan the Jebusite, might so indifferently, rather disdainfully, have disregarded even the mention of the proper name of this place throughout the narrative!

Fl. Josephus has also afforded a narrative of the event in his 'Antiquities', which will further elaborate the point:

> When God heard his [David's] supplication, he caused the pestilence to cease; and sent Gad the prophet to him, and commanded him to go up immediately to the threshing-floor of Araunah the Jebosite, and build an altar there to God, and offer sacrifices. When David heard that, he did not neglect his duty, but made haste to the place appointed him. Now Araunah was threshing wheat; and when he saw the king and all his servants coming to him, he ran before, and came to him (...). Now Araunah inquired, Wherefore is my lord come to his servant? He answered, To buy of him the threshing-floor, that he might therein build an altar to God, and offer a sacrifice. He replied, That he freely gave him both the threshing-floor, and the ploughs and the oxen for a burnt offering; and he besought God graciously to accept his sacrifice; (...); and when Araunah said he would do as he pleased, he bought the threshing-floor of him for fifty shekels; and when he had built an altar, he performed divine service, and brought a burnt offering, and offered peace-offerings also. (...). Now when king David saw that God had heard his prayer, and had graciously accepted of his sacrifices, he resolved to call that entire place The Altar of all the People, and to build a temple to God there;[4]

In the above passage, as in the previous one, the place allegedly named 'Moriah' by the Chronicler has been mentioned seven times; but has nowhere been mentioned with the name of 'Moriah'. Amazingly, when King David himself prescribes a name for the place, he gives it the name of 'The Altar of all the People'. Had it been the sacred place whose name had been 'Moriah' even before Abraham, having such a significant tradition attached to it as the sacrifice of Abraham's 'firstborn, and the only, and beloved son', king David would definitely have known it and would certainly have used it for the place. He could never have dared to ignore the mention of this important name and could never have dared to change it with a second rate name as 'The Altar of all the People'.

Another aspect of the proposition is also to be looked into. Abraham lived either at Hebron (Al-Khaleel of today), or at Mamre which is about three kilometer N. of Hebron. The pasture of his herds and flocks was at Beersheba, which is about twenty-five miles S of Hebron. The distance between Jerusalem and Hebron is not more than twenty miles. Abraham had set out for journey early in the morning, which shows his steadiness, eagerness, promptness, and sense of duty towards God. If he started his journey from Hebron, he had to travel twenty miles. If he started from Mamre, he had to travel only eighteen miles. If he started from Beersheba, he had to travel for about forty miles. Whatever the starting point of his journey be; as he was travelling on his donkey, and started the journey early in the morning, and undertook the journey earnestly;[5] it may have taken him merely a day or so to reach his destination, had it been in Jerusalem (which was between eighteen to about forty miles from his every possible place of residence). But the Bible asserts that even after three days' journey he was still 'afar off' from the appointed place. It means, as '*The New Jerome Biblical Commentary*' has well observed, that the total journey might have taken him well-nigh seven days to reach his destination,[6] which could in no case have been Jerusalem, because the actual destination was at such a long distance as to require such a long time. One may not agree with the '*New Jerome BC*', but nobody can deny the fact that after three consecutive days'[7] earnest journey they had not reached their destination and were still 'afar off' their destination. It rules out the idea of the 'Moriah' being situated at the hilltop at Jerusalem, which was almost one, or, at the most, two day's journey. This ambiguity has also been noted by the scholars of the Bible. *The Illustrated Bible Dic.* explains:

> The only other mention of the name occurs in 2 Ch. 3:1, where the site of Solomon's Temple is said to be on mount Moriah, on the threshingfloor of Ornan the Jebusite where God appeared to David (...). It should be noted that no reference is made here to Abraham in connection with this site. It has been objected that Jerusalem is not sufficiently distant from S Philistia to have required a 3 day's journey to get there,[8] and that one of the characteristics of Jerusalem is that the Temple hill is not visible until the traveler is quite close, so that the correctness of the Biblical identification is called in question.[9]

Peake's *Com. on the Bible* has also discussed the theme in a reasonable way. It asserts:

> In v. 2 the scene of the episode is said to be a mountain 'in the land of Moriah', and it is possible that these words and the obscure phrase in v. 14, 'in the Mount (i.e., the Temple Mount) where Yahweh is seen.' (where the Hebrew text has evidently suffered some corruption), may have been inserted by the Priestly editor to carry back the sanctity of the Temple site to the age of Abraham. But it is impossible that the Temple Mount at Jerusalem could have been the scene of the incident for various reasons.[10]

In the light of the above information, it can be asserted that the name of the hilltop on which the Solomon's Temple was built, had been 'the threshing-floor of Ornan the Jebusite', and not 'Moriah'; and it had wrongly been ascribed to it by the Chronicler to attach sanctity and significance to the site of the 'Temple'. The concept of some 'Moriah' at the site of the Solomon's Temple is completely void of any ground reality and is merely a fabrication. S.R. Driver observes in *Hastings DB* that the location of 'Moriah' at Jerusalem is the idea of the Chronicler. He asserts that it is obviously a matter of doubtful nature. He rules out the possibility of Jerusalem being the place of Moriah due to the fact that it cannot be seen from a distance, whereas the Bible asserts, 'Then on the third day Abraham lifted up his eyes, and saw the place afar off.' His observations are being recorded hereunder:

> What was originally denoted by this designation is very obscure. It is indeed evident that in 2Ch 3:1 the Temple hill is referred to; but this does not settle the sense of the expression 'land of Moriah' in Gn 22:2: the Chronicler may, in common with the later Jews, have supposed that that was the scene of the sacrifice of Isaac, and borrowed the expression from Gn 22:2—perhaps to suggest that the spot was chosen already by J" in the patriarchal age. (...). It is remarkable that, though it is here implied that it is well known to Abraham, the region is not mentioned elsewhere in the OT. It is difficult, under the circumstances, not to doubt the originality of the text; (...); Gerizim, moreover, is an elevation which a traveler approaching from the S. might 'lift up his eyes' (22:4) and see conspicuously at a distance, which is not the case with Jerusalem.[11]

L. Reed and A. H. McNeile in their article on 'Moriah' in the *Hastings' Revised (One Volume) Dic. of Bible* assert that the tradition of identifying 'Moriah' with the site of the Solomon's Temple is not traceable:

> The Chronicler (2 Ch 3:1) leaves no doubt concerning the Jewish tradition that Mount Moriah was the Temple hill where Solomon built the house of the Lord in Jerusalem and the place of David's theophany. Efforts to identify the source of this tradition have been unsuccessful.[12]

Michael Avi-Yonah observes in the *Encyclopedia Judaica* that the identification of Moriah with the threshingfloor of Ornan the Jebusite at Jerusalem is farfetched and is aimed to attach importance to the Solomon's Temple:

> The assumption that Abraham intended to sacrifice Isaac on the threshing floor of Jebus (Jerusalem), in full view of the Canaanite city, is farfetched; nor is the Temple Mount visible from afar, as it is hidden by the higher mountains around it. It seems more

probable that the biblical story left the location of Moriah deliberately vague; the importance of the sacrifice of Isaac in the series of covenants between God and Israel made it natural [to the later redactors of the Bible] that at an early time this supreme act of faith was located on the site destined to become the most holy sanctuary of Israel, the Temple of Solomon, just as the Samaritans transferred the act to their holy mountain, Mt. Gerizim.[13]

International Standard Bible Encyclopedia observes:

This land is mentioned only here [Gen. 22:2], and there is little to guide us in trying to identify it. A late writer (2 Chronicles 3:1) applies the name of Moriah to the mount on which Solomon's Temple was built, possibly associating it with the sacrifice of Isaac. A similar association with this mountain may have been in the mind of the writer of Genesis 22 (see 22:14), who, of course, wrote long after the events described (Driver). (…). The description could hardly apply to Jerusalem in any case, as it could not be seen 'afar off' by one approaching either from the South or the West. (…). With our present knowledge we must be content to leave the question open (W. Ewing).[14]

It is only the book of Chronicles in the whole of the Bible, which designates 'Moriah' as the site for the Solomon's Temple (II Chr. 3:1). Curiously, as already stated, the Chronicler, while narrating earlier the purchase of the site by David from Ornan the Jebusite in his I Chr. 21:15-28, does not mention the name of 'Moriah' for the place where the Solomon's Temple was to be built later. He simply uses the 'thresingfloor of Ornan the Jebusite' as the name of the place throughout the narrative for a number of times. Had 'Moriah' been the name of the place, he must have used this name categorically. Actually the source of the Chronicler for this narrative is II Samuel and he retells the incident from II Sam. 24:16-25. There too the name 'Moriah' has nowhere been mentioned for the place, as can be appreciated from the following quotation:

And when the angel stretched out his hand upon Jerusalem to destroy it, the Lord repented him of the evil, and said to the angel that destroyed the people, It is enough: stay now thine hand. And the angel of the Lord was by the threshingplace of Araunah the Jebusite. (17) And David spake unto the Lord when he saw the angel that smote the people, and said, Lo, I have sinned, and I have done wickedly: but these sheep, what have they done? let thine hand, I pray thee, be against me, and against my father's house. (18) And Gad came that day to David, and said unto him, Go up, rear an altar unto the Lord in the threshingfloor of Araunah the Jebusite. (19) And David, according to the saying of Gad, went up as the Lord commanded. (20) And Araunah looked, and saw the king and his servants coming on towards him: and Araunah went out, and bowed himself before the king on his face upon the ground. (21) And Araunah said, Wherefore is my lord the king come to his servant? And David said, To buy the threshingfloor of thee, to build an altar unto the Lord, that the plague may be stayed from the people. (22) And Araunah said unto David, Let my lord the king take and offer of what *seemeth* good unto him: behold, *here be* oxen for burnt sacrifice, and threshing instruments and *other* instruments of the oxen for wood. (23) All these *things* did Araunah, *as* a king, give unto the king. And Araunah said unto the king, The Lord thy God accept thee. (24) And the king said unto Araunah, Nay; but I will surely buy *it* of thee at a price: neither will I offer burnt offerings unto the Lord my God of that which doth cost me nothing. So David bought the threshingfloor and the oxen for fifty shekels of silver.[15] (25) And David built there an altar unto the Lord, and offered burnt offerings and peace offerings. So the Lord was intreated[16] for the land, and the plague was stayed from Israel.[17]

Prior to the Chronicler, the details of the plan of the Temple, the stages and style of the construction with meticulous drawings, measurements and other details of the building, had been recorded in I Kings vi-viii and Ezekiel xl-xlvii. The word 'Moriah' has nowhere been used in both of these accounts. The Chronicler was not an eye-witness of the event. He wrote the details after the lapse of seven centuries of the event as elaborated later. He gave the name 'Moriah' to the place to sanctify the site of the Temple. Nobody else had ever used the word 'Moriah' for the site of the Temple before him.

Afterwards, any one else who used the name 'Moriah' for the site of the Temple, copied it from the 'Chronicles'. It was the sole source of all the later credulous writers of so called 'histories', who eagerly picked it up without undertaking any objective and analytical appraisal of the statement and its sources. This is not 'history'. 'Wishful thinking and imaginative creativity' may be good qualities for the writer of a piece of literature, but they are plainly a demerit for a sober and genuine historian and are bound to damage his credibility.

Instead of Moriah, the Bible locates the Temple at mount Zion at some places, but it is not a unanimous opinion.[18]

The sole place in the whole of the Bible where the site of the Solomon's Temple has been attached to 'Moriah' is the book of Chronicles (II Ch. 3:1). It has been explained above that it was not based on any objective reality or historical facts. It was a 'theological invention' and was fabricated to attach reverence and importance to the 'House of the Lord'.[19]

It is hoped that the reader of this chapter of the book and the relevant Appendix III at the end of the book would face no hardship in concluding that:

(a) The statement of the Solomon's Temple having been built at 'Moriah' is a blatant forgery of the Chronicler; and

(b) The status, canonicity, historicity, and credibility of the Chronicler is not above board.

The claim that 'Moriah' was the site of Solomon's Temple is quite baseless, absurd and arbitrary; and the mention of Moriah in II Chronicles (3:1) should be considered as null and void, being a baseless invention of the Chronicler.

As the last four locations (according to the above categorization) claimed by the Bible scholars to be the spot of Abraham's offering his 'only son' for sacrifice stand ruled out through ample argumentation, there remains only one site in the whole of the Bible (Gen. 22:2); which can be claimed as the genuine 'Moriah' where Abraham had offered his 'only son' for sacrifice. A detailed study on the subject is being undertaken in the next chapter.

References

1. John L. McKenzie's *Dic. of Bible*, 586.
2. *The Interpreter's Dic. of Bible*, 3:438-9.
3. I Chr. 21:15-28 KJV. Originally the story had been recorded in II Samuel 24:16-25, which is the source of the Chronicler. Some of its excerpts have been afforded in this chapter below to enable the reader to make a comparative study. It will be appreciated that II Samuel has referred to this place for a number of times, but he has never used the word 'Moriah' for it.
4. *The Works of Flavius Josephus*, Tr. William Whiston (Boston: D Lothrop & Co., n.d.): Antiquities XIII: 4, pp. 203-4.
5. W. Gunther Plaut, *The Torah, A Modern Com.* (NY: Union of Am. Heb. Congregations, 1981), 154 explains:

   Abraham and his followers rose 'early in the morning' and 'went unto' the place of which God had told him; (...); it is as if, while he traveled on, Abraham had looked neither to the right nor to the left, had suppressed any sign of life in his followers and himself save only their footfalls.
6. Raymond E. Brown, *The New Jerome Bible Com.*, (Bangalore, India: TPI, 1994), 25 explains:

   This may be the halfway point of a seven-day journey ending in the arrival at the mountain.
7. John Fawcett, *The D. Family Bible*, 1811, Vol. I, no paging, notes:

   and after that long journey (...) the place was far distant: Mount Moriah; (...). He travels three successive days.
8. Not to say of three days, the actual journey which is allegedly claimed to be undertaken, was of not less than a week, as observed by the *New Jerome Biblical Com.* (p. 25); whereas, in view of the earnestness of Abraham and the distance to be covered being small, it could not have taken him more than about one day, had the destination been Jerusalem.
9. T. C. Mitchell, *The Illustrated Bible Dic.*, 2:1025.
10. *Peake's Com. on the Bible*, 193.
11. *Hastings Dic. of Bible*, 3: 437, s.v. 'Moriah' by S.R. Driver.
12. *Hastings Dic. of Bible*, Revised Single volume edn., 674-5.

13. *Enc Judaica* 1997 ed. CD-ROM. Version 1.0, Judaica Multimedia (Israel) Ltd., s.v. 'Moriah'.

14. *International Standard Bible Encyclopedia*, OR USA: Books For The Ages, AGES Software, Versioin 1.0 © 1997, 7:924,25.

15. The Chronicler (I Chr. 21:25) says: 'So David gave to Ornan for the place six hundred shekels of gold by weight', which is obviously an exaggeration of the Chronicler, which is his common feature—the discrepancy in the two statements is also to be noted.

16. Archaic form of 'entreat'. The NKJV makes the sense clear through his translation: 'So the Lord heeded the prayers for the land,'. NIV translates it as: 'Then the Lord answered prayer in behalf of the land, and the plague on Israel was stopped.'

17. II Sam. 24:16-25 KJV.

18. *Hastings' Dic. of the Bible* (4:983) writes:

    Throughout the OT there are passages which have no meaning, if Zion and the temple hill were two separate topographical features. Zion is the holy hill or mountain (Ps26), the chosen habitation of Jahweh (Ps 911 742 762 847 13213, Is 818 6014, Jer 810, Zec 83). There He manifests Himself (Ps 147202 536 1285 1343, Am 12); and there He must be worshipped and praised (Ps 651,2, Jer 316). (....). In 1 Maccabees, written c. BC 100 by some one who was well acquaited with the localities, Zion is identified with the temple hill (437,38 534 733 etc), and so it is in 1Es 881 2Es525 Sir2410, and Jth 913 [See also Ps 78 68,69 and Jer 50 28].

19. It would be quite pertinent to make an objective assessment of the canonicity, authenticity, and historicity of the book. It has been afforded at the end of this book as Appendix III under the title of: 'The Status of the Book of Chronicles'

7

The Actual Site of Moriah or Al-Marwah

As regards *this Moriah*, which is pronounced by the 'Arabs as 'al-Marwah', it is the only one genuine 'Moriah' (Gen. 22:2); that is the actual place where Abraham was asked to offer his 'only son' for sacrifice. The fact is that the site of Abraham's offering his 'only son' for sacrifice is unknown to the scholars of the Bible. An objective and analytic study has been undertaken in the following lines to thrash out the real position of the theme.

THE ACTUAL SITE OF MORIAH IS UNKNOWN TO THE SCHOLARS OF THE BIBLE

Some of the quotations from the authorities on Biblical literature are being afforded hereunder, which show that the scholars of the Bible are at a loss to locate the actual place where Abraham had offered his only son for sacrifice:

(i) W.Gunther Plaut, observes in '*The Torah, A Modern Commentary*':

> The original name is obscure and the actual location unknown.[1]

(ii) L. Reed and A. H. McNeile in their article on 'Moriah' in Hastings' *Revised Dic. of Bible* assert that 'evidence is not available for locating Moriah of Abraham's time':

> Because the place of origin of the journey is not stated in Genesis, it is best to conclude that evidence is not available for locating Moriah of Abraham's time.[2]

(iii) *New Jerusalem Bible* states that the site of 'Moriah' is unknown:

> But the text speaks of a 'land of Moriah', of which the name is otherwise unattested: the site of the sacrifice is unknown.[3]

(iv) *A New Commentary on Holy Scripture* explains:

> The land of Moriah is an unknown locality.[4]

(v) *The 7th Day Adventist Bible Com.* observes:

> The name seems to have been rather uncommon.[5]

(vi) The *New Oxford Annotated Bible* asserts that the place is unknown:

> The mountain in the land of Moriah is unknown.[6]

(vii) *Dummelow's Com. on the Holy Bible* indicates the uncertainty regarding the identification of both the places:

> The land of Moriah] only mentioned again 2 Ch 3:1, 'Then Solomon began to build the house of the Lord at Jerusalem in Mount Moriah.' It is uncertain whether the two places are to be identified.[7]

(viii) The *New Bible Com.* states that there is no ground reality to certify the exact location of this place:

> *The land of Moriah* (2). There is nothing in ancient topography to certify the exact location of this place, nor yet the mountain itself,[8]

(ix) *The Wycliffe Bible Com.'s* remarks are:

> The place of the sacrifice cannot be positively_identified.[9]

(x) The *Interpreter's Dic. of Bible* asserts:

> The location is otherwise unspecified.[10]

(xi) The '*Harper's Bible Dic.* has recorded the similar views about it:

> An unidentified site in rugged terrain three day's travel from Beersheba where Abraham was to sacrifice Isaac.[11]

(xii) T. K. Cheyne observes in the *Enc. Biblica*:

> Great obscurity hangs about this name,[12]

(xiii) Rev, B. Vawter, Professor of Sacred Scripture, De Paul University, Chicago, has asserted in *A New Catholic Commentary*:

'The land of Moriah' has never been identified.[13]

(xiv) Michael Avi-Yonah has also recorded the same viewpoint in the *Encyclopedia Judaica*:

MORIAH (Heb. הירומ), an unidentified locality mentioned in the Bible.[14]

(xv) *The Encyclopedia of Judaism* has also made the similar observation:

> Moriah; a place, originally unidentified, to which God sent Abraham:[15]

(xvi) *The Jerome Bible Com.* has observed:

The 'district of Moriah' is unknown.[16]

(xvii) Peter R. Ackroyd, Samuel Davidson Professor of OT Studies, University of London, King's College, in his article 'The OT in the Making' has entered a footnote on his sentence 'So we have sanctuary legends (…) and a high place at Jebus (Jerusalem, 2 Sam. 24) subsequently rightly or wrongly identified with the site of the Jerusalem temple (I Chrn. 21-22:1)':

> The identification must remain uncertain, and indeed suspect, since the Chronicler also identifies the same site with Moriah (2 Chron. 3:1, cf. Gen. 22).[17]

(xviii) The same writer further asserts:

> What is clear, however, is that the Chronicler sees this narrative in I Chron. 21 as providing an appropriate introduction to his account of how David prepared for the building of the Temple by Solomon (I Chron. 22:2-19; 28-29:9. The intervening section, chs. 23-7, may well be a later insertion, but it too illuminates the ideas concerning David's organising of the worship of the Temple). Whereas the 2 Sam. narrative makes no link with the building of the Solomonic Temple–and this strongly suggests that the narrative originally had to do with another sacred place–the Chronicler identifies the site precisely (22:1), explains why David

could not go to Gibeon[18] where the Tabernacle was (21:29-30), and subsequently also identifies this site explicitly with the Mount Moriah of Gen. 22 (2 Chron. 3:1), an even more improbable identification.[19]

(xix) *International Standard Bible Encyclopedia* has also dilated upon the theme. It explains the site as follows:

> This land is mentioned only here Gen 22:2, and there is little to guide us in trying to identify it. A late writer (2 Chronicles 3:1) applies the name of Moriah to the mount on which Solomon's Temple was built, possibly associating it with the sacrifice of Isaac. A similar association with this mountain may have been in the mind of the writer of Genesis 22 (see 22:14), who, of course, wrote long after the events described (Driver). (...). The description could hardly apply to Jerusalem in any case, as it could not be seen "afar off" by one approaching either from the South or the West. (...). With our present knowledge we must be content to leave the question open. ***W. Ewing***[20]

No doubt it is an uninteresting practice to quote so many authorities on a theme; but it was essential to show that it is not a rare or minority opinion. That's why ample evidence has been afforded from almost every school of thought. It may also be noted that those who do not acknowledge the unidentified nature of the location of Moriah, locate it at various places and are dubiously confused. It would thus be appreciated that the objective study of most of the scholars of the Bible reveals that, according to the Bible, the location of Abraham's offering his 'only son' for sacrifice cannot be identified with exactness and certainty.

Having failed to locate the place in the written annals of history pertaining to the Bible, one should try to trace it through some ground realities or some perpetual traditions, commemorations, celebrations, rituals, sites, buildings, etc. of the relevant nations on the theme.

REFERENCES

1. W. Gunther Plaut, *The Torah, A Modern Commentary*, 146.
2. *Hastings Dic. of Bible*, Revised. Single volume edn., 674-5.

3. Henry Wansbrough, *The New Jerusalem Bible* (London: Darton, Longman & Todd Ltd., 1993), 41.
4. Charles Gore, Goudge, A Guillaume, *A New Com. on Holy Scripture*, (London: Society for Promoting Christian knowledge, 1928), 53.
5. *7th Day Adventist Bible Com.*, 1:349.
6. *The New Oxford Annotated Bible*, (NY: Oxford University Press, 1989), footnote on p. 27.
7. J. R. Dummelow, *Com. On Holy Bible*, (1956), 30.
8. *New Bible Com.*, ed. F. Davidson (Michigan: W M B. Eerdmans Publishing Co., Grand Rapids, 1953), 94.
9. *The Wycliffe Bible Com.*, Charles F. Pfeiffer (Chicago: Moody Press, 1983), 27.
10. *Interpreter's Dic. of Bible*, 3:438.
11. *Harper's Bible Dic.*, 654.
12. *Enc. Biblica*, 3:3200.
13. *A New Catholic Commentary on Holy Scripture*, 195.
14. *Enc. Judaica*, 1997 edn. CD-ROM. Version 1.0, Co, s.v. 'Moriah'.
15. *The Judaic CD ROM Reference Library* Vol. I, Contents. The Enc. of Judaism Copyright 1989-G. G. the Jerusalem Publishing House, 1993, DAVKA Corporation and the Institute for Computers in Jewish Life, s.v. 'Moriah'.
16. *The Jerome Bible Com.*, 23.
17. *The Cambridge History of the Bible*, (1970), 1:69.
18. Gibeon is the scene of the victory by David over the Philistines. Before the Temple was built the Tabernacle and brazen altar stood here (Collins Gem DB, 1974, p.195).
19. *The Cambridge History of the Bible*, 1:89.
20. *International Standard Bible Encyclopedia*, 1997, 7:924.

8

Some Questions to Trace the Actual Site of Moriah

Here are some questions, which would help in thrashing out the solution to the problem:

(1) Had Abraham any son who could genuinely have been claimed to be his 'only son' upto the age of his being circumstantially suitable to be offered for sacrifice?

(2) Did that 'only son' permanently live with his father Abraham or had he been shifted to somewhere else to be settled there? What was the name and location of that place?

(3) Is there any evidence of this 'only son's' progeny having been perpetuated at the place of his new settlement [Paran and Beersheba]?

(4) Is there any tradition related to this 'only son's' having been offered there for sacrifice by his father Abraham?

(5) Is this tradition of Abraham's offering his 'only son' for sacrifice related to any mountain in that land of Moriah?

(6) Are there any physical remains pertaining to the act of the sacrifice near this mount 'Moriah' of the Bible (al-Marwah of the Arabs)?

(7) Is there any Concrete, Physical, and Material evidence of the presence of Ishma'el, his mother Hagar, and his father Abraham at the site of this 'Moriah'?

(8) Are there any festivities having perpetually been celebrated to commemorate this great event of Abraham's offering his 'only son' for sacrifice there; and are these festivities related to some places around this 'Moriah'?

(9) Is there any other tradition among the Arabs that confirms their relation to Abraham and Ishmā'el?

(10) Is there any building or sanctuary in the vicinity of this 'al-Marwah' ('Moriah' of the Bible), whose construction has been assigned to the patriarchs Abraham and Ishmā'el; ?

(11) Are there any traces which confirm that the construction of al-Ka'bah had been undertaken by Abraham and Ishmā'el?

(12) Is there any evidence of Isaac or his progeny having ever been to some 'Moriah' to commemorate Isaac's having been offered for sacrifice?

(13) Does the Bible state where Ishmā'el and his mother Hagar had breathed their last and what is their burial site; in the way as it gives these details about Abraham, his wife Sarah, and his son Isaac; and why?

(14) Is there any established tradition regarding the burying place of Ishmā'el and his mother Hagar amongst the Arabs, who are the historically established progeny of Ishmā'el?

(15) Why has this ambiguity been created by the redactors of the Bible?

THE QUESTIONS ANSWERED

As regards the 1st question (Had Abraham any son who could genuinely have been claimed to be his 'only son' upto the age of his being circumstantially suitable to be offered for sacrifice?), Ishmā'el was Abraham's firstborn son, who remained his 'only son' for nearly fourteen years. The age of thirteen years circumstantially suits and is compatible to all considerations for his being offered for sacrifice.

As regards the 2nd question (Did that 'only son' permanently live with his father Abraham or had he been shifted to somewhere else to be settled there? What was the name and location of that place?),

Ishmā'el, together with his mother Hagar, had been shifted by his father Abraham to the wilderness of Paran in the land of Moriah, near Beersheba (Well of Seven[1]); and they had settled there permanently. Abraham himself, along with his first wife, Sarah, had settled in Hebron and Beersheba (Well of Oath[2]) in Southern Canaan. Beersheba (Well of Seven) has been explained in Supplement I and the wilderness of Paran has been discussed in detail by this writer elsewhere. As to Moriah, it has been discussed in detail in chapters V, VI, VII, and VIII of this book

As regards the 3rd question (Is there any evidence of this 'only son's' progeny having been perpetuated at the place of his new settlement [Paran and Beersheba]?), it is the factual position that Ishmā'el's progeny has been living in Makkah and other parts of Arabia since time immemorial, and is still living there. The Bible claims that Hagar and Ishmā'el had been settled by Abraham in the Wilderness of Paran and Beersheba, and both of these places have allegedly been claimed to be located in Sinai. But, even according to the Bible, there are no traces of any Ishmā'elites in Sinai. That they have been living around Makkah in Arabia, has been discussed in detail in the next chapter of this book.

As regards the 4th question (Is there any traditioin related to this 'only son' having been offered there for sacrifice by his father Abraham?), it is a ground reality that millions of pilgrims travel to Makkah in the lunar month of Dhu al-Ḥijjah to offer sacrifice in commemoration of Abraham's offering his 'only son', Ishmā'el, for sacrifice. Hundreds of millions of people offer the same sacrifice in their home-towns at the same time. This tradition has come down for centuries before the advent of Islām. Nowhere on earth is celebrated any such tradition to commemorate any so-called offering of Isaac for sacrifice by his father Abraham.

The horns of the ram offered in place of Ishmā'el remained preserved in al-Ka'bah until 64 AH/683 AD, when the Ka'bah was rebuilt by Abd Allah b. Zubayr. The *Enc. of Islām* has recorded:

The two horns of Abraham's ram did not crumble to dust until the rebuilding of the Ka'bah by 'Abd Allah b. al-Zubayr.[3]

It is recorded both in Biblical and Muslim tradition that the son going to be offered for sacrifice was ransomed with a ram. A renowned Muslim scholar and commentator of the Holy Qur'ān, Mawlānā Amīn Aḥsan Iṣlāḥī, while explaining the Quranic verse 37:107 in his magnum opus *Tadabbur-e-Qur'ān* asserts:

> Allah asserts: 'We ransomed Ishmā'el with a great sacrifice.' It indicates that We instructed Abraham to offer a ram as sacrifice in lieu of this son. And this act of offering shall perpetually be commemorated as the memorial to this great event in the form of a great ritual of offering throughout the nations of the world. It is this very offering which, being included in the rituals of pilgrimage, has been perpetuating the memory of the event since the times of Abraham and shall endure for ever till the doomsday — It should be borne in mind here that although the ritual of offering is being performed in all the religions of the world since the times of Adam, but no ritual of offering could achieve such significance, importance, expansion, and universality in the world; as Abraham's this act of offering.[4]

The event has been recorded in the Bible in the follwing words:

> And Abraham stretched forth his hand, and took the knife to slay his son. (11) And the angel of the Lord called unto him out of heaven, and said, Abraham, Abraham: and he said, Here *am* I. (12) And he said, Lay not thine hand upon the lad, neither do thou any thing upon him: for now I know that thou fearest God, seeing thou hast not withheld thy son, thine *only son* from me. (13) And Abraham lifted up his eyes, and looked, and behold behind *him* a ram caught in a thicket by his horns: and Abraham went and took the ram, and offered him up for a burnt offering in the stead of his son. (...). (15) And the angel of the Lord called unto Abraham out of heaven the second time, (16) And said, By myself have I sworn, saith the Lord, for because thou hast done this thing, and hast not withheld thy son, thine ***only son***: (17) That in blessing I will bless thee, and in multiplying I will multiply thy seed as the stars of the heaven, and as the sand which *is* upon the sea shore; and thy seed shall possess the gate

> of his enemies; (18) And in thy seed shall all the nations of the earth be blessed; because thou hast obeyed my voice.[5]

As regards the 5th question (Is this tradition of Abraham's offering his 'only son' for sacrifice related to any mountain in that land of Moriah?), it is only the mountainous region in the land of 'Moriah' at Makkah, to which the tradition of Abraham's offering his 'only son', Ishmā'el, for sacrifice is related. The Arabic word for Moriah (î₀˝éں) is Marwah (î˝₀ں). In Hebrew[6] 'Moriah' is composed of five letters, whereas 'Marwah' is composed of four letters. The first and the last letters, i.e., 'Meem' (M) and 'He' (H) are common in both the words. The middle letters 'R' [˝] (Res) and 'W' [₀] (Waw) are resembling letters in Hebrew, as can be appreciated through observing them. They are often interchanged by the scribes. As far as the letter 'Yodh' [é] or 'Y' is concerned, it is a very small letter in Hebrew alphabet and is likely to be omitted or inserted due to some negligence or misunderstanding of a scribe. It is quite probable that the actual word may have been 'Marwah', which would have been mistakenly recorded as 'Moriah' in the Bible by some scribe, because Moriah/Marwah was not a commonly used word in the Biblical literature. There can be another possibility: the difference in 'Moriah' and 'Marwah' may be the variations of pronunciation between the Arabic language and the Hebrew language due to the change of the geographic conditions; as is common in so many cases. A construing reader might be aware of some instances of such cases.

As regards the 6th question (Are there any physical remains pertaining to the act of the sacrifice near this Mount 'Moriah' of the Bible — al-Marwah of the Arab tradition?), it is interesting to note that the horns of the ram which was offered in the stead of Ishmā'el had been preserved in the Ka'bah and they remained there until 64 AH/ AD 683. Wensinck and Jomier have reported in the *Enc. of Islam* in their article on the 'Ka'bah' that at the time of the conquest of Makkah in 8/629:

> All the pagan trappings which had adhered to the Ka'ba were now thrust aside. (…). The two horns of Abraham's ram did not crumble to dust until the rebuilding of the Ka'ba by 'Abd Allāh b. Zubayr.[7]

As regards the 7th question (Is there any Concrete, Physical, and Material evidence of the presence of Ishmā'el, his mother Hagar, and his father Abraham at the site of this 'Moriah'?), there exists a lot of such evidence. There exist the Black Stone, the Mi'jan, Maqām Ibrāhīm, the well of Zamzam, and the Graves of Hagar and Ishmā'el in Ḥaṭīm in close vicinity of the Ka'bah.

About the *'Black Stone'*, which is claimed to have been fixed at a corner of the Ka'bah by the patriarchs, the *Encyclopaedia of Religion* states:

> The Black stone is of unknown pre-Islamic origin, possibly meteoric.[8]

There is the Mi'jan in very close vicinity of the Ka'bah. A.J. Wensinck has provided the following details about it:

> (...); a depression in it [the Ka'bah] just opposite the door has still to be mentioned; it is called *al-mi'djan* 'the trough'; according to legend, Ibrahim and Isma'il here mixed the mortar used in building the Ka'bah. [9]

There is the Maqām Ibrāhīm, about which 'The *Enc. of Religion*' explains:

> Near the Ka'bah stands a gilded glass case (replacing an earlier simple wooden framework) that contains a stone marking the station of Ibrahim (Abraham). This stone is said to have miraculously preserved the footprint of Ibrahim, Who stood on it in order to complete the construction of an earlier Ka'bah: it is, as it were, the builder's mark.[10]

A.J. Wensinck has explained the Maqām Ibrāhīm as follows:

> Between this archway [*al-Ḥaṭim*] and the facade (N.E.) is a little building with a small dome, the *makam Ibrahim*. In it is kept a stone bearing the prints of two human feet. The patriarch Ibrahim, father of Isma'il, is said to have stood on his feet when building the Ka'bah and the marks of his feet were miraculously preserved.[11]

There is *The well of Zamzam*, which stands quite close to the Ka'bah. '*The Enc. of Religion*', although arbitrarily names it as a myth, explains:

> Opposite the corner of the Black Stone is a small building housing the sacred well of Zamzam, from which pilgrims drink water at the conclusion of their circumambulations and prayers. Its origin is mythically associated with Hajar (Hagar) and Ismail (Ishmael), for whom God provided water in this desert place after commanding Ibrahim to abandon mother and child and promising to care for them in his place.[12]

Then there are the Graves of Hagar and Ishmā'el in Ḥaṭīm. A. J. Wensinck explaining the rituals and places of the Islāmic Pilgrimage in its article on the 'Ka'bah' in '*The Enc. of Islam*' has given the following details about it:

> Opposite the north-west wall, but not connected with it, is a semi-circular wall (*al-ḥaṭim*) (...). The semi-circular space between the *hatim* and the Ka'bah enjoys an especial consideration, because for a time it belonged to the Ka'bah; (...). The space bears the name *al-hidjr* or *hidjr Isma'il* [lap of Ishma'el]. Here are said to be the graves of the patriarch [Isma'il] and his mother Hagar.[13]

As regards the 8th question (Are there any festivities having perpetually been celebrated to commemorate this great event of Abraham's offering his 'only son' for sacrifice there; and are these festivities related to some places around this 'Moriah'?), there have been a number of festivities related to this offering having perpetually been celebrated by the Arabs centuries before the advent of Islām. These festivities are related to a number of places around this 'Moriah'. There are the seven rounds of running between 'al-Ṣafā' and 'al-Marwah' called sa'y. This sa'y is performed by millions of pilgrims undertaking Ḥajj in the month of Dhū al-Ḥijjah or performing 'Umrah the whole year through. It is performed to commemorate the similar running by Hagar in search of water for her son Ishmā'el. The ritual of sa'y so meticulously depicts and retains the event that in the course of their sa'y the pilgrims resort to jogging at a certain space, marked with green lights these days, where Hagar had resorted to it. It is in the declivity of the Mas'ā where Hagar had to run fast, because she could not see his son in that slope.[14] Then there is the offering for sacrifice of goats, sheep, rams, camels, etc. on the festival of 'Eid al-Aḍḥā' by hundreds of millions of Muslims throughout the world and by millions of Muslim pilgrims at Makkah during the days of Ḥajj. Again there is the water of 'Zamzam' or 'Beersheba' (Well of Seven) taken by the pilgrims as a sacred drink. It is the very spring which gushed out for the relief of Ishmā'el in that waterless terrain. It wonderfully supplies the water for a large population the whole year through and is also taken home by the millions of pilgrims throughout the world in large quantities as souvenir. Then again there is a ritual of the Islāmic Pilgrimage called 'Talbiyah'. According to it the pilgrims, when put on the proper uniform of the Pilgrimage called 'Iḥrām', begin to assert this 'Talbiyah' until they enter into the 'Holy Mosque':

> Here I am, O Allah, here I am; here I am, there is no associate to You, here I am; verily all the praise, and all the grace, and all the kingdom belong to You, there is no partner to You.

It is to commemorate the alacrity (quickness and readiness) of Abraham to offer his only son for sacrifice when God tempted him. When God called him, he said, 'Behold, *here* I *am*'[15] .

As regards the 9th question (Is there any other tradition among the Arabs that confirms their relation to Abraham and Ishmā'el?), there does exist the tradition of circumcision which had been strictly observed amongst the Arabs to represent the tradition of their ancestors, Abraham and Ishmā'el. Islām extended the continuation of this tradition amongst its followers in the same way as it has been observed amongst the Jews as a sign of Abraham's covenant. Had the Arabs not been the descendants of Abraham through his son Ishmā'el, there had been no question of their observing this tradition and their attributing it to Abraham and Ishmā'el. It is not without significance that the *Enc. Biblica* has observed that the rite of circumcision may have been the typification of the tradition of offering the firstborn:

> (...), and, indeed, the evidence goes to show that in exceptional cases the offering was actually made. However, just as the first-fruits were offered as a part of the whole, it is conceivable that originally the rite of circumcision was instituted upon the same principle to typify the offering of the firstborn.[16]

Flavius Josephus has also observed in his 'Antiquities' (written more than five hundred years before the advent of Islām) that the rite of *circumcision* had been exercised amongst the Arabians to commemorate the *circumcision* of the founder of their nation, Ishmā'el:

> And they circumcised him upon the eighth day. And from that time the Jews continue the custom of circumcising their sons within that number of days. *But as for the Arabians*, they circumcise after the thirteenth year, *because Ismael, the founder of their nation*, who was born to Abraham of the concubine, was circumcised at that age; [17]

As regards the 10th question (Is there any building or sanctuary in the vicinity of this 'al-Marwah' ['Moriah' of the Bible], whose construction has been assigned to the patriarchs, Abraham and Ishmā'el?), there is the sanctuary of 'al-Ka'bah' in the vicinity of this 'al-Marwah' or 'Moriah', whose construction has been assigned to the patriarchs, Abraham and Ishmā'el; and there is reasonable evidence of the perpetuity of this tradition. The renowned translator of the Qur'ān into English, George Sale, has recorded in his 'The Preliminary Discourse' the existence of this sanctuary of 'al-Ka'bah' at Makkah as follows:

> The temple of Mecca was a place of worship, and in singular veneration with the Arabs from great antiquity, and many centuries before Mohammed (...) the Mohammedans are generally persuaded that the Caaba (...) was rebuilt by Abraham and Ismael, at God's command, (...). After this edifice had undergone several reparations, it was a few years after the birth of Mohammed, rebuilt by the Koreish on the old foundation, (...). Before we leave the temple of Mecca, two or three particulars deserve further notice. One is the celebrated black stone, which is set in silver, and fixed in the south-east corner of the Caaba, (...). Another thing observable in this temple is the stone in Abraham's place, wherein they pretend to show his footsteps, telling us he stood on it when he built the Caaba, and that it served him for scaffold, (...). The last thing I shall take notice of the temple is the well Zem-zem, on the east side of the Caaba,

(...). The Mohammedans are persuaded that it is the very spring which gushed out for the relief of Ismael, when Hagar his mother wandered with him in the desert, and some pretend it was so named from her calling to him, when she spied it, in the Egyptian tongue, Zem, zem, that is, 'Stay, stay,' [18]

Professor Palmer, the well known translator of the Qur'ān into the English language, says in his introduction to the Qur'ān:

The traditions of Abraham the father of their race and the founder of Muhammad's own religion, as he always declared him to be, no doubt gave the ancient temple a peculiar sanctity in the Prophet's eyes, and although he had first settled upon Jerusalem as his Qiblah, he afterwards reverted to the Kaabah itself. Here, then, Muhammad found a shrine, to which, as well as at which, devotion had been paid from time immemorial; it was one thing which the scattered Arabian nation had in common—the one thing which gave them even the shadow of a national feeling; and to have dreamed of abolishing it, or even of diminishing the honours paid to it, would have been madness and ruin to his enterprise. He therefore did the next best thing, he cleared it of idols and dedicated it to the service of God.[19]

Some more evidence is being noted below which testifies the existence of al-Ka'bah at Makkah from times immemorial. C.E. Bosworth attests the antiquity of al-Ka'bah in *Enc. Americana* in the following words:

The Kaaba was almost certainly an important shrine of a well attested Semitic pattern, in pre-Islamic times. It is not clear when it was first associated with the rites of the Pilgrimage, which itself must be of pre-Islamic origin. Muslim tradition traces it to Abraham and Ishmael. The Prophet Mohammed cleansed the Kaaba of its idols and its pagan features in 630.[20]

Edward J. Jurji asserts in *Colliers Encyclopedia* that the Quraysh were the custodians of al-Ka'bah and preservers of the Ishmā'elite tradition:

As custodians of Kaaba and preservers of the Ishmaelite tradition, the Quraysh tribe presided over its pagan worship until Mohammed appropriated it for his new faith, [21]

The *Encyclopedia of Religion* states that the Ka'bah had undoubtedly existed for several centuries before the birth of Muḥammad:

> The historical origin of the Ka'bah is uncertain, but it had undoubtedly existed for several centuries before the birth of Muhammad (c. 570 CE). By his time it was the principal religious shrine of central Arabia and, located at the centre of a sacred territory (haram), had the characteristic of a Semitic sanctuary.[22]

The renowned Egyptian geographer of the ancient times, Claudius Ptolemaeus (commonly known as Ptolemy, c. 90-168 AD) has also mentioned the existence of a temple near Makkah, for which he uses the word 'Macoraba':

> It is to be noted that Ptolemy (*Geography*, vi.7) in place of Mecca mentions Macoraba, which is probably to be interpreted, as does Glaser, as the South Arabian or Ethiopic *mikrāb*, 'temple'. From this one may conclude that the Ka'ba already existed in the second century A. D.[23]

Shorter Enc. of Islam has noted some other evidence to it as well:

> The information available regarding the distribution of the offices among the sons of Ḳuṣaiy shows that the worship of the sanctuary had developed into a carefully regulated cult several generations before Muḥammad.[24]
>
> The Ka'ba had offerings dedicated to it in the heathen as well as the Muslim period. Al-Azraḳī devotes a detailed chapter to this subject (ed. Wustenfeld, p. 155 *sqq.*).[25]

As regards the 11th question (Are there any traces which confirm that the construction of al-Ka'bah had been undertaken by Abraham and Ishmā'el?), there had been a depression in the Maṭāf just opposite the door of the Ka'bah where Ishmā'el and Abraham mixed the mortar used in building the Ka'bah. The *Enc. of Islām* has recorded it as follows:

> The pavement on which the *ṭawāf* is performed is called *maṭāf*; a depression in it just opposite the door has still to be mentioned; it is called *al-mi'djan* 'the trough'; according to legend, Ibrāhim

and Ismā'il [q.v.] here mixed the mortar used in building the Ka'ba.[26]

Then there is the Maqām Ibrāhīm, which is another evidence of the Ka'bah having been built by Abraham. The *Enc. of Islām* explains:

> Between this archway and the facade (N.E.) is a little building with a small dome, the *maḳām Ibrāhīm*. In it is kept a stone bearing the prints of two human feet. The patriarch Ibrāhīm, father of Ismā'il, is said to have stood on this stone when building the Ka'ba and the marks of his feet were miraculously preserved.[27]

As regards the 12th question (Is there any evidence of Isaac or his progeny having ever been to some 'Moriah' to commemorate Isaac's having been offered for sacrifice?), there is neither in the Bible or in the traditions of the Arabs any evidence of Isaac having ever been to some 'Moriah'; nor is there any evidence in the Bible or the annals of history in favour of the progeny of Isaac having frequented to 'Moriah' for offering sacrifices and performing any pilgrimage. On the other hand this 'Marwah' is a celebrated spot of offering sacrifice by the pre-Islāmic Arabian tribes from the times immemorial and subsequently by the whole of the Muslim world, in memory of Abraham's offering his 'only son' for sacrifice. Of course, the descendents of Ishmā'el, the Arabs, have been observing the ritual centuries rather millennia before Islām, following their Ancestor's offerings.

As regards the 13th question (Does the Bible state where Ishmā'el and his mother Hagar had breathed their last and what is their burial site; in the manner as it gives these details about Abraham, his wife Sarah, and his son Isaac; and why?), it is interesting to note that the Bible is totally silent about Ishmā'el and Hagar's burying place; whereas it states categorically that the cave of Macphelah at Hebron in Canaan was the burial ground of Abraham[28], his wife Sarah[29], and his son Isaac[30]. As to the question 'why', it can only be assumed that it was due to the disregard, disinterest, unconcern, indifference, and apathy, rather rivalry and jealousy, of the Israelites towards their brethren or cousins, Ishmā'elites.

As regards the 14th question (Is there any established tradition regarding the burying place of Ishmā'el and his mother Hagar amongst the Arabs — who are the historically established progeny of Ishmā'el?), the answer is a positive 'Yes'. A. J. Wensinck and J. Jomier in their article on 'Ka'ba' in the '*Enc. of Islām*' write:

> The space (*al-ḥaṭim*) bears the name *al-ḥidjr* or *ḥidjr Isma'il.* Here are said to be the graves of the patriarch and his mother Hagar.[31]

The *New Standard Encyclopaedia* observes:

Ishmael Son of Abraham and Hagar. He was exiled with his mother to the wilderness on account of Sarah's jealousy of him. He married an Egyptian, was famed as an archer and was buried in Mecca. Mahomet claimed him as an ancestor.[32]

As regards the 15th question (Why has this ambiguity been created by the redactors of the Bible?), the answer is quite clear. It is merely because they wanted to attach reverence and respect to their forefather Isaac. The Chronicler forged for them the basis for this ambition through arbitrarily attributing the name of 'Moriah' to the site of the threshing floor of Araunah the Jebusite. This ambiguity would never have gained ground, had the Chronicler not fabricated and imposed it in his 'Chronicles' to attach sanctity to the Solomon's Temple. It is interesting to note that the 'Chronicles' had long been a non-canonical and rejected book.[33] There is another aspect of this theme. In fact Abraham's offering cannot be treated as a merit for the son, if the son is not taken into confidence for the task. Isaac did not know that he was going to be offered even to the last momet. That's why he asks his father Abraham, 'Behold the fire and the wood: but where is the lamb for a burnt offering?[34] ' Even then, Abraham did not think it advisable to disclose to him that it was him whom he was going to offer for the sacrifice; and rather says, 'My son, God will provide himself a lamb for a burnt offering.[35] ' Thus the act of offering could only have been to the credit of Abraham who was going to be 'tempted' by God; and no credit could have been attributed to Isaac who had been totally ignorant of his going to be offered for sacrifice by his father. But, as regards Ishmā'el, he was not only taken into full confidence by his father Abraham, but he willingly endorsed the idea, surrendered to the will of God, and offered himself for sacrifice at the hands of his father. The Qur'ān records the event as follows:

[illegible]

Said they, 'Build for him [Abraham] a pyre, and throw him into the flaming hell!' They desired to plot against him, but we made them inferior. Said he, 'Verily, I am going to my Lord, He will guide me. My Lord! Grant me (a son), one of the righteous;' and we gave him glad tidings of a clement and patient boy. And when he reached the age to work with him, he said, 'O my boy! Verily, I have seen in a dream that I should sacrifice thee[36] , look then what thou seest right.' Said he, 'O my sire! Do what thou art bidden; thou wilt find me, if please God, one of the patient!' And when they were resigned, and Abraham had thrown him down upon his forehead, we called to him, 'O Abraham! Thou hast verified the vision; verily, thus do we reward those who do well. This is surely an obvious trial.' And we ransomed him with a mighty victim; and we left for him amongst posterity, 'Peace upon Abraham; thus do we reward those who do well; verily, he was of our servants who believe!' And we gave him glad tidings of Isaac, a prophet among the righteous; and we blessed him and Isaac; – of their seed is one who does well, and one who obviously wrongs himself.[37]

References

1. Entry 875, p. 18: 'Jà˝ *be-ayr*; from 874; a *pit*; espec. a *well*.' Entry **874, p. 18: 'Jà˝ ba'ar**, *baw-ar* ; a prim. Root; to dig'; + Entry 7650, p. 112: '**ùJ shaba** *shaw-bah* ; a prim. Root; to *seven* oneself, i.e. *swear* (as if by repeating a declaration seven times).' (*A Concise Dic. of the words in The Heb. Bible* by J. Strong, NY: The Methodist Book Concern, 1984)
2. **Beer Sheba**. 'ùJ Jà˝ *be-ayr' sheh-bah*; from 875 and 7651 (in the

sense of 7650); *well of an oath.* : —adjure, charge (by an oath, with an oath), take an oath.' (J. Strong's Dic. of Heb. B, 1984, Entry 884; p.18).

3. *The Enc of Islam New Edition* ed. E. Van Donzel, B. Lewis and ch. Pellat, C. E. Bosworth (Leiden: E. J. Brill, 1978), 4:320.
4. Mawlānā Amīn Aḥsan Iṣlāḥī, 37:107 *Tadabbur-e-Qur'ān*, (Lahore: Faran Foundation, 1977), 5:485.
5. Gen. 22:11-18 KJV.
6. It may be noted that the Hebrew language is written from right to left like the script of her other sister Semitic languages (Syriac, Aramaic, Arabic, etc.).
7. *Enc. of Islam, New (1997) edn.*, s.v. 'Ka'ba', 4:320.
8. *The Enc. of Religion* (NY: Macmillan Publg. Co, 1987), 8:225,26.
9. *Enc. of Islam, New (1997) edn.*, s.v. 'Ka'ba', 4:318-20.
10. *The Enc. of Religion* (NY: Macmillan Publg. Co, 1987), 8:225,26.
11. *Enc. of Islam, New (1997) edn.*, s.v. 'Ka'ba', 4:318-20.
12. *The Enc. of Religion* (NY: Macmillan Publg. Co, 1987), 8:225,26.
13. *Enc. of Islam, New (1997) edn.*, s.v. 'Ka'ba' 4:318-20.
14. For a detailed refernce see pp 164-67 of this book.
15. Gen. 22:1 KJV.
16. *Encyclopaedia Biblica*, 2:1525-6.
17. Flavius Josephus, *Antiquities*, Book I, Ch. xii: 2, 4, p.41.
18. George Sale, '*The Preliminary Discourse*' to the 'ALKORAN OF MOHAMMED' (London: Frederick Warne & Co., n.d.), 90.
19. The QUR'ĀN, tr. E. H. Palmer (Delhi: Motilal Banarsidass, 1988), liii.
20. *The Enc. Americana International edn.* in 30 Vols. (Danbury, Connecticut: Grolier Incorporated, 1987), 16:254.
21. *Colliers Enc.* In 24 Vols. (NY: 1995), 13:695.
22. *The Enc. of Religion*, 8:225-6.
23. H.A.R. Gibb and J.H. Krammers, *Concise Enc. Of Islam* (Leiden: Brill Academic Publishers, Inc. 2001), s.v. 'Ka'ba', 193.
24. *Concise Enc. Of Islam*, 193.

25. *Concise Enc. Of Islam,* 193.
26. *The Enc. of Islam*, 4:318.
27. *The Enc. of Islām*, 4:318.
28. Gen. 25:9-10.
29. Gen. 25:10.
30. Gen. 49:29-30.
31. *The Enc. of Islām*, 4:318.
32. *The New Standard Enc. and World Atlas* (London: Odhams Press Ltd,, W. C. 2, 1932), 699.
33. See App. III.
34. Gen. 22:7 KJV.
35. Gen. 22:8 KJV.
36. The translator, Palmer, has inserted a footnote here as: 'The Mohammadan theory is that it was Ishmā'el and not Isaac who was taken as a sacrifice.'
37. The Qur'ān, Sūrah al-Ṣāffāt 37:95-113; as Tr. by E. H. Palmer (Delhi: Motilal Banarsidass, 1988), 171-2.

9

Makkah and Arabia As the House of the Progeny of Ishma‘el

Ishmā‘el's progeny has been living in *Makkah* and other parts of Arabia since time immemorial, and is still living there. The Bible claims that Hagar and Ishmā‘el had been settled by Abraham in the Wilderness of *Pārān* and *Beersheba*, both of which have been claimed to have located in *Sinai*. But, even according to the Bible, there are no traces of any Ishmā‘elites in *Sinai*. 'The *New English Bible*' has recorded:

> Ishma‘el's sons inhabited the land from Havilah to Shur, which is east of Egypt on the way to Asshur, having settled to the east of his brothers.[1]

'*King James Version*' has recorded the theme in the following words:

> And they [Ishmā‘el's sons] dwelt from Havilah unto Shur, that is before Egypt, as thou goest toward Assyria and he died in the presence of all his brethren.[2]

Almost all the translations and versions of the Bible have recorded the same statement about the settlement of the Ishmā‘eliṭes. There is no other statement about their settlement.

It means that, according to the Bible, the progeny of Ishmā‘el had settled in the area 'from Havilah unto Shūr'. To determine the dwelling place of the progeny of Ishmā'el, the exact location of 'Havilah' and 'Shūr' is to be explored. The word 'Havilah' was used for the land of Yemen and 'Shūr' was situated somewhere near the Gulf of 'Aqabah, at the north-eastern end of the Red Sea. It can thus be deduced that according the Bible the progeny of Ishmā'el had settled in the area of Al-Hijāz, which is a strip of land in the Western Arabia North of Yemen.

A brief account of the sites of Havilah and Shūr has been afforded hereunder:

Havilah

As far as 'Havilah' is concerned, it is the name of South Arabia or 'Yemen', which, in the ancient days was named 'Arabia Felix', as recorded by the renowned geographer of Alexandria, Ptolemy (d. 140 AD). Easton's BD asserts:

> A district in Arabia-Felix[3]. (...). It is the opinion of Kalisch, however, that Havilah 'in both instances, designates the same country, extending at least from the Persian to the Arabian Gulf, and on account of its vast extent easily divided into two distinct parts.' This opinion may be well vindicated. [4]

W. Smith has also expressed almost similar views in his BD:

> A district in Arabia Felix, Gen. 10:7, named from the second son of Cush; probably the district of Kualan, in the northwestern part of Yemen.[5]

Encyclopedia Judaica has noted that one of Havilah's location is in South Arabia:

> The latter Havilah, the son of Joktan, apparently stands for a locality in South Arabia as do Hadoram (Gen. 10:27), Sheba (Gen. 10:28), and Ophir (Gen. 10:29).[6]

The Jewish Encyclopedia has explained as below:

> HAVILAH: Name of a district, or districts, in Arabia. (...); the Ishmaelites are also placed in the same locality (Gen. xxv.18), (...). In Gen. x.29 and I Chron. i.23, Havilah is a son of Joktan, associated with Sheba and Ophir in the southern portion of the

> peninsula. (...). Havilah was identified by Bochart Niebuhr with Khaulan in Tehamah, between Mecca and Sana;[7]

All the above data make it quite clear that Havilah stands for Yemen, which is situated in the south-west of the Arabian Peninsula.

Shūr

'Shūr' can be located somewhere near the Gulf of 'Aqabah, i.e. north-eastern end of the Red Sea. W. Smith has explained it as follows:

> Shur may have been a fortified town east of the ancient head of the Red Sea; and from its being spoken of as a limit, it was probably the last Arabian town before entering Egypt.[8]

Most of the authorities locate it in *Sinai* to the SE of the Gulf of Suez. Whatever the case may be, it can safely be said that *Shūr* or the *Wilderness of Shūr* is situated somewhere outside the SW corner of Canaan, which may be in the vicinity of the NW corner of Arabia.

It means that, according to the Bible, Ishmā'el's descendants had settled in Arabia between *Shūr* (north western corner of Arabia) and *Havilah* (southern coast land of Arabia, i.e., *Yemen* and *Ḥaḍramawt*), which, according to the Arabs, is the region of al-Ḥijāz. The cities of *Makkah*, al-Madīnah, and Ṭāyef are also situated in this al- Ḥijāz. Most of the Ishmā'elite tribes (Arabs) had settled in and around this al-Ḥijāz. It has been noted above that, according to the Bible, Hagar and Ishmā'el had been settled by Abraham in the Wilderness of *Pārān* and *Beersheba*. It requires that the 'Wilderness of Pārān and Beersheba concerning Hagar and Ishmā'el, and the land of Moriah as well', must be located in *Arabia* and not in *Sinai*.

That most of the Arabs are the descendants of Ishmā'el, is a universally acknowledged historical fact and needs not to be discussed in detail. A few lines are reproduced below from the 'Antiquities' of Josephus:

> And they circumcised him upon the eighth day. And from that time the Jews continue the custom of circumcising their sons within that number of days. *But as for the Arabians,* they circumcise after the thirteenth year[9], *because Ismael, the founder*

of their nation, who was born to Abraham of the concubine, was circumcised at that age; (....). Of this wife were born to Ismael twelve sons; Nabaioth[10], Kedar[11], Abdeel[12], Mabsam [or Mibsam], Idumas[13], Masmaos[14], Massaos[15], Chadad[16], Theman[17], Jetur, Naphesus[18], Cadmas[19]. These inhabited all the country from Euphrates to the Red Sea, and called it Nabatene. They are an Arabian nation and name their tribes from these, both because of their own virtue, and because of the dignity of Abraham their father.[20]

The Book of Jubilees has also recorded that the progeny of Ishmā'el is of Arabian origin. Here is an excerpt to this effect:

And Ishma'el and his sons, and the sons of Keturah, and their sons, went together and dwelt from Paran to the entering of Babylon in all the land which is towards the East facing the desert. And these mingled with each other, and their name was called Arabs, and Ishma'elites.[21]

Lawrance Boadt, while explaining Gen 25:1-18, writes:

These names also represent a variety of Arabian Tribes.[22]

New Jerusalem Bible asserts:

Ishmael's descendents are the North Arabian tribes.[23]

McKenzie writes in his DB:

He is the ancestor of a number of Arabian tribes.[24]

It has also been abundantly recorded in the legends and poetry of the Arabs. The 'Quraysh' was one of the most important tribes of Ishmā'el's progeny from the line of his second son Kedār; and it had been living in *Makkah* for centuries, rather millennia, before the advent of Islām.

References

1. Gen. 25:18 NEB.
2. Gen. 25:18 KJV.
3. 'Arabia Felix' is the classical name of SW Arabia or the 'Yemen'. J. A, Thompson explains in the *Interpreter's Dic. of Bible*, 1:179-80:

Classical geographers, following Ptolemy (2nd century A.D.), divided the country into three parts: [1] Arabia Patrea, whose main city was Petra and which included Sinai,, Edom, Moab, and E. Trans-Jordan; [2] Arabia Deserta, the Syrian Desert; and [3] Arabia Felix, 'Fortunate Arabia,' the S portion.

4. *Easton's 1897 Bible Dic.* in 'Power Bible' CD. ROM Version.
5. *W. Smith's Bible Dic.*, 235.
6. *Enc. Judaica*, CD-ROM Version.
7. *The Jewish Enc.*, 6:266.
8. *W. Smith's Bible Dic.*, 627.
9. It may be noted here that the writer of this '*Antiquities*', Flavius Josephus (c.37-c.100), had died more than five centuries before the advent of Islām. F. L. Cross writes in his *Oxford Dic. of the Christian Church* (London: Oxford University Press, 1974), 759:

   He brought out c. 94 his second great work, the 'Antiquities of the Jews', the 20 books of which trace the history of the Jews from the creation of the world to the beginning of the Jewish war.

   It shows that his observation '*But as for the Arabians,* they circumcise after the thirteenth year', if it be so, might have been true regarding the pre-Islāmic Arabs, whereas the Muslims generally get their children circumcised in their early days, preferably on the seventh day, as the Propohet of Islām had got his grand children, al-Ḥasan and al-Ḥusayn circumcised on the 7th day of their birth (Ḥākim and al-Bayhiquī reported by 'Ā'ishah) .
10. Nabaioth was the firstborn of Ishmā'el and may be the ancestor of the Nabatians of Petrea, after whom the northern Arabia was named 'Arabia Petrea' by the ancient geographers like Ptolemy.
11. Kedar was the ancestor of the great Arabian tribe of Quraysh, to whom belonged the Prophet of Islām. (See The Jewish Enc. n.d., 7:462, s.v. 'Kedar')
12. 'Abdeel' means 'the slave of God'; which, in Arabic, is 'Abd Allah'; but the Bible has named it as 'Ad-beel' (Gen. 25:13 KJV), which might have been a scribal mistake.
13. Which, according to the Bible, is 'Dumah' (Gen. 25:14 KJV); after whom was named the famous Arabian town of 'Dūmat al-Jandal', which was besieged by the Prophet of Islām himself during the adventure of 'Tabūk'.

14. Which, in the Bible, is 'Mish-ma' (Gen. 25:14 KJV).
15. Which, in the Bible, is 'Mas-sa' (Gen. 25:14 KJV).
16. Which, in the Bible, is 'Ha-dar' (Gen. 25:15 KJV).
17. Which, in the Bible, is 'Te-ma' (Gen. 25:15 KJV).
18. Which, in the Bible, is 'Na'-phish' (Gen. 25:15 KJV).
19. Which, in the Bible, is 'Ke-de-mah' (Gen. 25:15 KJV).
20. Flavius, *Antiquities*, Book I, Ch. xii: 2, 4, p. 41.
21. *The Apocrypha and Pseudepigrapha of the OT*, Volume II: *Pseudepigrapha*, ed. Dr. R. H. Charles (Oxford: at the Clarendon Press, 1968), 43.
22. *International BC*, Ed. William R. Farmer (Bangalore: TPI, 2004), 431.
23. Footnote 'b' on Gen 25:18 *New Jerusalem Bible*, p. 47.
24. McKenzie, *Dic. of Bible*, 1984, s.v. 'Ishmael', p. 403.

10

The Mention of the Offering of Sacrifices at Makkah
In the Book of Isaiah

This prophecy recorded in chapter LX of the Book of Isaiah[1] of the Bible is reproduced below. A renowned Muslim scholar, Qāḍī Sulaymān Manṣūrpuri, has quoted this prophecy in his magnum opus *Raḥmatulli'l-'Ālamīn* and has explained it in a few lines there.[2] It is pertinent to undertake a thorough study of it. Exhaustive footnotes having sufficient references and relevant excerpts have been afforded on the spot, so that it may not be said that the evidence is scanty. They are to be carefully studied along with the text to appreciate the significance of the observations recorded at the end of the passage. In some cases they may not be directly relevant to the theme, but they are important to make the concept clear. It would be advisable that after initially going through the whole of this theme, the verses alongwith their footnotes be studied once again. It would thus be appreciated that the conclusions drawn from the verses are absolutely pertinent:

[3] Arise, shine; for thy light is come[4], and the glory of the Lord
is risen upon thee. (2) For, behold, the darkness shall cover the earth,
and gross darkness the people; but the Lord shall arise upon thee,
and his glory shall be seen upon thee. (3) And the gentiles[5] shall
come to thy light[6], and kings[7] to the brightness of thy rising.[8] (4)
Lift up thine eyes round about, and see: all they gather themselves
together, they come to thee[9]; thy sons shall come from afar, and thy

daughters shall be nursed at *thy* side.[10] (5) Then thou shalt see, and flow together, and thine heart shall *fear, and be enlarged* [NKJV translates these italicized words as: 'swell with joy']; because the abundance of the sea shall be converted unto thee,[11] the forces of the Gentiles shall come unto thee. (6) The multitude of camels[12] shall cover thee, the dromedaries [young camels] of Midian[13] and Ephah[14]; all they from Sheba[15] shall come; they shall bring gold and incense and they shall shew forth the praises of the Lord. (7) All[16] the flocks of Kedar shall be gathered together unto thee, the rams of Nebaioth[17] shall minister[18] unto thee; they shall come up with acceptance[19] on mine altar,[20] and I will glorify the house of my glory.[21] (8) Who *are* these *that* fly as a cloud[22], and as the doves to their windows? (9) Surely the islands shall wait for me, and the ships of Tarshish[23] first, to bring thy sons from far, (...). (11) Therefore thy gates shall be open continually; they shall not be shut day nor night[24]; that *men* may bring unto thee the forces of the Gentiles, and *that* their kings *may* be brought. (12) For the nation and kingdom that will not serve thee shall perish; yea, those nations shall be utterly wasted.[25] (...). (14) The sons also of them that afflicted thee shall come bending unto thee; and all they that despised thee shall bow themselves down at the soles of thy feet; and they shall call thee, The city of the Lord, The Zion[26] of the Holy One of Israel.[27] (15) Whereas thou hast been forsaken[28] and hated, so that no man went through *thee*, I will make thee an eternal excellence, a joy of many generations[29]. (...). (18) Violence shall no more be heard in thy land, wasting nor destruction within thy borders; but thou shalt call thy walls Salvation, and thy gates Praise. (...). (20) Thy sun shall no more go down [30]; neither shall thy moon withdraw itself; for the Lord shall be thine everlasting light, and the days of thy mourning shall be ended. (21) Thy people also shall be all righteous; they shall inherit the land forever, the branch of my planting[31], the work of my hands, that I may be glorified. [32]

Here are some observations which would help the reader to appreciate the real status of the above verses and their implications:

1. Changes have been made in the above passage by the redactors of the Bible, as is evident from the New Jerusalem

Bible's observation on verse 12 and 14 reproduced in the relevant footnotes above. Each and every verse, therefore, should be considered on its own merit.

2. Most of the commentators of the Bible attach these verses to the rebuilding of the Solomon's Temple that is generally called the 'Second Temple' or the 'Temple of Zerubbabel'.[33] (A brief account of the history of the 'Solomon's Temple' has been afforded under 'Appendix IV' at the end of this book.)

3. Most of the scholars of the Bible hold that according to the above passage this 'Second Temple' had to be more magnificent than the 'First One'[34]. The New Oxford Annotated Bible remarks: 'The new Jerusalem will surpass Solomon's city in beauty and tranquillity.[35]' The actual position is quite contrary to it. McKenzie's *Dic. of Bible* explains:

It [The Second Temple] was no doubt of the same dimensions and structure as the temple of Solomon but much inferior in the richness of its decorations (Ezr 3:12; Hg 2:3).[36]

W. Smith's *Dic. of Bible* asserts:

> From these dimensions we gather that if the priests and Levites and elders of families were disconsolate [i.e. unhappy, downcast] at seeing how much more sumptuous [i.e. lavish, magnificent, costly] the old temple was than the one which on account of their poverty they had hardly been able to erect, Ezra 3:12, it certainly was not because it was smaller; but it may have been that the carving and the gold and the other ornaments of Solomon's temple far surpassed this, and the pillars of the portico [i.e. covered walk; row of columns] and the veils may all have been far more splendid; so also probably were the vessels; and all this is what a Jew would mourn over far more than mere architectural splendor.[37]

R. J. McKelvey explains, 'but even the foundations showed that it [the Second Temple] would be inferior to Solomon's Temple.'[38] *The 7th Day Adventist Bible Dic.* explains that it was of poorer construction as compared to the Solomon's Temple.[39] Prof. Dr George A. Barton asserts:

> The dimensions of the building were probably the same as those of Solomon's Temple, though the edifice was apparently at first lacking in ornament. It was probably because the building was less ornate that the old men who had seen the former Temple wept at the sight of its successor.[40]

4. If someone undertakes a sincere and objective analytic study to ascertain the implications and purport of the verses, he will reach only one conclusion: these verses plainly and obviously relate only to the sacrifices offered since time immemorial by the pilgrims of the Ka'bah at Makkah. These verses can in no way be attached to the Second (or Zerubbabel's) Temple because: (i) It was not more glorious or magnificent than the Solomon's Temple, even if the glory be considered to be the spiritual glory as some of the scholars take it to be. (ii) The Gentiles and kings never came to the 'light' and 'the brightness of the rising' of the Second Temple (v.3). It were only a small number of Jews who visited it after they were allowed to return from their exile, for only the period of 515 BC to AD 70, whereafter the Jewish Second Temple had been destroyed and it does not exist there for almost the last twenty centuries. Even during this period of 515 BC to 70 AD the Temple and the Jews had to suffer great distress (see App.V) for a number of times. (iii) Neither the abundance of the sea was ever converted unto the Jewish clan; nor the forces of Gentiles ever came or entered to the fold of the Jews or their Second Temple (v. 5). The wealth of the nations was never brought to this Second Temple on the seas. (iv) There is no tradition that any herds of camels of the Arabian pilgrims (the people of Midian, Ephah, and Sheba, the progenies of Abraham through his wife Keturah) ever visited this Second Temple for pilgrimage 'proclaiming the praise of the Lord' (v. 6).[41] (v) There is no tradition that Abraham's progenies from Ishma#'el's sons Kedar and Nebaioth (the people of Arabia) ever gathered around the

Second Temple or offered any sacrifices of flocks and rams on the Second Temple, which would be accepted as offerings on God's altar (v.7). (vi) It is in no way applicable to the Second Temple that 'thy gates shall be open continually; they shall not be shut day nor night; that men may bring unto thee the forces of the Gentiles, and that their kings may be brought.' (v.11). Not to say of the gates, there is not even a building of the Temple on earth for the last two thousand years. (vii) It never happened at any time in the history of nations that 'The sons also of them [the Babylonians] that afflicted thee [the Jews] shall come bending unto thee; and all they that despised thee shall bow themselves down at the soles of thy feet.', as the verse 14 claims; whereas the Yemeni forces that were utterly wasted due to their ill-will towards Ka'bah but their descendants regularly visit the sanctuary with respect and fervour. (viii) It can in no way be said of the Second Temple or the Jews 'I will make you an object of eternal pride,[42] and the joy of all generations.[43]' (v.15). (ix) It is also not true about the 'Second Temple' that 'Violence shall no more be heard in thy land, wasting nor destruction within thy borders; but thou shalt call thy walls Salvation, and thy gates Praise.' (v.18). (x) It can also not be claimed about the 'Second Temple' or the Israelites that 'Thy sun shall no more go down; neither shall thy moon withdraw itself; for the Lord shall be thine everlasting light, and the days of thy mourning shall be ended' (v.20); for the 'Second Temple' and the Israelites have undergone so many vicissitudes and misfortunes that plainly belie the assertion 'the Lord shall be thine everlasting light,' (xi) The conduct and status of the Israelites is quite contrary to the claim made in v. 21 'Thy people also shall be all righteous; they shall inherit the land forever,'. Whereas the actual fact is that instead of being 'righteous' they became evildoers, usurers, and wealth-worshippers; and instead of 'inheriting the land forever' they had been thrown out of it disgracefully. Now, that they have again been given the control of their land, they have resorted to cruelty, plunder, corruption, and sin, instead of sympathy, God-cautiousness, and virtuousness. It can by no means be attributed as righteousness.

From the analytical study undertaken above it can be concluded that the words of Ch. LX of the book of Isaiah, with all shades of their meanings and implications have nothing to do with the 'Second Temple' or the Israelites.

5. The application of chapter LX of the book of Isaiah to the Jews or the 'Second Temple' being categorically ruled out, a probe into its exact significance is to be made. If someone undertakes a sincere and objective study to ascertain the implications and purport of the verses, he will reach only one conclusion: these verses plainly and obviously relate only to the sacrifices offered since time immemorial by the pilgrims of the Ka'bah at Makkah to commemorate the offering of Abraham his only son Ishmā'el. Here are some observations based on the analytic study of the verses that will be useful in appreciating their real status, purport, and significance. **(a)** Verse 3 asserts, 'And the Gentiles [according to NIV and many other translations: 'Nations'] shall come to thy light, and kings[44] to the brightness of thy rising.' It is to be noted that as long as the Temple belonged to the Jews, the Gentiles were not permitted to enter the main Temple, and if some Gentile dared to enter the sanctuary, he was to be sentenced to death. No doubt there existed a 'Court of the Gentiles' with the Temple, but it lay outside the sanctuary. 'The court of the Gentiles was accessible to anyone. It was separated from the temple and the other courts by a balustrade (row of short pillars surmounted by rail) with inscriptions prohibiting Gentiles from entering the interior courts under pain of death.'[45] When the Jews got ejected from the temple for good, its building was also destroyed and there does not exist any temple on this planet for the last twenty centuries. If the Government of Israel gets the temple reconstructed, for which it is trying hard, and there are reasons to believe that it may succeed in it, its main sanctuary would again become prohibited for the Gentiles.

It is only the sanctuary of Makkah, where Muslims of all nations from all over the world have been coming regularly since time immemorial. **(b)** The contents of v.4, 'Lift up thine eyes round about, and see: all they gather themselves together, they come to thee; thy sons shall come from far, and thy daughters shall be nursed at thy side. [GNB has well translated it as, 'Your daughters will be carried like children']' had never been applicable to the 'Second Temple'. But as far as the Ka'bah is concerned, they are fully applicable to it in every sense of the words. It would be interesting to note that the Qur'ān has described the phenomenon of the Pilgrimage and the sacrifices to be offered there as:

And when We settled for Abraham the place of the House [the Ka'bah]: 'Thou shall not associate with Me anything. And do thou purify My House for those that shall go about it and those that stand, for those that bow and prostrate themselves; and proclaim among men the Pilgrimage, and they shall come unto thee on foot and upon every lean beast, they shall come from every deep ravine that they may witness things profitable to them and mention God's Name on days well-known over such beasts of the flocks as He has provided them: So eat thereof, and feed the wretched poor. Let them then finish with their self-neglect and let them fulfil their vows, and go about [circumambulate] the Ancient House.'[46] (…). 'Such (is the Pilgrimage): Whoever honours the sacred Rites of God, for him it is good in the sight of his Lord'[47]

(c) It can by no means be said of the 'Second Temple' as the v. 5 claims, 'the abundance of the sea shall be converted unto thee, the forces of the Gentiles shall come unto thee.' It is true only of the Ka'bah at Makkah, that although it is situated in a barren land, yet it is abundantly provided with every sort of the provisions of the world. Again it is Makkah that the faithful Muslim Gentiles (men and women) from all over the world assemble there together with all their utilities through sea routes, land routes, and by air. It has been recorded in verse 8: 'Who *are* these *that* fly as a cloud, and as the doves to their windows?' The landings of the aeroplanes carrying the millions of pilgrims for the sanctuary of Makkah depict the exact picture of the verse. No planes coming to any sanctuary on earth present this phenomenon. **(d)** Who can claim about the Second Temple as has been asserted in v.6, 'The multitude of camels shall cover your land, The dromedaries [young camels] of Midian and Ephah; All they from Sheba shall come: They shall bring gold and incense; and they shall proclaim the praises of the Lord.[48]' It never happened at any stage of the history of the world that such great multitudes of the Arabian people might have visited the sanctuary of Jerusalem in the form of the camel caravans. As regards the sanctuary of Makkah and the sacrifices being offered there, it is true to the letter. It will also be appreciated that the pilgrims utter the 'Talbiyah' (a part of which is 'All praise belongs to you, O God.') loudly as the Bible has noted 'they shall proclaim or shew forth [i.e. declare loudly or openly] the praises of the Lord.' **(e)** No man on earth can endorse to the claim of v.7 regarding the 'Second Temple' that: 'All the flocks of Kedar shall be gathered together unto thee, the rams of Nebaioth shall minister unto thee: they shall come up with acceptance on mine altar, and I will glorify the house of my glory.' Kedar and Nebaioth are the sons of Ishmā'el and their descendants have been living in Arabia for thousands of years. There had been no tradition amongst them to visit Jerusalem and to offer sacrifices there. On the other hand every informed citizen of the modern world knows that they have been coming to the sanctuary at Makkah for Pilgrimage since time immemorial. Isn't it a sufficient proof of the fact that the above verses of chapter LX of the book of Isaiah exclusively refer to the offering of sacrifices at the sanctuary of Makkah by the descendants of Abraham's son Ishmā'el. It is further to be considered how God can glorify the house that does not even exist on earth. It is only the house of God's glory at Makkah that has been safely existing since time immemorial which can be glorified and is physically glorified in every sense of the word. Page H. Kelley has explained this verse as, 'The tribes of Arabia also bring sacrificial offerings of flocks and rams.'[49] And the fact is that the tribes of Arabia never took their sacrifices to Jerusalem. The tradition amongst them has prevailed to bring sacrificial offerings to Makkah, which is an important ritual during their Pilgrimage. **(f)** It has been claimed in v. 9 that, 'Surely the isles shall wait for me, and the ships of Tarshish first, to bring thy sons from far.' Tarshish was situated on the south coast of Spain, as explained in the relevant footnote (No.210) above. As long as the Jerusalem Temple existed, there was no question of any Spaniards coming to it for offering any sacrifices. On the other hand, Spain had been conquered by the Arabs in the first century of Hijrah and they had settled there. These sons of Abraham through his son Ishmā'el, as the Arabs are, regularly visited the sanctuary of Makkah to perform Umrah (small Pilgrimage, which is performed the whole year through) and Pilgrimage and offered their sacrifices there to commemorate Abraham's offering their fore-father Ishmā'el for sacrifice. **(g)** As regards v.11, 'thy gates shall be open continually; they shall not be shut day nor night', this writer has himself visited the sanctuary at Makkah. It has been noted that it remains open around the clock. It has been a perpetually celebrated tradition through the ages. As regards the 'Second Temple', when there does not exist any building thereof, how the gates can remain open day or night. **(h)** Verse 14 asserts, 'The sons also of them that afflicted thee shall come bending unto thee; and all they that despised thee shall bow themselves down at the soles of thy feet; and they shall call thee, the city of the Lord, the Zion of the Holy One of Israel.' It is true of the sanctuary of Makkah *verbatim et literatim*. It physically happened in January, 630 at the time of the Conquest of Makkah by the Prophet of Islām. As regards the phrase 'The Zion of the Holy One of Israel', it does not fit in the context. It is obviously an interpolation by some redactor or a gloss by some commentator. 'The city of the Lord' is the exact translation of 'Baytullah' which is the Arabic name of 'Ka'bah' **(i)** The opening clause of v. 15, 'Whereas thou hast been forsaken and hated,' plainly refers to Hagar. In the relevant footnote above, it has been noted with reference to Dummelow and the 7th Day Adventist Bible Com. that 'The figure is that of a forsaken wife.' As regards the last sentence of the verse, 'I will make thee an eternal excellency, a joy of many [in fact this word should have been 'all' as has been translated by NIV, etc.] generations' the words 'eternal excellency' and 'a joy of all generations' can in no way be applied to the temple. of Jerusalem. It is only the sanctuary of Makkah that the words can be attributed to in true sense. **(j)** Verse 18 reads as, 'Violence shall no more be heard in thy land, wasting nor destruction within thy borders; but thou shalt call thy walls Salvation, and thy gates Praise.' Not to say of Jerusalem's Temple being secured from 'violence, wasting, and destruction' it does not even exist on earth for the last two thousand years. The contents of this verse can in no way be applied to the Temple of Jerusalem. A brief sketch of the history of Jerusalem's Temple has been afforded in 'Appendix IV' and it can be confirmed there. On the other hand it is applicable to the sanctuary of Makkah in true sense of the words. **(k)** V.21 says, 'Thy people also *shall be* all righteous; they shall inherit the land for ever.' Who can claim the Jewish people to have inherited the land of Jerusalem forever? On the other hand every knowledgeable person knows that the Arabs have been holding the land of the sanctuary of Makkah since time immemorial. As to the last clause of the verse, 'that I may be glorified', anybody who has happened to perform a Pilgrimage or Umrah at the sanctuary of Ka'bah, would verify the statement.

References

1. Dr. W. Fitch, Minister, Church of Scotland, Glasgow, remarks in his Commentary to the book of Isaiah in the *New Bible Com.* (p.604):

   This is a prophecy of great beauty, thrilling [make someone feel excited and happy] with the joy of a great assurance that the purpose of God is so triumphantly to be fulfilled in the earth.

2. Qāḍī Sulaymān Manṣūrpuri, *Raḥmatulli'l-'Ālamīn* (Delhi: I'tiqād Publishing House, 2001), 1:196.

3. Carroll Stuhlmueller asserts in *The Jerome Bible Com.* (p.382):

   These chapters (60-62), especially ch. 60 according to Dhorme (op. cit., xlvii), are a lyrical description of the new Jerusalem.

   He assigns the explanation of Chapter 60 the title of 'GLORY OF THE NEW JERUSALEM'. It means that this Chapter 60 is considered to be related to the 'Second Temple'. A brief account of the history of the Solomon's Temple has been afforded in App. IV at the end of the book.

   It may be noted here that Jerusalem is a meaningful word comprising of two segments: Jeru = city or place; and Salem = peace. As such Jerusalem means: 'city or abode of peace'. The Bible mentions two Jerusalems without any explanation. In fact the first and the ancient 'City of Peace' is the Jerusalem of Canaan which existed there even before Abraham. The second and the new 'City of Peace' is Makkah which was founded by Abraham and has been mentioned in the Qur'an as 'al-Balad al-Amin'. It is only Makkah which is Jerusalem (City of Peace) in the true sense of word. A detailed study on the theme has been undertaken in this writer's book '*Muḥammad Foretold in the Bible by Name*'.

4. The Jewish Com. *Soncino Chumash*'s footnote (p.1134) is:

   This is addressed to Jerusalem. Light being the symbol of joy and salvation, Jerusalem is told that the light had been rekindled (K).

   For the history of Jerusalem see Appendix V at the end of the book.

5. NIV translates it as: 'Nations'. Generally this word 'gentile' means all the nations and people other than the Jews.

6. The Rev. Dr. I. W. Slotki, *Eng. Trans. & Com on Isaiah* (London: The Soncino Press, 1949), p. 292 has recorded a footnote on it:

   The nations will learn the ways of God, religion and morality, from [you].

7. *Matthew Henry's An Exposition of the O & NT* (5:351), explains:

   'kings' means: 'men of figure, power, and influence'.

8. Dr. W. Fitch asserts in *New Bible Commentary* (p. 604):

   Then will the city be the centre of the world's light, for the glory of the everlasting God will rest upon her and will radiate around the world.

   It may be noted here that after Isaiah the 2nd Temple never gained such glory as has been indicated here. It is only the Temple of Makkah which can claim this glory through the advent of the Prophet of Islām.

9. Matthew Henry asserts in his *An Exposition of the O & NT* (NY: Robert Carter & Bros., 530, Broadway, 1712), 5:350:

   When the *Jews were settled again in their own land*' after their captivity, many of the people of the land joined themselves to them; but it does not appear that there ever was any such numerous accession to them as would answer the fulness of this prophecy; and therefore we must conclude that this looks further, to the bringing of the Gentiles into the [naturally, the forthcoming words should have been '*fold of that altar or sanctuary*'; but it is the dexterity and adroitness of the worthy commentator that he manipulates to interpret it in the following terms] gospel church, not their flocking to one particular place, though under that type it is here described. There is no place now that is the centre of the church's unity; but the promise respects their flocking to Christ, and coming by faith, and hope, and the holy love, into that society which is incorporated by the charter of his gospel, and of the unity of which he only is the centre.

   This is an example how the Christian scholars mould any simple statement of the OT to be applied to Jesus Christ or the 'Church'.

10. NEB: 'your daughters walking beside them leading the way.' Matth. Henry's *An Exposition of the O & NT*, 5:351: 'Sons and daughters shall come in the most dutiful manner'. Both of these translations make a reasonable sense in this context. It depicts the true picture

of the caravans and groups of men and women coming together for the pilgrimage of this sanctuary of Makkah.

11. *New Jerusalem Bible* (p.1282) translates it as:

    since the riches of the sea will flow to you, the wealth of the nations come to you;

    NIV (p. 779) has translated it as:

    the wealth on the seas will be brought to you, to you the riches of the nations will come.

    The Soncino Chumash (p.1134) has recorded a footnote here:

    Whereas in the past the Land of Israel was desolate and forsaken, it will now be crowded with multitudes like a roaring sea (K).

    But it could never come true as far as the Second Temple is concerned.

12. *The Wycliffe Bible Com.* explains (p.651):

    It is quite remarkable that, in origin, all these offered treasures are preponderantly [being superior in power, numbers, etc] Arabian.

    But, in his wishful thinking, he interprets it as:

    Perhaps there is a suggestion here that Islam will some day turn to the Cross.

    This remains a mere dream and wishful thinking of the worthy scholar.

13. *7th Day Adventist BC* (4:314) explains the word 'Midian' as 'A region in the desert of Arabia (Ex. 2:15).' In fact Midian was one of the six sons of Abraham from his wife Keturah (whom he had taken as wife after the death of Sarah). Abraham had settled these Keturah's sons (Zimran, Jokshan, Medan, Midian, Ishbak and Shuah) in Arabia.

14. *7th Day Adventist Bible Com.* (4:314) explains the word 'Ephah' as:

    A Midianite tribe (Gen. 25:4; 1 Chron. 1:33), and here the region they inhabited.

    In fact Ephah was one of the five sons of Midian (Ehpah, Epher, Hanoch, Abida and Eldaah). Midian was one of his sons from Keturah.

15. *The New Jerusalem Bible* (p.1283) explains:

    Midian, Ephah and Sheba are peoples of Arabia.

    The 7th Day Adventist Bible Dic. (p.1015) explains:

(...) it is now generally held that it was a queen of this Arabian Sheba, in the area now called Yemen, who made a visit to Solomon (1Ki 10:1-13). The Sabeans were one of the most important peoples of all Arabia. (...). They built large dams and an extensive irrigation system, which made their country the most fertile in ancient Arabia. This is why it was known in classical times as Arabia Felix, 'Happy Arabia.'

16. Derek Kidner, Warden of Tyndale House, Cambridge, in his *Commentary on the Book of Isaiah* in the NBC Revised (p. 621) asserts:

    v. 7 is crucial to the understanding of the chapter [60].

17. Dummelow (p.450) has explained the word 'Nebaioth' in his commentary as: 'a tribe allied to Kedar, descended from Ishmael (Gn 2513).' *The New Jerusalem Bible* (p.1283) explains Nebaioth as 'an Arabian people, see Gn. 25:13; 28:9; 36:3.' *A New Catholic Com. on Holy Scripture* (p.597) explains:

    The tribes of 'Kedar' and of 'Nebaioth' were of Ishmaelite origin, and were mainly shepherds.

    The Wycliffe Bible Com. (p.651), after remarking that:

    It is quite remarkable that, in origin, all these offered treasures are preponderantly Arabian.

    makes a wishfully predictive assertion:

    Perhaps there is a suggestion here that Islam will some day turn to the Cross.

18. The actual Hebrew word for this 'minister' or 'serve' is **ù˜** 'sharath' or 'shareth', which, according to Strong's *Dic. of the Hebrew Bible*, p. 122, entry 8334, 35, means:

    to attend as a menial or worshipper; fig. to contribute to, minister, wait on; or service (in the temple).

    J. H. Hertz' *The (Jewish Commentary) Pentateuch and Haftorahs* (p. 875), translates the Hebrew Word as 'minister'; and explains it in his footnote as 'By providing animals for sacrifices '.

19. NIV (p. 779) translates it as:

    They will be accepted as offerings on my altar, and I will adorn my glorious temple.

20. Dummelow (p. 450) has recorded a footnote here in his Com. on B:

The nations are pictured as coming in a long train, to bring their riches for the service of the sanctuary.

Matthew Henry's *An Exposition of the O & NT*, 5:351 notes:

Great numbers of sacrifices shall be brought to God's altar, acceptable sacrifices, and, though brought by Gentiles, they shall find acceptance.

If related to the Second Temple, these are mere wishful imaginations.

21. NIV (p. 779) translates it as: 'and I will adorn my glorious temple.' *The Soncino Chumash* (p. 1134) has recorded a footnote here: 'By causing the nations to bring their gifts and offerings to it (K).'
22. It depicts a true picture of thousands of aeroplanes coming and landing at the airport of Jeddah daily like clouds, with hundreds of thousands of pilgrims on board who come here to perform 'Umrah (short Ḥajj), and during the Ḥajj season in even greater multitude.
23. Carroll Stuhlmueller explains the word 'Tarshish' in *The Jerome Bible Com.* (p. 383) as: 'A Phoenician colony in southern Spain (Jon 1:3).' It is to be noted here that it had been ruled by Muslim Arabs for about eight centuries. These Muslims travelled in ships to the sanctuary of Makkah to perform pilgrimage.
24. Dr. W. Fitch, Minister, Church of Scotland, Glasgow, remarks in his *Commentary to the book of Isaiah in the NBC* (p. 604):

    The gates will not be shut by day nor night, a symbol of absolute security under the blessing of her God.

    But, under any stretch of sense, they cannot be applied to the Second Temple. On the other hand it is exactly true of the sanctuary at Makkah, whose gates remain open day and night and the pilgrims, most of which are gentile, and their kings as well, keep circumambulating around Ka'bah without any break of even a single minute during day and night with absolute security and under the blessings of their God.
25. *The New Jerusalem Bible* (p. 1283) has inserted a footnote on V. 12:

    Interrupting the continuity, [v. 12] is very probably additional.

    A New Catholic Com. on Holy Scripture (p. 597) has also recorded similar observation on this verse:

    In a context of this kind, the threat mentioned in 12 is astonishing, *and is probably a gloss inserted later.*

26. A brief account of the word 'Zion' has been afforded at the end of ch. XI of this book.
27. In the words of *The New Jerusalem Bible* (p. 1283) it may also be, like v. 12, '*very probably additional*'. But even if vv 12 and 14 be not additional, interpolated, and corrupt in entirety and their theme be intact and unpolluted, it is safely applicable to the sanctuary of Makkah and depict the true picture of the conquest of Makkah at the hands of the Prophet of Islām.
28. Dummelow (p. 450) has recorded a footnote here in his commentary: 'The figure is that of a forsaken wife (546)₂'. *The 7th Day Adventist Bible Com.* (4:315) notes, 'Like a forsaken wife.' It clearly relates to Hagar, the mother of Ismā'el.
29. *The Nelson Study Bible* asserts in the footnote to v.15 (p.1209):

    The new sanctuary will be greater than the old one because it is eternal, rich, and spiritual (vv. 17, 18);

    which is exactly true of the sanctuary of Makkah.
30. *The Soncino Chumash* (p.1137) has recorded a footnote here:

    Israel's sovereignty and glory will never again depart (K).

    It is nothing more than a wishful expectation, which could never be materialized . On the other hand it is exactly true of the sanctuary of Makkah.
31. *The Soncino Chumash* (p. 1137) has recorded a footnote here:

    Israel's national glory will endure for ever, because the restoration will be the work of God (K).

    It also remained a mere dream, because even after the construction of the Second Temple, the restoration of the glory of Israel, which is mentioned here as 'the work of God', was not materialized. They could only enjoy a limited 'Internal Autonomy' under the Persian, Greek, Syrian, or Roman empires and, subsequently, the Temple was completely destroyed in AD 70 for good; and the dream of '*Israel's national glory will endure for ever*' remained a mere dream, as it was.
32. Isa. 60:1-21 KJV.
33. Dr. W. Fitch in his *Com. on Isaiah in the NBC* (p. 604) asserts:

    Jerusalem is to be rebuilt (...). Then will the city be the centre of the world's light [unfortunately the city could never become 'the centre of the world's light'], for the glory of everlasting God will rest upon her and will radiate around the world [the world never saw this dream come true]. (...) **iii.** *Jerusalem to be built again.* (lx. 10-14). (...). When rebuilt the gates will not be shut by day nor night (11), a symbol of absolute security under the blessing of her God [of course, it is quite true that 'the gates will not be shut by day nor night' because they do not even physically exist on earth. As such, the question of their being ever shut does not arise, because it is 'a symbol of absolute security under the blessing of her God.' How can someone dare to comment on it!], and also implying the warmth of the welcome that will be given to those that seek an entrance therein.

See also the first footnote on the above passage.

34. See footnotes on vv. 5, 15, 20, 21 above.
35. Footnote on Isa. 60:17-18 NOAB, p. 950.
36. J.L. McKenzie's *Dic. of Bible*, 875.
37. W. Smith's *Dic. of Bible*, 680.
38. *New Bible Dic.*, 1170.
39. See *7th Day Adventist Bible Dic.*, 1100.
40. *The Jewish Enc*, 12: 97.
41. Isa. 60:6f GNB:

    Great caravans of camels will come, from Midian and Ephah. They will come from Sheba (...)! All the sheep of Kedar and Nebaioth Will be brought to you as sacrifices And [*sic.*] offered on the altar to please the Lord.

    Isa. 60:6f CEV:

    Your country will be covered with caravans of young camels from Midian and Ephah. The people of Sheba will bring gold and spices in praise of me, the Lord. Every sheep of Kedar will come to you; rams of Nebaioth will be yours as well. I will accept them as offerings and bring honor to my temple.

    The contents of the above statement are merely a wishful imagination as far as the Second Temple is concerned. The phenomena of the above verse are only a dream of some credulous redactor of the Bible, which could never turn into a ground reality to console the poor person!
42. *New Jerusalem Bible*, 1283.

43. NIV (p. 780).
44. It may be noted here that According to Matth. Henry's *An Exposition of the O & NT*, 5:351, 'kings' means: 'men of figure, power, and influence'.
45. Mckenzie's *Dic. of Bible*, 875.
46. A. J. Arberry, *The Koran Interpreted*, p. 336, (Sūrah al-Ḥajj 22:26-29).
47. A Yūsuf Ali, *The Holy Qur'ān*, p. 858, (Sūrah al-Ḥajj 22:32).
48. *The Nelson's Study Bible*, 1208.
49. Page H. Kelley in the *Broadman Bible Com.*, ed. Clifton J. Allen etc., (Nashville, Tennessee: Broadman Press, 1971), 5:360.

11

The Pilgrimage of Bakkah in the Psalms of David

King David has mentioned the Pilgrimage of Bakkah in his 84th Psalm. He wishes that he could also have the opportunity of accompanying the pilgrims. He envies at the birds who make nests and reside there in the house of the Lord, whereas he cannot even pay a visit to it. He longs for the Lord and the courts of His house and exclaims, 'A day in thine courts *is* better than a thousand. I had rather be a doorkeeper in the house of my God.' What an ardent desire! An objective study of the Psalm has been undertaken in this chapter.[1] Most of the points have been explained at the spot in the footnotes. The Psalm is reproduced hereunder:

1. How amiable *are* thy tabernacles[2] , O Lord of hosts![3]
2. My soul longeth, yea, even fainteth for the courts of the Lord[4] : my heart and my flesh crieth out for the living God.
3. Yea[5] , the sparrow hath found an house, and a swallow a nest for herself, where she may lay her young[6] , Even thy altars, O Lord of hosts, my king, and my God.[7]
4. Blessed *are* they that dwell in thy house: they will be still[8] praising thee.[9] Selah.[10]
5. Blessed *is* the man whose strength *is* in thee;[11] in whose heart *are* the ways *of them*.[12]
6. *Who* passing through the valley of Baca[13] make it a well[14] ; the rain also filleth the pools.[15]

7. They go from strength[16] to strength, *every one of them* in Zion appeareth before God.
8. O Lord God of hosts, hear my prayer: give ear, O God of Jacob. Selah.
9. Behold, O God our shield, and look upon the face of thine anointed.
10. For a day in thine courts *is* better than a thousand. I had rather be a doorkeeper in the house of my God, than to dwell in the tents of wickedness.[17]
11. For the Lord God is a sun and shield[18] : the Lord will give grace and glory: no good *thing* will he withhold from them that walk uprightly.
12. O Lord of hosts, blessed *is* the man that trusteth in thee.[19]

It would be advisable that a verse to verse study be undertaken to ascertain the theme of the Psalm.

Verse 1, as translated by NIV (p. 621) and NOAB (p. 747) asserts, 'How lovely is your dwelling place, O Lord Almighty! (NOAB: O Lord of hosts!)' It means that the Psalm relates to some dwelling place of the Lord Almighty, which physically existed at that time. The Arabic version of the 'dwelling place of the Lord Almighty' is 'Bayt Allah', which means the 'House of the Lord'. It had been built by his primogenitor Abraham and physically existed there in Makkah with the same name as a ground reality. It was, however, also called 'The Ka'bah' by the Arabs. On the other hand, there existed no 'dwelling place' of the 'Lord Almighty' or 'Bayt Allah' anywhere else on earth at that time. The 'Solomon's Temple' did not exist at that time. It was built almost half a century later. Its construction could not even be started during the lifetime of King David. So there obviously remains no option but to consider this 'dwelling place' of the 'Lord Almighty' as the 'Bayt Allah' or 'The Ka'bah' situated at Makkah. And there are other reasonable grounds as well in the body of this very Psalm which make the proposition quite certain.

Verse 2 shows the passionate earnestness of the king for the courts of the Lord, the Living God. It reveals that the 'courts of the

Living Lord' already existed somewhere, but are not situated within his empire, and, as such, he cannot visit them. Therefore he can only long for 'the courts of the Lord'.

As regards vv. 3-4, the comments recorded in the relevant footnotes above sufficiently make the theme clear. NOAB (p. 747) has afforded a very beautiful footnote on vv. 3-4, 'Envy of the birds and servitors[20] who live there.' The comments by the *Collegeville Bible Com.* (p. 772) on these vv. 3-4 are also noteworthy, 'All living things are safe from threat in the presence of the Lord.' *The 7th Day Adventist Bible Com.* (3:828) explains these verses in the following words:

> The general meaning of the verse, whose conclusion the poet only implies, is that *even the birds have free access to the sacred precincts of the sanctuary, they make their homes there undisturbed, while the psalmist is exiled from the source of his joy, is denied the privilege of worshipping within the sacred enclosure* [stress added]. The nostalgic appeal of this verse is one of the most delicately beautiful expressions of homesickness in the whole realm of literature.

Verses 1-4 can be summed up as follows:

1. King David is paying homage to such a sanctuary which pertained to God and which physically existed there as a ground reality.
2. King David had an earnest desire to visit this sanctuary, but he could not accomplish it. Obviously, it could have been due to the fact that this sanctuary might have been outside the territorial boundaries of his state.
3. Solomon's Temple had not so far been built. There existed only one sanctuary on earth devoted to the worship of the only one God whose construction was attributed to Abraham, i.e. the Ka'bah at Makkah, and there did not exist any such other sanctuary on earth by that time.
4. King David expresses his yearnings that even the birds can set their dwellings in the courts of the Lord, but he is

deprived of the privilege of the pilgrimage of this house of the Lord.

The translation of the second clause of v. 5 in the KJV ('in whose heart are the ways of them') is not clear. Most of the other translations have rendered the theme as *who have set their hearts on pilgrimage* or the like. Here is a list of some translations, versions, and commentaries of the Bible which relate the theme of the verse and the Psalm with pilgrimage:

(i) *Bible Knowledge Com.*, p. 855.

(ii) *Christian Community Bible*, p. 1000.

(iii) *Collegeville Bible Com.*, p.772.

(iv) *Contemporary English Version*, p. 707.

(v) *Good News Bible*, p. 900.

(vi) *Jerome Bible Com.*, p. 591.

(vii) *New American Bible*, p. 615.

(viii) *New Bible Com.*, p. 472.

(ix) *New Bible Com., (Rvd)*, p. 504.

(x) *New Catholic Com.*, p. 473.

(xi) *New Com. on Holy Scripture*, p. 264.

(xii) *New English Version*, p. 441.

(xiii) *New International Version.*, p. 621.

(xiv) *New Jerome Commentary*, p.540.

(xv) *New Jerusalem Bible*, p.900.

(xvi) *New KJV (Nelson Study Bible)*, p. 966.

(xvii) *Peake's Bible Com.*, p. 431.

(xviii) *Today's English Version*, p. 607.

(xix) *Wycliffe Bible Com.*, p. 526.

(xx) *7th Day Adventist Bible Com.*, p. 828.

(xxi) *The Holy Bible (Old and New. Testament)*: An Improved edn. (American Baptist Publication Society), as quoted by '*The Old Testament Books of Poetry from 26 Translations*', p. 334.

(xxii) *A New Trans. of the Bible* (James Moffatt), as quoted by '*The OT Books of Poetry from 26 Trans.*', p. 334.

It can be appreciated from the above data that the Psalm refers to some pilgrimage which has traditionally been performed at some sanctuary for a long time. First of all King David is bestowing the blessings in this psalm upon those 'that dwell permanently in the house of the Lord and are ever praising Him.' Secondly he is bestowing the blessings upon those 'who have set their hearts on pilgrimage [but are not the permanent residents of it].' It shows that the sanctuary physically exists there. It is practically dedicated to the Lord and not to any thing else whatsoever. People travel to it to perform 'Pilgrimage'.

It is to be noted that the sanctuary of Jerusalem, the Solomon's Temple, did not exist there by that time. It was built about half a century later. The sanctuary of Ka'bah, called the 'Bayt Allah' or the 'House of the Lord' by the Arabs, existed there at Makkah in Arabia as a ground reality for the last about one thousand years (before King David). The descendants of his primogenitor Abraham through his son Ishmā'el and the tribes of the whole of the Arabian Peninsula travelled to perform pilgrimage there in large multitudes. They pronounced (which they still pronounce) the praise of the Lord during their pilgrimage saying,

I am present, O my Lord, I am present; (...); of course, all praise is for you, and all grace, and all sovereignty; there is no partner to you.

David should have had deep love, longing, and reverence for it, because it had been built by his primogenitor, Abraham. But it was outside his empire and, being a king of another land and engaged in constant battles, he could not visit it then. So he wishes he could have attended the sanctuary and performed pilgrimage there with offering sacrifice on it. There was another genuine reason for David's longing for the Pilgrimage of Bakkah, which is being stated under the next heading.

BAKKAH HAD PROVIDED REFUGE TO DAVID DURING HIS DAYS OF TROUBLE

David had rendered great services to King Saul but, according to the Bible, Saul, seeing David's popularity and power, became jealous of him and wanted to kill him. *Smith's Bible Dic.* explains:

> Unfortunately David's fame proved the foundation of that unhappy jealousy of Saul towards him which, mingling with the king's constitutional malady [illness], poisoned his whole future relations to David. (...). He [David] also still performed from time to time the office of minstrel [singer or musician of the king's court]; but the successive attempts of Saul upon his life convinced him that he was in constant danger. (...), he escaped by night, (...). David's life for the next few years was made up of a succession of startling incidents. (...); he is hunted by Saul from place to place like a partridge.[21]

In the mean time David's patron, Prophet Samuel died. David fled to the wilderness of Pārān to remain out of Saul's reach, as is recorded in the Bible:

> Then Samuel died; and the Israelites gathered together and lamented for him, and buried him at his home in Ramah. And David arose and went down to the Wilderness of Paran.[22]

This Pārān can obviously be the place where Ishmā'el and Hagar settled after Abraham had left them there. Had it been the other Paran (of Sinai), it would have been in approach of Saul; and David would not have been safe therte. It can thus only be that Paran which has been described in the Bible in the following words:

> And God heard the voice of the lad; and the angel of God Called to Hagar out of heaven, and said unto her, What aileth thee, Hagar? fear not; for God hath heard the voice of the lad where he *is*. Arise, lift up the lad, and hold him in thine hand; for I will make him a great nation. And God opened her eyes, and she saw a well of water; and she went, and filled the bottle with

> water, and gave the lad drink. And God was with the lad; and he grew, and dwelt in the wilderness, and became an archer. And he dwelt in the wilderness of Paran: and his mother took him a wife out of the land of Egypt.[23]

Had it been the other Pārān (of Sinai), it would have been quite in approach of Saul, and David would not have been safe there.

It is a historically admitted fact and ground reality that the Ka'bah was built by Abraham and Ishmā'el. The Ishmā'elite Arabs performed pilgrimage there. David had the opportunity to live there and perform the pilgrimage of al-Ka'bah during his stay at Bakkah in the wilderness of Paran. That's why he yearns to have the opportunity to visit the place of his refuge and perform its pilgrimage once again.

THE EXACT PROPER NAME BACA/BAKKAH

Verse 6 '*Who* passing through the valley of Baca make it a well; the rain also filleth the pools.' points out the exact proper name of the place from which the pilgrims have to pass through for the accomplishment of their pilgrimage at 'Arafāt. It is to be noted that some of the translations have changed the word 'Baca' with some other word. *The New Jerusalem Bible* (p. 900, 901) has translated it as 'Balsam' and has remarked in the footnote:

> In seven MSS and in versions, 'the valley of Tears' (the Heb. words for these two words are identical when spoken).

Some other translations have not taken the word 'Baca' as a proper noun and have translated it to 'misery'[24], 'Weary-glen'[25], 'thirsty valley'[26], etc. All the 26 translations of Dr. Curtis Vaughan's '*The OT Books of Poetry from 26 Translations*' have basically considered the original Hebrew word as 'Baca'. *The 7th Day Adventist Bible Com.* reports:

> The LXX[27] and the Vulgate[28] translate the phrase 'valley of Baca' as 'valley of Tears.'[29]

It means that according to these Greek and Latin translations of the Bible as well, the original Hebrew word here is 'Baca'. Here is a list of some more translations, versions, and commentaries of the Bible that have used the word 'Baca' at this place:

1. *Bible Knowledge Com.*, p. 855.
2. *Dummelow's Bible Com.*, p. 363.
3. GNB, p. 585.
4. *Gray & Adams Bible Com.*, 1:612.
5. *Matthew Henry's Exposition*, 4:324.
6. NAB, p. 615.
7. NASB, p. 747.
8. NBC, p. 472.
9. NBC (Rvd), p. 504.
10. *New Catholic Com.*, p. 473, (Baka).
11. *New Com. on Holy Scripture*, p. 364.
12. NIV, p. 621.
13. NKJV (*Nelson Study Bible*), p. 966.
14. *New Oxford Annotated Bible*, p. 747.
15. *Paragraph Bible*, p. 621.
16. *Peake's Bible Com.*, p. 431.
17. *Readers Digest Bible*, p. 306.
18. RSV, p. 539.
19. TEV, p. 607.
20. *Thompson's Bible*, p. 666.
21. *7th Day Adventist Bible Com.*, 3:827.

THE SITE OF BAKKAH IS UNKNOWN TO THE SCHOLARS OF THE BIBLE

The fact is that most of the scholars of the Bible do not know the location of Bakkah/Baca and they clearly admit this fact. Some observations of some of these authorities are reproduced hereunder:

1. Contemporary English Version (p. 707) has recorded a footnote to it:

   Dry Valley: Or 'Balsam Tree Valley.' The exact location is not known.

2. The New American Bible (p. 615) says in its footnote to the verse:

   Baca valley: Hebrew obscure; probably a valley on the way to Jerusalem.

3. The Jerome Biblical Com. (p. 591), taking vv. 7-8 collectively, has afforded the footnote:

   A description of the pilgrim's journey. The MT is uncertain.

4. 7th Day Adventist Bible Dic. has afforded a fairly detailed explanation of the word. Concluding his remarks he could not help asserting its uncertainty:

   Baca (baka). [Heb. *Baka*, possibly 'balsam tree.'] The name of a valley in Palestine (Ps 84:6), possibly so named because balsam trees grew there. Some have thought that it is another name for the Valley of Rephaim, where trees of that species were found, but this is pure conjecture. There were doubtless many valleys in which balsam trees grew. Another interpretation names it the valley of 'weeping' from the Hebrew *bakah*, 'to weep,' a word that differs only slightly from baka. However, neither interpretation helps to identify this place.[30]

5. The *New Oxford Annotated Bible* (p. 747) in the footnote to vv.5-7 indicates:

   Baca, some unknown, desolate place through which the pilgrims must go.

6. The *Harper's Bible Dic.* also holds the similar opinion:

   Baca [bay'kuh], unidentified valley associated with weeping or balsam [Ps. 84:6]. The term is derived from the verb 'to drip,' hence its association with weeping.[31]

7. W. Smith's A *Dic. of Bible* although calls it 'a valley in Palestine', yet the air of uncertainty can be smelt from its following remarks:

   That it was a real locality is most probable from the use of the definite article before the name.[32]

8. *Collins Gem Dic. of Bible* has also expressed the similar views about it:

   It may simply be a valley in Palestine (Ps. 84,6). It may simply be the Valley of the balsam trees, or it may be the Valley of Weeping (Heb. *Bakah*) or the Valley of little water.[33]

9. J. Hasting's *Dic. of the Bible Revised One Vol. edn.* throws a shadow of doubt on it:

   An allegorical place-name, found only in Ps. 84^6 (AV, RSV), where RV renders 'Valley of Weeping.' Most probably it is no more an actual locality than is the 'Valley of the Shadow of Death' in Ps 23^4.[34]

10. A. S. Aglen, in his article on 'Baca' in Hasting's *Dic. of Bible*, discovers nothing but uncertainties about the valley:

    If an actual valley (the article is not quite conclusive), it may be identified either with 'the valley of Achor, i.e. *trouble*'; 'the valley of Rephaim'; a Sinaitic valley with a similar name (Burckhardt); or the last station of the caravan route from the north to Jerusalem.

    Perseverance and trust not only overcome difficulties, but turn them into blessings; this is the lesson, whether the valley be real or only (as the Vulg. *Vallis lacrymarum* has become) an emblem of life.[35]

11. W. H. Morton is also of almost the similar views. In his article on 'Baca' in *Interpreter's Dic. of Bible* he observes:

    No valley of such a name has yet been identified, (....). In the same vein, it is quite possible that the valley was entirely symbolic.[36]

12. Dr. Frants Buhl (Copenhagen Univ.) and Dr. Morris Jastrow (Univ. of Pennsylvania), have noted:

    (...); but it signifies rather any valley lacking water.[37]

13. *A New Com. on Holy Scripture* is also not certain as to where this valley of Baca is to be found:

    Baca was the name of some valley [Note the air of uncertainty regarding the location of the valley!] on the way to the city.[38]

14. Peake's *Com. On Bible* observes:

    The valley of Baca; this rendering is better than 'valley of weeping' (LXX, RV). The location of the valley is unknown. Baca may mean 'balsam tree', which grows in dry soil. The point at all events seems to be that the valley is arid.[39]

The above information makes it quite clear that the scholars of the Bible cannot confidently claim to locate the exact site of the 'Valley of Baca'. It is because they relate it to the pilgrimage of the sanctuary at Jerusalem and don't try to trace it somewhere else. It is to be regretted that they either forget or knowingly ignore that:

(a) This Psalm was written by King David.

(b) There did not exist any sanctuary during the lifetime of King David.

(c) The language and the composition of the Psalm reveal that King David is mentioning some sanctuary which physically existed there.

(d) King David passionately desired to visit the sanctuary but it being outside his empire, he was unable to attend it.

Had they not ignored the plain words and the purport of the Psalm, and had they sincerely tried to locate the place, they would have easily located it.

THE ACTUAL SITE OF BACA/BAKKAH

It is unanimously accepted that the original word in the Hebrew Bible is 'Baca'. The context clearly indicates that it has been used as a proper noun and most of the versions and translations of the Bible have retained this status. Some of the translations and versions have misconceived its status and have taken it to be a common word. Then they tried to translate it whimsically as: weeping, tears, balsam tree, mulberry, some of the other trees, dry valley, etc. It does not seem to be a proper approach and is based on some misunderstanding.

The Hebrew word 'Baca' is composed of three alphabetical letters = Jëà (b?k?a). According to the Strong's Dic. of the Heb. Bible it means:

> 'weeping'[40] or 'the weeping tree (some gum-distilling tree, perhaps the balsam,):—mulberry tree.'[41]. 'Bakah' is also composed of three alphabetical letters = Jëɔ, meaning 'to weep; gen. to bemoan, to bewail, complain, mourn, with tears, weep'[42].

The vowel symbols had not been introduced in the Hebrew writing system until the seventh/eighth century AD.[43] It was only after their introduction in the Qur'ān in the 7th century AD that some proper vocalization system for the Bible was developed somewhere in the beginning of the seventh century. As far as its usage is concerned, the fact is that 'Bakkah' was the ancient name of 'Makkah'. Originally the city was called by this name ('Bakkah'). Here are some of the Arab authorities to explain its meanings:

> *'Lisān al-'*Arab' (the language of the 'Arabs), a renowned Arabic Dictionary in 18 volumes, explains:

Ya'qūb says, 'Bakkah is what is situated in between the two mountains of Makkah, because the people crushed one another during the circumambulation or overcrowded there. (…). It is said that Bakkah is the name of the interior of Makkah and it was given this name due to the crowding and swarming of the people. The tradition of Mujāhid states, 'Bakkah is among the names of Makkah.' And it is said, 'Bakkah is the site of the House of the Lord, and Makkah is the whole of the city.' It is also said, 'Both [Makkah and Bakkah] are the names of the city; and [the alphabetical letters] "B" and "M" succeed (can replace) one another.'[44]

Tahdhīb al-Lughah (in 16 volumes) is one of the most reliable dictionaries of the 'Arabic language. It explains the word as follows:

> Al-Layth says: al-bakk means breaking the neck. It is said that Makkah was named Bakkah because it broke the necks of oppressors when they deviated from the right course. And it is said that Bakkah was named Bakkah because the people crushed or pushed away one another in the paths. 'Amr reports from his father: Bakka something, i.e. tore or disjointed it; and from it was derived Bakkah, because it broke the necks of the oppressors and tyrants when they transgressed in it. It is also said that it was named Bakkah because people crushed one another in its routes. (…).

Zajjāj says: It is said that Bakkah is the site of the sanctuary, and what is all around it, is Makkah. He [Zajjāj] said: and there is consensus on it that Makkah and Bakkah are the place where the people resort for pilgrimage; and it is the city. And he [Zajjāj] said: And as far as its derivation in the lexicon is concerned it would be appropriate to say that 'the people crushed one another in the circumambulation, i.e. pushed away one another.' And it is said: Bakkah was given this name, because it crushed the necks of the tyrants.[45]

'Mu'jam al-Wasīṭ' says, 'Bakkah = Makkah'.[46]

Al-Ṣiḥāḥ explains:

> 'Bakkah' is the name of the inner portion of 'Makkah'. It was thus named because of the overcrowding of the people [in it]. It is also said that it was thus named because it crushed and broke the necks of the oppressors.[47]

Tartīb al-Qāmūs al-Muḥīṭ has also explained 'Bakkah' in a fair detail:

> 'Bakkah' stands either for 'Makkah'; or for what lies between its two mountains; or for the field of circumambulation [Maṭāf], because it crushes and breaks the necks of the arrogant or because of the overcrowding of the people in it.[48]

Muḥīṭ al-Muḥīṭ is also one of the authorities of the 'Arabic lexicons. It is a revised and advanced version of Firūzābādī's renowned '*Qāmūs*'. It has also recorded similar explanation of the word:

> It is the name of what lies between the two mountains of Makkah or of the circumambulation field [Maṭāf]. It is said that it was so named because it crushes and breaks the necks of the arrogant or because of the overcrowding of the people in it.[49]

Mu'jam Maqāyīs al-Lughah is an authority as regards the basic roots of the Arabic words. It explains the word as follows:

> 'Al-Khalīl' *says 'Al-Bakku:* crushing the neck', and it is said that 'Bakkah' was named so because it used to crush the necks of the oppressors. When they inclined towards oppression, they were erased from the scene. It is also said that it was named 'Bakkah' because the people crush one another during the circiumambulation or pushed them away.[50]

Al-Khalīl bin Aḥmad (100-175 A.H.) is one of the greatest, if not the greatest, authorities on Arabic lexicon. The first Arabic lexicon, *Kitāb al-'Ayn*, was compiled by him. He explains:

> Al-Bakku: to crush the neck. Makkah was named Bakkah because people crush one another in the Ṭawāf (circumambulation of Ka'bah), or push one another due to overcrowding. It is also said that it was so named because it crushed the necks of tyrants when they deviated (from the right path) in it by way of oppression.[51]

'Akhbār Makkah' is a detailed history of 'Makkah' in six volumes in the Arabic language. Here are some excerpts from its section on 'Names of Makkah':

> One of the residents of Makkah (...) gave me a book written by some of his forefathers. In it were stated the names of Makkah which the residents of Makkah claimed to be, i.e., Makkah, Bakkah, Barrah, Bassāsah, Umm al-Qurā, al-Ḥaram, al-Masjid al-Ḥarām, and al-Balad al-Amīn. Some people say that 'Ṣalāhī' is also among its names. Some of the Makkans claim that 'Kūthā' is also one of its names.[52]

It is written beneath 'al-Maqām', I am Allāh, Lord of 'Bakkah'. I sanctified it on the day when the heavens and the earth were brought into existence.[53]

The Qur'ān has used both 'Makkah' and 'Bakkah' for the name of the place. When it is mentioned as a place of the ancient times it has been named as 'Bakkah', as it has been used in sūrah Āl 'Imrān (3) of the Qur'ān:

ة مُبَارَكًا وَهُدًى لِّلْعَالَمِينَ فِيهِ آيَاتٌ بَيِّنَاتٌ مَّقَامُ

مَن وَلِلَّهِ عَلَى النَّاسِ حِجُّ الْبَيْتِ مَنِ اسْتَطَاعَ إِلَيْهِ سَبِيلًا وَمَن

كَفَرَ فَإِنَّ اللَّهَ غَنِيٌّ عَنِ الْعَالَمِينَ [54]

The first House ever to be built (as sanctuary) for men was that at Bakkah (Makkah), a blessed place, a beacon for the nations. In it, there are clear signs and the spot where Ibrahim stood. Whoever enters it is safe. Pilgrimage to the House is a duty to Allah for all who can make the journey.[55]

There is another occasion in the Qur'ān where it has been mentioned in the perspective of the period contemporary with the Prophet of Islām:

مْ عَنكُمْ وَأَيْدِيَكُمْ عَنْهُم بِبَطْنِ مَكَّةَ مِن بَعْدِ أَنْ

اللَّهُ بِمَا تَعْمَلُونَ بَصِيرًا [56]

It was He who restrained their hands from you and your hands from them in the valley of Makkah after He had given you victory over them. Allah was watching over all your actions.[57]

Here it has been mentioned with the name of 'Makkah', which shows that in the times of the Prophet of Islām the city was named as 'Makkah'.

The source of the sounds (vocal organ) of the alphabetical letters 'b' and 'm' is one and the same: the lips. So by the passage of time 'Makkah' replaced 'Bakkah'. It can thus be appreciated that the original and ancient name of the place was 'Bakkah'. King David used this ancient name as it was in vogue during his days. It was only in the later centuries that it was replaced by Makkah.

The verse says, 'passing through the valley of Baca [they] make it a well;' Hagar passed through the valley of Baca in search of water for her son Ishmā'el. Consequently she was given a well [Beersheba or Zamzam]. Those who have happened to visit this valley of Bakkah know it well that 'Ka'bah' is situated in a low lying area. Previously, when there was a heavy rain it turned into a pond. Now, a very sophisticated drainage system has been constructed there and the rain-water is quickly swept away. So every clause of the verse is perfectly pertinent to the ground realities of Makkah.

Verse 7 asserts, 'They go from strength to strength.' It depicts the zeal of the pilgrims. As they draw nearer and nearer to the sanctuary, their fervour is increased, which gives them new strength and impetus instead of fatigue.

The second clause of the verse is, '*every one of them* in Zion appeareth before God' or, as NIV states, 'till each appears before God in Zion.' The word 'Zion' needs to be studied in a fair detail.

As regards its meanings, *Encyclopaedia Biblica* observes:

> Various explanations of the name have been given. Gesenius (*Thes*. 1164) and Lagarde (*Übers*. 84. n) derive from [a Hebrew word meaning] 'to be dry' (...) Wetzstein derives from 'to protect' so that the name would mean '*arx*, citadel'; cp Zin.[58]

Interpreter's Dic. of Bible explains:

> The etymology of the name is uncertain. It may be related to the Hebrew (sayon), 'dry place' 'parched ground' (Isa. 25:5; 32:2).'[59]

It would be appreciated that 'dry place' or 'parched ground' can be only applied to arid, barren, and sterile land of 'Makkah'. It can by no means be applied to the verdant and fertile land of 'Jerusalem'.

Like other Bible names 'Zion' may also have more than one significations. There may have been a 'Zion' of Makkah and the other of Jerusalem. But in the sense of 'dry place,' or 'parched ground' it can only be applied to 'Makkah' in the present context. It is not possible for the writer of this book to dilate upon this theme here. It may, however, be noted that the implication of the Zion of Jerusalem is to be ruled out due to the fact that there did not exist any sanctuary at Jerusalem at that time. The rest of the Psalm depicts the strong yearnings of King David to have some opportunity to visit the sanctuary of the Lord like other pilgrims.

It can thus be appreciated that as far back as the annals of history and tradition can be traced, there has been perpetually commemorated the act of Abraham's offering his genuinely 'only son', Ishmā'el, for sacrifice at the mountainous area in the land of Moriah (a mountain situated in Makkah). But there is not even a single place, or a ritual, or a festivity, or a trace, or a building amongst the Jewish people or the Christians to commemorate the event of the offering of Abraham his 'only son' for sacrifice. It is now unto the reader to derive an objective conclusion.

From the perusal of the material of the chapter it would easily be appreciated that:

(i) Some 'House of the Lord of nations' already existed during the days of King David.

(ii) It was a sanctuary and was abundanatly visited by pilgrims from far and near.

(iii) King David had happened to stay there for a considerable period of time.

(iv) It was situated in the valley of Bakkah.

(v) After going back to his motherland he could not have an opportunity to visit this sanctuary due to some reasons.

(vi) He expressed his earnest desire to visit this sanctuary.

(vii) He envies the birds which uninterruptedly make their nests in this sanctuary and reside there.

(viii) He is so fond of this 'house of the Lord' that he would prefer to be a doorkeeper there than to live in his own homeland, whom he calls the land of wickedness as compared to the sanctuary.

(ix) According to him 'a day in the court of Lord' is better than a thousand (else-where).

(x) The Jewish sanctuary (i.e. the Solomon's Temple) did not exist at that time. It was built by his son Solomon after his death. By that time there existed only the sanctuary of Ka'bah at Makkah, which was built by his primogenitor Abraham, and Ishma#'el about ten centuries earlier and hundreds of thousands of people visited it all the year through.

References

1. As to the authorship of this song, it can safely be considered as a genuine work of King David himself. Some of the authorities are given here. Matthew Henry's *An Exposition of the O&NT*, (4:324) explains in its introduction:

   Though David's name be not in the title of this song, yet we have reasons to think he was the penman of it, because it breathes so much of his excellent spirit and is so much like the sixty-third psalm which was penned by him; (...), witness this psalm, which contains the pious breathing of a gracious soul after God and communion with him.

   7th Day Adventist Bible Com. (3:827) writes in its introduction to this psalm:

   Ps 84 was composed by David, the Lord's 'anointed'(...). It is a passionate lyrical expression of devotion and love for the house of Jehovah and His worship. The psalm seems to describe the blessedness of those who dwell in the sacred precincts (vs. 1-4, 9-11); the blessedness of those who make pilgrimages to the sanctuary (vs. 5-8).

   Peake's Com. on the Bible (p. 431) observes:

   The period of its composition is clearly that of the monarchy.

   It shows that the commentators take it to be written by David himself.

2. The actual Hebrew word used here is îùëï 'mishkawn' which is the exact synonym for the Arabic word 'maskan', i.e., residence. According to the *Strong's Dictionary* (Entry 4908, p. 74), it means: '*a residence; dwelling (place), habitation.*' So 'thy tabernacles, O Lord of hosts' would literally mean: 'Your house O Lord of nations.' It would be 'Baytullah' in Arabic, which is al-Ka'bah of Makkah. Keeping in view the fact that the Solomon's Temple had not so far

been built, it becomes certain that it refers to only Ka'bah of Makkah, as there did not exist any 'House of Lord' on earth except it by that time.

3. 'Lord of hosts' may imply here that He is not the Lord of Israel only; but He is the Lord of all the nations.

4. *Gray & Adams Bible Com.*, 2:611 explains:

   David says not, Oh how I long for my palace, my crown, my sceptre, my kingdom; but oh how I long to return to the house of God! [the word 'return' shows that King David had previously been to this place.]

   It may, however, be noted that the construction of Solomon's Temple had not yet begun. By the time of King David, there existed only one 'House of God', which had been built at Bakkah (the name of Makkah at that time), by his forefathers, Abraham and Ishmā'el.

5. *NOAB* (p. 747) has afforded a very beautiful footnote on vv. 3-4, 'Envy of the birds and servitors [a male servant] who live there.' The comments by the *Collegeville Bible Com.* (p. 772) on these vv 3-4 are also noteworthy, 'All living things are safe from threat in the presence of the Lord.'

6. Matthew Henry's *An Exposition of the O&NT*, (4:24, 25) observes at this point:

   He would rather live in a bird's nest nigh God's altars than in a palace at a distance from them. It is better to be serving God in solitude than serving sin with a multitude. (...). Observe, David envies the happiness not of those birds that flew over the altars, and had only transient view of God's courts, but of those that had nests for themselves there. David will not think it enough to sojourn in God's house *as a way-faring man that turns aside to tarry for a night*; but let this be his rest, his home; here he will dwell.

7. *The 7th Day Adv. Bible Com.* (3:28) explains the verse:

   The general meaning of the verse, whose conclusion the poet only implies, is that even the birds have free access to the sacred precincts of the sanctuary, they make their homes there undisturbed, while the psalmist is exiled from the source of his joy, is denied the privilege of worshipping within the sacred enclosure. The nostalgic appeal of this verse is one of the most delicately beautiful expressions of homesickness in the whole realm of literature.

8. According to *Gray & Adams Bible Com.*, 2:611, 'still' here means, 'all the day long'.
9. NIV, (p. 621) translates it as: 'they are ever praising you', instead of: 'they will be still praising thee.'
10. *A New Catholic Com. on Hebrew Scripture* (p. 473) renders this v. as, 'Blessed [be] those who dwell in thy house, still they praise thee.' It further observes, 'Yet the idea of "They are pilgrims at heart" is consistent with the theme of the psalm.'
11. NIV, (p. 621) has well translated it as: 'who have set their hearts on pilgrimage', instead of: 'in whose heart *are* the ways *of them*.'
12. *The 7th Day Adventist Bible Com.* (3:828) explains the verse:

    The second blessing is bestowed on those who hold God in their hearts as they make the pilgrimage.

    It may be noted at this point that some of the translations have arbitrarily inserted the word 'Zion' here; e.g. *NOAB* (p. 849) and *Praise Songs of Israel: a Rendering of the Book of Psalms* (John DeWitt), as recorded in *OT books of poertry from 26 translations*, ed. Curtis Vaughan (Michigan: Zondervan Bible Publishers, 1973), p. 334, write: 'in whose heart are the highways to Zion.' *NOAB* has also recorded a footnote to it saying, 'Heb. lacks *to Zion*' (p. 849). But this word 'Zion' does not exist in most of the English translations. The original Hebrew also lacks it as quoted above with refence to *NOAB*. On the contrary most of the translations use here the word of 'pilgrimage' or 'pilgrim'.

    The Holy Bible Containing O & N T: An Improved Edition (American Baptist Publication Society), as recorded in *OT books of poertry from 26 translations*), p. 334, translates it as, 'In their heart the pilgrim-way.'

    James Moffatt translates it in his *'A New Translation of the Bible'* (London: Hodder and Stoughton, Ltd. At St Paul's House, 1941, p.660) as, 'Set out on pilgrimage!'

    New English Bible translates (p. 441) it as, 'Whose hearts are set on the pilgrim-ways'

    NIV translates it as, 'Who have set their hearts on pilgrimage.'

    CEV (p. 707) translates it as:

    You bless all who depend on you for their strength and all who deeply desire to visit your temple.

And the Temple of the Lord, by that time, was only the Ka'bah at Makkah.

It clearly shows that the theme of the Psalm 84 is the 'Pilgrimage'.

13. Matthew Henry's *An Exposition of the O&NT*, (4:326) here observes:

    Our way to heaven lies through a valley of Baca, but even that may be made a well if we make due improvement of the comforts God has provided for the pilgrims of the heavenly city.

14. *Gray & Adams Bible Com.*, 2:612 explains:

    To such a one, whose soul is athirst for God, the valley of Baca becomes a well, while the hot rock pours out its streams of blessing.

    It portrays a true state of mind of a Pilgrim to Makkah.

15. *The Peshitta*, (p.628):

    They have passed through the valley of weeping [the word 'weeping' shows that the actual word here was 'Baca', because its meaning, if not taken as a proper noun, is 'weeping'], and have made it a dwelling place; the Lawgiver shall cover it with blessings.

16. The actual Hebrew word used here in the Bible is çéى *'khahyil'*. According to *Strong's Dictionary*, (Entry 2428, p. 39), it means, 'an army, strength, band of men, company.'

17. *Gray & Adams Bible Com.*, 2:612 explains:

    The poet would rather be the humblest of the guests of Jehovah than dwell at ease among the heathen.

    It depicts the honour and esteem which the poet attaches to the 'House of God'.

18. *The Peshitta* (p. 628) presents it as:

    For the Lord God is our supply and our helper;

19. Ps. 84: 1-12 KJV.
20. *Servitor* means: A man servant (*Chambers Eng. Dic.*, 1989; 1345).
21. Smith's Bible Dic., 138.
22. I Sam, 25:1 NKJV.
23. Gen, 21:17-21 KJV.
24. From the Psalms in the *Book of Common Prayer of the Anglican Church* (as quoted by *OT Poetry 26 Tr*; 334).

25. James Moffatt, *A New Trans. of the Bible,* quoted in *OT Poetry 26 Tr*; 334 ('glen' means 'deep narrow valley').
26. NEB, p. 441.
27. 'Septuagint' or 'LXX' (meaning 'seventy', the number of the scholars who undertook the translation task), the Greek translation of the MT [Massoretic Text] of the Bible made at Alexandria during the 3rd and 2nd centuries BC.
28. 'Vulgate' means 'common'. It is the name of the Latin translation of the Bible made by St. Jerome and was commonly used by the Christians of that time. It was completed in ca. AD 450.
29. *The 7th Day Adventist Bible Com.*, 3:828.
30. *7th Day Adventist Bible Dic.* Revised 1979 edn., 114.
31. *Harper's Bible Dic.*, 89.
32. William Smith, *A Dic. of the Bible*, 73.
33. Rev. James L. Dow, *Collins Gem Dic. of the Bible*, 54.
34. J. Hasting's *Dic. of the Bible Revised One Vol. edn.*, 84.
35. J. Hastings, *A Dictionary of the Bible*, 1:230.
36. *Interpreter's Dic. of Bible*, 1:338.
37. *Jewish Encyclopaedia*, 2:415.
38. *A New Commentary on Holy Scripture*, 364.
39. *Peake's Com. on Bible*, 431.
40. *Strong's Dic. of the Hebrew Bible*, p. 21, entry 1056.
41. *Strong's Dic. of the Hebrew Bible*, p. 21, entry 1057.
42. *Strong's Dic. of the Hebrew Bible*, p. 21, entry 1058.
43. A detailed study on this subject has been undertaken by this writer in the Appendix 'Recording of the Vocalization Signs to the Text of the OT' to his work '*Muhammad Foretold in the Bible by Name*'.
44. Ibn al-Manẓūr, *Lisān al-'Arab* (Beirūt: Dār Ṣādir, 1300 AH), 10: 402.
45. Abū Manṣūr Muḥammad bin Aḥmad al-Azharī, *Tahdhīb al-Lughah* (al-Qāhirah: Al-Dār al-Miṣriyah littālīf wattarjamah, n.d.), 9:463,64.
46. *Mu'jam al-Wasīṭ* (Beirūt: Dār Iḥyā al-Turāth al-'Arabī, 1972), 1:67.
47. Ismāīl bin Ḥammād al-Jawharī, *Tāj al-Lughat wa Ṣiḥāḥ al-'Arabiyyah* (Beirūt: Dār al-'Ilm lil Malāyīn, 1984), 4:1576.

48. Al-Ustādh al-Ṭāhir Aḥmad al-zāvī, *Tartīb al-Qāmūs al-Muḥīṭ 'ala Ṭariqah al-Miṣbāḥ al- Munīr*, 1979, 1:308.
49. Al-Mu'allim Buṭrus al-Bustānī, *Muḥīṭ al-Muḥīṭ* (Beirūt: Maktabah Lubnān Nāshirūn, 1993), 50.
50. Aḥmad bin Fāris, *Mu'jam Maqāyīs al-Lughah* (Beirūt: Dār Iḥyā al-turāth al-'Arabī, 2001), 92.
51. Al-Khalīl bin Ahmad, *Kitāb al-'Ayn*, (Beirūt: Dār Iḥyā al-turāth al-'Arabī, 2001), 84.
52. Al-Imām Abī 'Abd Allāh Muḥammad bin Isḥāq al-Fākihī, *Akhbār Makkah fī Qadīm al-Dahr wa Ḥadīthihī* (Makkah: Maktabah al-Nahḍat al-Ḥadīthah, 1987), 2:282-3.
53. *Akhbār Makkah,* 2:293.
54. The Qurān, sūrah Āl 'Imrān 3:96,7.
55. *The Quran, An Eng. Trans.*, tr. N. J. Dawood, revd. Dr. Zayid, (Beirūt: Dar Al-Choura, 1980), 3:96,7; p. 43.
56. The Qur'ān al-Fatḥ 48:24.
57. *The Quran, An Eng. Trans.*, tr. N. J. Dawood, al-Fatḥ 48:24; p.43.
57. The Qur'ān al-Fatḥ 48:24.
58. *Enc. Biblica*, 4:5421.
59. *The Interpreter's Dic. of Bible*, 4:959.

Appendix-I

Beersheba (The Well of Seven or the Well of Zamzam)

'Beersheba' has been referred to in the body of the book a number of times. It required a detailed study, which could not have been undertaken there. It is discussed in detail in this appendix. The names of persons or places and their spellings have mostly been recorded in accordance with the Bible or the source books. The scheme of the symbols of transliteration of the present work has not been applied in the quotations. Generally, the scheme of the symbols of the source of the quotations has been followed. The salient features of this Appendix are:

(1) Abraham had settled his elder son, Ishmā'el, together with his mother Hagar, at the 'Wilderness of Beersheba', 'Wilderness of Pārān', or 'Moriah' (Zamzam, al-Ḥijāz, and al-Marwah) under the command of God: and not as a result of some so called jealousy or dispute between Hagar and Sarah[1].

(2) The event of settling Ishmā'el and Hagar at Beersheba took place in the childhood of Ishmā'el—when Isaac had not even been born yet—and the story of the weaning feast and the alleged jealousy of Sarah and her heinous cruelties towards Hagar are mere fables.

(3) Hagar and Ishmā'el were not cast away out of the door to wander helplessly in some wild wilderness without any

guidance. Such a ruthless and inconsiderate treatment is unbecoming and inconceivable of a common gentleman rather than of a benign and benevolent Apostle of Abraham's calibre. Abraham must himself have taken them to the destination appointed by God for their settlement, which he actually did.

(4) 'Beersheba' is a meaningful word and means (i) 'the Well of Seven' and (ii) 'the Well of an Oath'

(5) According to the record of the Bible 'Beersheba' can be located at more than one places. It has occurred in the Bible 34 times, but it is only once that it has been preceded by the qualifying word 'wilderness'.

(6) This singular use of the qualifying word 'wilderness' before 'Beersheba' singles out the 'Beersheba of the Well of Seven' from the rest of the 'Beersheba's' and signifies exactly the region of Makkah.

(7) In this context it denotes the well given to Hagar as a result of her seven rounds of running between the mounts of 'al-Ṣafā' and 'al-Marwah' in search of water.

(8) As such, this 'Beersheba' is the well of 'Zamzam' in Makkah.

(9) It is quite different from the 'Beersheba of the Well of Oath', which is at the SW of Canaan[2].

(10) The story of the Bible is a blend of various traditions and has a lot of objectionable and self-contradictory material in it. Therefore any of its statement is to be taken only after due scrutiny, and on its own merit.

The 'wilderness of Beersheba', where Hagar 'wandered' with her child, Ishmā'el, after Abraham had left her there, is mentioned in the Bible as below (Most of the points regarding this forthcoming passage have been discussed in a pretty detail, at the spot, in the footnotes. Therefore, no detailed discussion has been undertaken regarding them in the body of the article. These footnotes should be perused side by side with the following text of the Bible.):

And the child [Isaac] grew, and was weaned[3] : and Abraham made a great feast the *same* day that Isaac was weaned. And Sarah saw the son of Hagar[4] the Egyptian, which she had born unto Abraham, mocking[5] . Wherefore she said unto Abraham, *cast out*[6] *this bondwoman*[7] *and her son*[8] *: for the son of this bondwoman shall not be heir with my son*[9] [stress added], *even* with Isaac.[10] And the thing was very grievous in Abraham's sight[11] because of his son[12] . And God said unto Abraham, Let it not be grievous in thy sight because of the lad[13] , and because of thy bondwoman;[14] in all that Sarah hath said unto thee, hearken unto her voice; for in Isaac shall thy seed be called. And also of the son of the bondwoman will I make a [great] nation[15] , because he is thy seed[16] . And Abraham rose up early in the morning, and took bread, and a bottle[17] of water, and gave *it* unto Hagar, putting *it* on her shoulder, and the child to Hagar[18] and sent her away[19] : and she departed, *and wandered in the wilderness of Beer-sheba*[20] [stress added]. And the water was spent in the bottle, *and she cast the child under one of the shrubs*[21] [stress added]. And she went, and sat her down over against *him* a good way off, as it were a bowshot: for she said, Let me not see the death of the child. And she sat over against *him*, and lift up her voice, and wept. And God heard the voice of the lad[22] ; and the angel of God[23] called to Hagar out of heaven[24] , and said unto her, What aileth thee, Hagar?[25] Fear not[26] ; for God hath heard the voice of the lad where he *is*[27] . Arise, lift up the lad, and hold him in thine hand[28] ; for I will make him a great nation. *And God opened her eyes, and she saw a well of water; and she went, and filled the bottle with water, and gave the lad drink* [stress added][29] . And God was with the lad[30] ; and he grew, and dwelt in the wilderness, and became an archer. And he dwelt in the wilderness of Paran[31] : and his mother took him a wife out of the land of Egypt.[32]

Some important points of, or related to, this 'wilderness of Beersheba', are explained below:

(a) To ascertain the location of the *wilderness of Beersheba* it is to be noted that Chapter 21 of the book of Genesis of the Bible, from which this narrative has been taken, is a mixture of the three intricately interwoven traditions (Yahwistic, Priestly, and Elohistic).[33]

(b) As to the narrative reproduced above (Gen. 21:8-21), it is solely an Elohist Version.[34] This is mainly a narrative of the story of Hagar and Ishmā'el and ends with v.21. From v.22 to the end of the chapter, there is another story (regarding a treaty at certain other Beersheba [Well of Oath] between Abraham and Abimelech). It is quite a separate narrative and has nothing to do with the story of Hagar and Ishmā'el near Beersheba (Well of Seven). Scholars differ as to whether it is Elohistic or Yahwistic.[35]

(c) The word *Beersheba* has been used at 34 places in the Bible. It is only once in the whole of the Bible that it is preceded by the qualifying word *wilderness* (Gen. 21:14) and Abraham had settled Hagar and her son Ishmā'el in it. It is for the first time that the word *Beersheba* has been introduced in the Bible. At the same time it is the sole place in the whole of the Bible where the word *Beersheba* is related to Hagar and Ishmā'el both. The 'Beersheba' related to the treaty between Abraham and Abimelech is quite a different place, hundreds of miles away from it, and having nothing to do with it.

(d) 'Wilderness' means 'uncultivated, barren, uneven, and mountainous land or desert'. The word has also been used in the Bible figuratively in the sense of 'uninhabited', though it is not its literal sense. The original Hebrew word used in the Bible for this 'wilderness' is 'Midbār'. In the English Bible, the Hebrew word 'Midbār' has been translated either with the word 'wilderness' or with 'desert'. The use of this word 'Midbār' in the Bible in the sense of 'uncultivated and uninhabited place' is obvious from: 'Yet the defenced city shall be desolate[36], and left like a wilderness [in Hebrew 'midbār']'.[37] It has also been applied to convey other senses or implications in the Bible. Stanley A. Cook explains in *Enc. Biblica*:

The English word 'desert' ordinarily means a sterile sandy plain without vegetation and water–a 'sea of sand' such as, e.g., parts of the Sahara. This is not the meaning of the Hebrew word. No desert of this kind was known to Israel either before or after the occupation of Canaan. (…) *midbār*; AV 'desert,' RV 'wilderness'; (…). It is commonly employed to denote the wilderness of wanderings, which itself is a mountainous region, (…). The most prominent is that which was the scene of the wandering of Israel. It is commonly called *ham-Midbār;* (…), and with this agrees the circumstance that it is only in the later writings that the horror and lonesomeness of the 'wilderness' is referred to (e.g., Dt. 8:15).[38]

In the OT (according to the 'Authorized' and 'Revised' English Versions), the English word 'wilderness' has been used 270 times, out of which it has been used 256 times as the translation of 'Midbār'. In the Hebrew Bible (OT), there are different words for it (e.g. 'Midbār', 'Sarab', 'Arabah', 'Yasheemon', 'Tohoo', 'Kharabah', etc.). The Heb. word 'Midbār', is the most commonly used word for 'wilderness' and 'desert', and has been used in the OT for 269 times (256 times in the meaning of 'wilderness'; and 13 times in the meaning of 'desert'). Another Hebrew word for 'wilderness' is 'Arabah', which has been used for 59 times in different meanings (e.g. 5 times in the meaning of 'wilderness'; and 8 times in the meaning of 'desert', etc.). This 'Arabah' signifies a barren and sterile land, hence 'Arabia'. Other Hebrew words (e.g. Tohoo, Yasheemon, etc.) have also been used for this 'wilderness' for a number of times. The word used here is 'Midbār'. It has been explained by Shemaryahu Talmon, Professor, Bible Stuidies and Dean, Faculty of Humanities in the Hebrew Univ. of Jerusalem, in his detailed article 'Wilderness' in the Supplementary Volume of the *Interpreter's Dic. of Bible*, according to which it refers to:

> (…) arid or semiarid areas which are not suited for permanent settlement but in part can be utilized as pasture lands for small stock. (….). In the majority of occurrences, 'wilderness' carries negative overtones, referring to parched, inhospitable, and dangerous places. (….). No trees or other vegetation grow in this barren void, and no husbanded animals or civilized men live there. Anyone who ventures into this wilderness suffers hunger and thirst. (…). This wilderness is synonymous with utter

distress, a place cut off from life. (...). The Mesopotamian, for which Arabian desert lay to the W, where the sun sets, identified the wilderness as the area which leads to the nether [in a lower place or position] world. This idea appears to be reflected in scriptures in which *midhbar, `ᵃrabha, sᵉ*mama contrast with the Garden of Eden, the source of life and abundant growth[39] .

W.L. Reed explains in the same *Dic. of the Bible*:

The translation of several different words [he has written here in Heb. script: Midbar, Yasheemon, 'arabah, etc.]; often used interchangeably with 'DESERT.' An accurate translation is difficult, because the so-called wilderness regions included arid and semiarid territory as well as sandy desert, rocky plateaus, pasture lands, and desolate mountain terrain. Such regions existed in Canaan and beyond its E and S borders.[40]

Smith's *Dic. of Bible* explains:

MIDBAR. (...). It is most frequently used for those tracts of waste land which lie beyond the cultivated ground,[41]

Harper's *Bible Dic.* explains:

> Wilderness, a desolate or deserted area devoid of civilization. One Hebrew word above all others is used for 'wilderness,' or 'desert,' in the OT: midbar, indicating both 'that which is desolate and deserted' and 'that which is beyond,' i.e., beyond the limits of settlement and therefore of government control, perceived by both city dwellers and villagers as being essentially disorderly and dangerous, the home of wild beasts and savage wandering tribes. In time of war or repression refugees would flee to the midbar; (....). Midbar was for them, as 'wilderness' was originally in English, the wild, alarming wasteland, where men and women find themselves bewildered and disoriented.[42]

It means that the word 'midbār' used in the Hebrew Bible for 'wilderness' signifies a mountainous, sandy, desolate, inarable place, which is quite similar to the wilderness of Beersheba and Paran.

(e) 'Beersheba'[43] is a meaningful word.[44] It has literally two different meanings which are: (i) 'a well of seven'[45]; and (ii) 'a well of an oath or covenant'[46]. The 'Beersheba' related to the oath of Abraham and Abimelech, next to this story of Hagar and Ishma#'el, which starts with v. 22 of this chapter, is 'the well of the oath', from which it took its name[47].

(f) In this paragraph a study of the 'Beersheba' related to the 'the well of the oath' is being undertaken. Some important authorities are being quoted here to elaborate these second meanings. *Hasting's Revd. Dic. of Bible* explains that it was a place:

> where he [Abraham] made a covenant with Abimelech, from which the place is alleged to take its name ('well of the covenant,' according to one interpretation).[48]

J. Hasting's *Dic. of the Bible* explains:

> It (...) received its name ('Well of the oath') as having been the place, marked by a well, where Abraham entered into covenant with Abimelech, king of Gerar (Gn 21:31 E).[49]

According to McKenzie, it is:

> about 28 mi [miles] S [South; according to *Interpreter's Dic. of Bible* 'SW' (1:375)] of Hebron.[50]

Hebron (which is now called 'Al-Khalīl') lies twenty miles south (SSW) of Jerusalem[51]. This Hebron was the place where Abraham had permanently settled with his first wife Sarah; but he spent most of his own time at Beer-sheba, with his large number of flocks and herds, on his land, which was offered to him by Abimelech (Gen. 20:15); and dictionaries of the Bible have recorded the fact that it was a suitable pasture for the herds and flocks, for example *Harper's B.D.* explains:

> The Beer-sheba plain with its ample winter pasturage is well suited for seminomadic living; thus it served as the principal homestead of Israel's patriarchs.[52].

F. F. Bruce asserts that it had been a green grassy valley with human settlements in it, as back as 4th millennium BC:

On both sides of the Beer-sheba valley, in the Negeb, there is evidence of human settlement going back to the Chalcolithic Age (later fourth millennium BC [Gr. Chalkos = copper + lithos + stone]). (….). The Beer-sheba valley and its neighborhood were frequented by pastoralists like Abraham because the water-table was sufficiently high to be tapped by the digging of wells.[53]

E. Hull has described its present condition in similar way in the Hasting's *Dic. of Bible*:

> The soil in the valleys where there is some moisture is exceedingly rich, and is rudely cultivated by the fellahin, who succeed in producing fine crops of wheat and barley. In the tracts around Beer-sheba the Bedawin find ample pasturage for their flocks and herds, which towards evening assemble in crowds around the wells as they did three thousand years ago.[54]

It was quite a different place from the 'Wilderness of Beersheba', where Abraham had settled Hagar and Ishmā'el.

g) A detailed account of the 'Wilderness of Beersheba' related to Hagar and Ishmā'el is being afforded in the next paragraph. This Beersheba of Hagar and Ishmā'el was, in true sense of word, a 'wilderness': being a desolate, mountainous, sandy, sterile, uneven, and uncultivated land. In the present paragraph some points about the 'well of Oath' are being noted briefly. This 'well of Oath' was situated in a beautiful valley with thick green pastures. Archaeologists have traced human settlements at this place as early as the fourth millennium BC. According to the Bible a 'city' existed here in Isaac's times (Gen. 26:33). As such it could not have been the place where Abraham had settled Hagar and her son Ishmā'el, which had been a Midbār, *i.e.*, a desolate, uneven, mountainous, sandy, sterile, and uncultivated 'wilderness' in true sense of word.

h) The '*Beersheba*' in the first sense (the 'well of seven,'[55]), related to Ishmā'el and Hagar, is being dealt with in this paragraph. In the ancient times a name was given to a place due to the settlement of some tribe there or due to some remarkable event which happened there, or due to some conspicuous qualities of its location or the surroundings etc. The same is the case with both these *Beer-sheba's*.

Both the places, which were subsequently given the name of 'Beer-sheba', previously bore no particular name. So they were named due to the events that took place there. The first was called 'Beer-sheba' (the well of an oath or a covenant), because an oath had been carried out there between Abraham and Abīmelech. The second was given the name 'Beer-sheba' (the well of seven) after the seven rounds of running between al-Ṣafā and al-Marwah (Moriah of the Bible) by Hagar as a result of which she was made to discover this 'well of seven' by God through His angel; and this well had been commonly called by the Arabs as 'Zamzam'[56], hence the uncultivated and uninhabited area, surrounding this 'Well of Seven', was given the name of the 'Wilderness of Beersheba'. *Shorter Encyclopaedia of Islām* explains:

> Hadjar, cast off by Abraham and seeing Ishmā'el perishing of thirst, ran in despair seven times from one hill to the other;[57]

David Kerr explains:

> This [the circumambulation around the Ka'bah] is followed by running seven times between two small hills [al-Safa and al-Marwah], recalling the plight of Hagar and her son Ishmael who, in Islamic, Jewish and Christian tradition, were saved from certain death by a spring of water which God caused to break through the desert sands. This well is named in Islamic tradition as Zamzam,[58]

After a detailed study of Arabic and Biblical accounts, a summary of the event can be stated something like that:

> An extraordinary event happened there. Leaving Hagar and her child Ishmā'el in the mountainous, uncultivated, and sandy wilderness of Beer-sheba (Well of Seven) under the word of God, Abraham returned to his flocks and herds at Beersheba (Well of Oath) and his abode at Hebron. The food and water left by Abraham with her was used up in a few days. She was much perplexed and distressed. Nearby stood the hillocks of al-Ṣafā and al-Marwah (Moriah of the Bible). She ran from one hillock to the other in search of some food or drink, or somebody to help her; but in vain. After seven rounds of running between al-

Ṣafā and al-Marwah, a well was provided there for Hagar and her son in a strange manner. So the place was given the name of 'Beer-sheba'–'the well of seven'. Close by stood perhaps the remnants of the Sanctuary of the Ka'bah (or Bayt-Allah, i.e. House of Allah, which, in Hebrew, is Beth-el), on which the building was to be raised by Abraham and Ishmā'el in the near future.

It had been an established and well-known tradition among the Arabs since remote pre-Islāmic times that while performing the Pilgrimage of Makkah, they ran (performed Sa'y, according to the terminology of the Islāmic Pilgrimage) between the Mounts of al-Ṣafā and al-Marwah 'seven times'. Islām has retained this tradition, which came down from the times of Abraham, to remind the believers of Abraham's firm faith in and his total submission to Allah, and Hagar's trust in her Master; and to make them follow the spirit of the event. Al-Bukhārī has reported the event in detail:

> Narrated Ibn 'Abbās: 'Ibrāhīm (Abraham) brought her and her son Ishmā'el while she used to nurse him at her breast, to a place near the Ka'bah under a tree on the spot of *Zamzam*, at the highest place in the mosque. During those days there was nobody in Makkah nor was there any water. So he made them sit over there and placed near them a leather bag containing some dates, and a small water-skin containing some water, and set out homeward. Ishmā'el's mother followed him saying, 'O Ibrāhīm! Where are you going, leaving us in this valley where there is no person whose company we may enjoy, nor there is anything?' She repeated that to him many times, but he did not look back at her. Then she asked him, 'Has Allah ordered you to do so?' He said, 'Yes.' She said, 'Then He will not neglect us,'[59] and returned while Ibrahim proceeded onwards, and on reaching the Thaniya where they could not see him, he faced the Ka'bah, and raising both hands, invoked Allah saying the following supplication:

O our Lord! I have made some of my offspring to dwell in an uncultivated valley, by Your Sacred House (...) so that they may give thanks. (v. 14: 37).

Ishmā'el's mother went on suckling Ishmā'el and drinking from the water (she had). When the water in the water-skin had all been used up, she became [felt] thirsty and her child also became [felt] thirsty. She started looking at him (i.e., Ishmā'el) tossing in agony. She left him, for she could not endure looking at him, and found that the mount of al-Ṣafā was the nearest mountain to her on that land. She stood on it and started looking at the valley keenly so that she might see somebody, but she could not see anybody. Then she descended from al-Ṣafā and when she reached the valley, she tucked up her robe and ran in the valley like a person in distress and trouble, till she crossed the valley and reached al-Marwah mountain, where she stood and started looking, expecting to see somebody, but she could not see anybody. She repeated that (running between al-Ṣafā and al-Marwah) *seven times* [stress added].

Ibn 'Abbās told: The Prophet (Pbuh) said, 'This is the source of the tradition of Sa'y (the [briskly] walking) of people between them (i.e., al-Ṣafā and Al-Marwah).'

[The Prophet continued] 'When she reached Al-Marwah (for the last time) she heard a voice and she asked herself to be quite and listened attentively. She heard the voice again and said: 'O, (whoever you may be)! You have made me hear your voice; have you got something to help me?' And behold! She saw an angel at the place of *Zamzam*, digging the earth with his heel (or his wing), till water flowed from that place. She started to make something like a basin around it, using her hands in this way, and started filling her water-skin with water with her hands, and the water was flowing out after she had scooped some of it.'

The Prophet (Pbuh) added, 'May Allah bestow mercy on Ishmā'el's mother! Had she let the *Zamzam* (flow without trying to control it) (or had she not scooped from that water) (to fill her water skin), *Zamzam* would have been a stream flowing on the surface of the earth.'

The Prophet [pbuh] further added, 'Then she drank (water) and suckled her child. The angel said to her, "Don't be afraid of being neglected, for this is the House of Allah, which will be built by this boy and his father, and Allah never neglects His people." The House (i.e., Ka'bah) at that time was on a high place resembling a hillock, and when torrents came, they flowed to its right and left. She lived in that way till some people from the tribe of Jurham or a family from Jurham passed by her and her child, as they (i.e., the Jurham people) were coming through the way of Kada, they landed in the lower part of Makkah where they saw a bird that had the habit of flying around water and not leaving it. They said, "This bird must be flying around water, though we know that there is no water in this valley." They sent one or two messengers who discovered the source of water, and returned to inform them of the water. So they all came (towards the water).'

The Prophet (Pbuh) added: 'Ishmā'el's mother was sitting near the water. They asked her, "Do you allow us to stay with you?" She replied, "Yes, but you will have no right to possess the water." They agreed to that.'

The Prophet (Pbuh) further said, 'Ishmā'el's mother was pleased with the whole situation (...). So, they settled there, and later on they sent for their families who came and settled with them so that some families became permanent residents there. The child (i.e., Ishmā'el) grew up and learnt Arabic from them and (his virtues) caused them to love and admire him as he grew up, and when he reached the age of puberty they made him marry a woman from amongst them.'[60] (*Ṣaḥīḥ al-Bukhārī*, Kitāb Ahādīth al-Anbiā, Bāb Qawl Allah Ta'ālā 'Ittakhadhallahu Ibrāhīma Khalīla' Ḥadīth 3113).

It may be appreciated by a construing mind how clear, compact, consistent, spontaneous, flawless, and logical, is the statement of the event in this tradition.

(i) It has been recorded above that some well already existed, and was quite visible, at the site of the 'Beersheba of the Well of Oath', where the oath was carried out between Abraham and Abimelech; but it was without any name. It was named 'Beersheba or the Well of Oath' after the oath which was administered there between Abraham and Abimelech. Whereas *prima facie* there existed no well at the site of the 'Wilderness of Beersheba of the Well of

Seven', and the well was subsequently provided there in an unusual way, after Abraham had gone away, leaving Hagar and Ishmā'el in the 'Wilderness of Beersheba and Paran'. It shows that the Beersheba of 'the Well of Seven' and the Beersheba of 'the Well of Oath' are quite different places.

(j) There is the mention of a third 'Beersheba' as well in the Bible as recorded hereunder:

> Abimelech came to him from Gerar with Ahuzzath his friend and Phicol the commander of his army. Isaac said to them, 'Why have you come here? You hate me and you sent me away.' They answered, 'We have seen plainly that the Lord is with you, so we thought, Let the two of us put each other to the oath and make a treaty that will bind us. We have not attacked you, we have done you nothing but good, and we let you go away peaceably. Swear that you will do us no harm, now that the Lord has blessed you.' So Isaac gave a feast and they ate and drank. They rose early in the morning and exchanged oaths. Then Isaac bade them farewell, and they parted from him in peace. The same day Isaac's slaves came and told him about a well that they had dug: 'We have found water', they said. He named the well Shibah [there is a footnote 'x' on it: 'That is Oath']. This is why the city is called Beersheba [there is a footnote y on it: 'i.e. Well of an Oath'] to this day.[61]

According to most of the commentators and lexicographers of the Bible, the Beersheba concerning Abraham and the Beersheba concerning Isaac are one and the same place. There are others who believe they are different. There are, again, some others, who observe that it was a mere fabrication of the redactors of the Bible. Whatever the case may be, there is a special point to be noted here. Isaac did not find Hagar or any of the member of Ishmā'el family there. Had it been the same Beersheba (Well of Seven) related to Hagar and Ishmā'el story:

(i) It must have already existed there,

(ii) The well genuinely being the property of Hagar and Ishmā'el, they should have been very much there.

(iii) Ishmā'el being a hospitable person, must have entertained his younger brother Isaac there.

But to the utter disappointment of the writer and the readers, nothing of this sort had been witnessed there. The well did not exist there before this event. It was dug out there by the slaves of Isaac. There was neither Hagar nor the Ishmā'el family on the spot to entertain Isaac. Then it was Isaac who named it the well Shibah according to the Bible. It means that it was a well that came into being through digging it out by the slaves of Isaac and it was not the well that was provided and brought to the sight of Hagar through some extra-ordinary process.

From the above data it has become quite clear that the *wilderness of Beersheba* mentioned in the relevant passage of the Bible relates to the *uncultivated, mountainous, sandy, sterile and desolate land of Makkah and the well of Zamzam.* It, in no way, has anything to do with the cultivatable *Beersheba of the Well of Oath*, which is near the S. boundary of Canaan, where Abraham frequented to look after his herds and flocks which he had kept there.

To recapitulate and sum up the whole of the above theme, some conspicuous points are given below:

1. There are some interpolations, additions, deletions, and alterations in the passage, which render the whole story quite doubtful. Any of its statement should, therefore, be judged on its own merit after examining it critically.
2. The story depicts Sarah as a jealous, revengeful, spiteful, and mean-spirited woman. It is quite unbecoming and unbelievable of a lady of Sarah's calibre, and as such the whole of this episode looks to be a fabrication.
3. Hagar was the daughter of the king of Egypt and as such a princess. She was given to Abraham and Sarah to be reared up and educated and for learning noble and godly etiquette under the guidance of Abraham and Sarah, and to serve the family, as an acknowledgement of its piety and godliness. She was not a 'bondwoman' sold by his father, the king of Egypt. As such all the stories of Sarah's maltreatment to

Hagar are simply fabrications. Even if Hagar had been a slave-girl, it was not proper for Sarah's grace to injure her feelings by reminding her of her inferior status and to subject her to such ill treatment.

4. When Hagar and Ishmā'el were settled at Beersheba, Ishmā'el was a child of very young age which is obvious from the clauses that Abraham: 'took some bread and a skin of water and, giving them to Hagar, put the child on her shoulder'; and Hagar 'cast the child under one of the shrubs'; and the angel of God said to Hagar, 'lift up the lad, and hold him in thine hand.' On the other hand it occurred as a result of the 'mocking' of Ishmā'el to Isaac at the time of the weaning feast of Isaac. The weaning took place when Isaac was either two years old or three. He was younger than Ishmā'el by fourteen years. It means that Ishmā'el was a youth of not less than sixteen or seventeen years at that time. Hagar could not have 'put him on her shoulder' or 'cast him under one of the shrubs' or 'lift up the lad, and hold him in her hand.' All this makes quite clear that the episode of the weaning feast, in its present form, is inconsistent and incredible; and the noble Sarah stands exonerated of all the charges of jealousy etc., and this episode of the story is also to be rejected on merit.

5. Abraham had abandoned Hagar and Ishmā'el in the wilderness of Beersheba to be settled there under the orders of God. He should not have worried, as he was doing it under the command of God, and he had previously witnessed that God was the Sustainer of the family.

6. The word 'Beersheba' has been used at 34 places in the Bible. It is only in connection with both Hagar and Ishmā'el that it has been preceded by the word 'wilderness'. It is due to the fact that this 'Beersheba' is a 'wilderness' in true sense of word; whereas the other 'Beersheba' is a green and fertile place abounding in water.

7. 'Beersheba' is a meaningful word which means the 'Well of Seven'; or the 'Well of Seven Rounds of Running between

the Mounts of al-Ṣafā and al-Marwah (Moriah of the Bible)'; or the 'Well which was given to Hagar as a result of her Seven Rounds of Running between the Mounts of al-Ṣafā and al-Marwah'.

8. 'Beersheba' also means the 'Well of Oath', which relates to the covenant between Abraham and Abimelech, and to the covenant between Isaac and Abimelech, carried out in the SW end of Canaan. It has nothing to do with the former 'Beersheba' or the 'Well of Seven [Rounds of Running between the Mounts of al-Ṣafā and al-Marwah]'.

9. 'Wilderness' is the English rendering of the Hebrew word 'Midbār' [in Heb. character 'îãáø'], which means: 'sandy, barren, uneven, uncultivated, and mountainous land or desert'. These qualities are promptly relevant to the 'Beersheba' of the 'Well of Seven' i.e., Makkah and its environment. As to the 'Beersheba' of the 'Well of Oath', they cannot be applied to it.

10. 'Beersheba of the Well of Oath', already existed at the place where the oath was carried out between Abraham and Abimelech (or, in the case of the oath between Isaac and Abimelech, it was dug out by the slaves of Isaac); Whereas no well was visible or dug out at the site of the 'Wilderness of Beersheba of the Well of Seven'. It makes clear that the 'Beersheba of the Well of Oath' and the 'Beersheba of the Well of Seven' are quite different places. The 'Beersheba of the Well of Seven' is the 'Well of Zamzam', which was given to Hagar as a result of her running seven times between the hillocks of al-Ṣafā and al-Marwah in search of water.

References

1. *Chambers Biographical Dictionary* explains (p.1633):

   Sarah, whose name means 'princess' in Hebrew, was the wife of Abraham and mother of Isaac. She accompanied Abraham from Ur to Canaan (Gen 12-23) and *pretended to be Abraham's sister before Pharaoh in Egypt and Abimelech in Gerar, since her beauty and their desire for her might have endangered Abraham's life. Pharaoh took her as his wife, and Abraham prospered, but when the truth was revealed, Pharaoh banished them both* [stress added]. Long barren, she eventually gave birth to Isaac in her old age, fulfilling God's promise that she would be the ancestor of nations (Gen 17.16). She died at the age of 127 in Kiriath-arba.

This account of Sarah has been reproduced to show how shameful a character is depicted of the great patriarch.

2. *New Shorter Oxf. Eng. Dic.*, 1:325 s.v. 'Canaan', explains:

   Ancient name of western Palestine, promised in the OT and Hebrew Scriptures to the children of Israel (Exod. 3:17 etc.)

3. Chambers *Essential English Dic.*, 1998, p. 1115 explains:

   A mother weans her baby when she gradually stops feeding it with milk from her breast and gives it increasing amounts of other kinds of food.

   R.J. Clifford and R. E. Murphy have noted in their commentary to the book of Genesis in '*The New Jerome Bible Com.*', ed. R. E. Brown, etc, (Bangalore: T.P.I., 1994), 24:

   The age of weaning was three years.

   The Soncino Chumash, a Jewish Commentary to the Torah, p.103, has quoted Rabbi Shelomoh Yitschaki (1040-1105) that it took place 'At the age of two years.' *J. Hastings Dic. of Bible.*, 2:277 explains:

   [In Gen. 21] We are told of the birth of Isaac (vv. 1-7). On the occasion of the festival which was held perhaps two or three years later.

   In its Vol. I, it has been told by H. A. White (p.301):

   It was not fully weaned for two or three years.

   It shows that a child was weaned at the age of two or three years. According to Gen. 16:16:

   Abraham was eighty-six years old when Hagar bore him Ishmael.

   According to Gen. 21:5:

   Abraham was a hundred years old when his son Isaac was born to him.

   It means that there is a difference of fourteen years in the ages of the two brothers; and when Isaac is said to be weaned, his elder brother, Ishma'el, should have been a teenager of sixteen (14+2) or seventeen (14+3) years. Having grown up in open-air tough life and fed mainly on milk and meat, he would have been a stout, strong, and sturdy youth. But according to the forthcoming verses he looks to be a suckling baby or having just been weaned. These self-contradictory statements make the weaning feast episode incredible. The commentators of the Bible have also noted the discrepancy. Eugene H. Maly, in his commentary on the book of Genesis in The Jerome Bible Com., p. 22, notes:

From 17:25 and 21:8 we can deduce that Ishmael would be about 16 years old, which clashes with the present account (cf. vv. 14-17).

It shows that the statements of the Bible about the age of Ishmā'el at the time of his being settled in the wilderness of Beersheba/Paran are self-contradictory. One should, therefore, judge every part of the story analytically on its own merit.

4. This phrase explicitly signifies that Ishmā'el was the son of Hagar, whom she had born unto Abraham, and Sarah had no right to claim him her son. Whereas it is noted:

   Now Sarai, Abram's wife, had borne him no children. And she had an Egyptian maidservant whose name was Hagar. 2 So Sarai said to Abram, 'See now, the LORD has restrained me from bearing *children*. Please, go in to my maid; perhaps I shall obtain children by her.' [How queer that a lady can 'obtain children by' some other lady for herself!] And Abram heeded the voice of Sarai. 3 Then Sarai, Abram's wife, took Hagar her maid, the Egyptian, and gave her to her husband Abram to be his wife, after Abram had dwelt ten years in the land of Canaan. (Gen. 16:1-3 NKJV). So he went in to Hagar, and she conceived. (...). And when Sarai dealt harshly with her, she fled from her presence. [So Sarai ill-treated her and she ran away (Gen. 16:6 NEB)]. (...). And the Angel of the Lord said to her: 'Behold, you are with child. And you shall bear a son. You shall call his name Ishmael, because the Lord has heard your affliction ['ill-treatment' (Gen. 16:11 NEB)].' (...). So Hagar bore Abram a son; and Abram named his son, whom Hagar bore, Ishmael. (*Nelson Study Bible,* Gen. 16:1,3,4,6,11,15; p. 33f).

   This statement does not seem to be true. As is explained in a later footnote (302) on 'bondwoman' of v 10, Hagar was not Sarah's maidservant. She was a princess and was offered to Sarah and Abraham by her father, the king of Egypt. [see Chapter II, footnote

No. 19 above] Even if she was a maidservant of Sarah, she had ceased to be so when Sarah gave her to Abraham as his wife. It is a matter of natural Justice that the status of motherhood should go only to that lady, who actually gives birth to the child in question. No woman, who is not the actual mother of the child, should be allowed to usurp the motherhood of this child from the woman who physically gave birth to it. No lady, irrespective of her social status, should be allowed to exploit another lady, who happens to be poor, weak or helpless. Whosoever commits this heinous act is a cruel criminal. Had there been any such unjust local tradition contrary to this natural justice, it was not desirable and becoming of the patriarch prophet Abraham to follow it. He ought to have amended it according to the canons of divine and natural justice. A prophet of Abraham's status is not meant to follow the prevailing inequities of the society. He is sent to root out all the inequities and establish and maintain divinely natural justice in the whole of his jurisdiction, not to say of his own family. So the above story cannot be treated as correct; and, by all canons of justice and equity, Ishma`el was the genuine and legitimate first-born son of Abraham from his legitimate wife Hagar, enjoying full rights of a first-born son. On the Biblical clause 'Now Sarai, Abram's wife, had borne him no *children'* Nelson Study Bible (p. 33) remarks:

In the world of the OT, infertility caused great distress (see 25:21). At that time, the woman was always blamed. When a woman was not able to conceive a child, her husband might divorce her.

Had Abraham observed the customs of the time, he would have unjustly punished Sarah by divorcing her on the charge of infertility, for which she was not to blame according to natural justice. It shows that (i) Ishmā'el was Abraham's legitimate son from Hagar for all purposes; (ii) Hagar was Abraham's legitimate wife when she gave birth to Ishmā'el; and it can only be *mala fide* asserted that she did not enjoy the full status of a wife. (iii) It is baseless to claim that Ishmā'el did not hold the full status of being Abraham's son. As a Prophet of the Lord, Abraham was not bound to; and did not observe; and was not supposed to observe; the unjust customs of the prevailing pagan societies. It was rather mandatory for him to change all such oppressive customs.

5. *The New Jerome Bible Com.*, 24 here observes:

with her son Isaac: This phrase seems to have dropped out of the MT by haplography [the inadvertent writing once, of what should have been written twice (*The Chambers Dic.*, 1995, s.v. 'haplography' p.762)]; the phrase is preserved by the LXX and the Vg [Vulgate, i.e. the Latin Version].

It shows a form of 'omission' in the text of the Bible by its redactors. Such errors are not an uncommon phenomenon in the Bible.

Another point to be noted under the word translated here as 'mocking' is that in Hebrew it is öç÷, i.e., in Arabic characters, ṣ+ḥ+q = 'ṣaḥaqa' or 'zaḥaqa', or exactly transliterated 'ḍaḥaka'. There does not exist the letter 'ḍ' in the Hebrew alphabet; and it uses the letter 'ṣ' in lieu of it. According to the *Strong's Dic. of Heb. Bible* entry. 6711, p. 99, it means, as a prim. root:

to *laugh* outright (in merriment or scorn); by impl. to sport:—¾ laugh, mock, play, make sport.

That's why Gunther Plaut's '*The Torah, A Modern Com.*' p.139 translates it:

Sarah saw the son, whom Hagar the Egyptian had borne to Abraham, playing.

Some of the other translations of the Bible have also used here the word 'playing' instead of 'mocking', e.g., *New Jerusalem Bible*, NOAB [it writes here 'playing with her son Isaac' and gives in note 'g' below 'Gk Vg: Heb lacks *with her son Isaac*.'], The Torah MT, NAB, RSV (Catholic edn.), TEV, GNB, New Catholic Com. on Holy Scripture, *Soncino Chumash* [making sport], etc. *The Wycliffe Bible Com.*, (1987), p.26, has explained the episode as follows:

It has been translated 'mocking', 'sporting', 'playing', and 'making sport.' There is no good reason here to introduce the idea of mocking. What Ishmael was doing does not matter so much as the fact that it infuriated Sarah. Perhaps she simply could not bear to see her son playing with Ishmael as with an equal. Or it may be that green-eyed ['green-eyed' was used by Shakespeare in Othello 3:3 to mean 'very jealous'] jealousy took full control. Sarah may have feared that Abraham, out of love for Ishmael, would give the older lad the prominent place in the inheritance.

How grimly the character of noble Sarah has been depicted. It is quite unbecoming of the lady, who has left her homeland and her family; and who has undertaken the troublesome journeys of thousands of miles for the sake of her faith and her loyalty to her husband; and for whose protection God had done miracles: that she would treat so ruthlessly to the second wife of her husband and the mother of her husband's son. And, moreover, that she would so indifferently injure the feelings of her godly husband at his such an old age. It is quite unbelievable and renders this part of the story as fabricated.

6. Eugene H. Maly has noted here in the *Jerome Bible Com.*, 22:

   Ancient law ordinarily forbade the expulsion of a slave wife and her child, and no justification for it is indicated here as in 16:4; Abraham accordingly hesitates (v.11).

   But the redactor of the Bible does not hesitate to smear Abraham with the innocent blood of this so-called 'slave wife and her child' by throwing them out of his door helplessly, possibly to fall a victim to any quite foreseeable misfortune. It means that Abraham not only violates the natural and religious duties towards his child and his wife and acts ruthlessly and inhumanely, but also disregards the prevailing ancient laws, which were genuinely good to be observed to the letter, as the may be formulated by some prohet. Can a man on earth believe it?

7. It looks not to be true that Hagar was a maid, or a slave-girl, or a bond-woman of Sarah. She was a princess, being the daughter of the Egyptian king, who offered her to Abraham to serve him and his wife Sarah, and to be brought and reared up in a pious atmosphere. She had been purposely described by the redactors of the Bible as a slave girl, as can be appreciated from the following excerpts:

   That Hagar appears as a slave-woman is a necessary consequence of the theory on which the Hebrew myth is based, the notion being that Ishma'el was of inferior origin. (*Enc. Biblica*, p. 1933).

   It purports that slavery was attributed to Hagar to prove Ishmā'el inferior to Isaac. Whereas the fact is that she was an Egyptian princess; as is clear from the following quotation of *the Jewish Encyclopedia*:

   According to the Midrash (Gen. R. xiv.), Hagar was the daughter of Pharaoh, who, seeing what great miracles God had done for Sarah's sake (Gen. xii, 17), said: 'It is better for Hagar to be a slave in Sarah's house than mistress in her own.' In this sense Hagar's name is interpreted as 'reward' ('Ha-Agar' = 'this is reward'). (...). Hagar is held up as an example of the high degree of godliness prevalent in Abraham's time, (...). Her fidelity is praised, for even after Abraham sent her away she kept her marriage vow, (...). Another explanation of the same name is 'to adorn,' because she was adorned with piety and good deeds (l.c.). (*Jewish Enc.*, 6:138).

H. E. Ryle has also reproduced the same opinion in his article on 'Hagar':

Rashi, in his commentary on 6:1, records the belief that Hagar was a daughter of Pharaoh, who, after seeing the wonders that had been done for Sarah, declared that it was better for his daughter to be a bondservant in the house of Abraham than a mistress in the palace of another. (J. Hastings, *Dic. of Bible*, 2:278.)

8. *The New Jerome Bible Com.*, here observes:

Sarah in her anger brands her rival 'that slave woman and her son,' not even mentioning their names (p. 24).

It depicts Sarah so spiteful a woman, as cannot be believed and the story based on it cannot be treated as credible one. The following excerpt shows what natural but shameful and unbelievable conclusions the scholars of the Bible draw from these verses. *Jewish Enc.* explains:

Sarah took revenge (Gen. xvi) by preventing her intercourse with Abraham, by whipping her with her slipper, and by exacting humiliating services, such as carrying her bathing-materials to the bath (l.c.); she further caused Hagar by an evil eye to miscarry, and Ishma'el, therefore, was her second child. (*Jewish Enc.*, 6: 138).

What an ugly fabrication! Only a devil can believe it! It shows the unbelievable mean-spiritedness of Sarah towards Hagar and her son Ishmā'el; of which, even some learned Christian scholars are forced to blame her (see next footnote).

9. *The Collegeville Bible Com., OT*, ed. Dianne Bergant, 1992, observes:

It is Sarah's jealousy, not Hagar's arrogance, that leads her to demand that Abraham expel the two. She fears that Isaac's future inheritance is threatened by Ishmael's presence in the home. (p.60).

This is obviously unjust and cannot be expected from noble Sarah. It renders the story unbelievable. Some heart-rending excerpts are afforded here from the *Expositor's Bible*, which pose a serious question mark to the credibility of the story:

The act of expulsion was itself unaccountably harsh. (…). There may have been some law giving Sarah absolute power over her maid; but if any law gave her power to do what was now done, it was a thoroughly barbarous one, and she was a barbarous woman who used it. It was one of those painful cases in which one poor creature, clothed with a little brief authority, stretches it to the utmost in vindictive maltreatment of another. Sarah happened to be mistress, and, instead of using her position to make those under her happy, she used it for her own convenience, for the gratification of her own spite, and to make those beneath her conscious of her power by their suffering. (...). She breathed freely when Hagar and Ishmael were fairly out of sight. A smile of satisfied malice betrayed her bitter spirit. No thought of the sufferings to which she had committed a woman who had served her well for years, who had yielded everything to her will, and who had no other natural protector but her, no glimpses of Abraham's saddened face, visited her with any relentings. It mattered not to her what came of the woman and the boy to whom she really owed a more loving and careful regard than to any except Abraham and Isaac. It is a story often repeated. One who has been a member of the household for many years is at last dismissed at the dictate of some petty pique [i.e. 'a feeling of annoyance and displeasure, esp. caused by the hurting of one's pride.' (*Longman's Dic. of Eng. Language and Culture*, 1992, p. 999)] or spite [i.e. to deliberately annoy or upset someone] as remorselessly and inhumanly as a piece of old furniture might be parted with. Some thoroughly good servant, who has made sacrifices to forward his employer's interest, is at last, through no offence of his own, found to be in his employer's way, and at once all old services are forgotten, all old ties broken, and the authority of the employer, legal but inhuman, is exercised. It is often those who can least defend themselves who are thus treated; no resistance is possible, and also, alas! the party is too weak to face the wilderness on which she is thrown out, and if any [i.e. any one] cares to follow her history, we may find her at the last gasp under a bush. Still, both for Abraham and for Ishmael it was better this severance should take place. (....). For Ishmael himself, too, wronged as he was in the mode of his expulsion, it was yet far better that he should go. (...). All he required to call out his latent powers was to be thrown thus on his own resources. (...). But the two fugitives are soon reminded that, though expelled from Abraham's tents and protection, they are not expelled from his God. Ishmael finds it true that when father and mother forsake him, the Lord takes him up. At the very outset of his desert life he is made conscious that God is still his God, mindful of his wants, responsive to his cry of distress. (...). God still 'heard the voice of the lad, and the angel of God called to Hagar out of heaven.' It is this voice of God to Hagar that so speedily, and apparently once for all, lifts her out of despair to cheerful hope. It would appear as if her despair had been needless; at least from the words addressed to her, 'What aileth thee, Hagar?' (....). When Ishmael turned his back on the familiar tents, and flung his last gibe at Sarah, he was really setting out to a far richer inheritance, so far as this world goes, than ever fell to Isaac and his sons. [*The Expositor's Bible* {a Com. in 25 Volumes}, ed. W. Robertson Nicoll (NY: A. C. Armstrong & Son, 1903), 1: 214-15, 17-19].

Of course this account of the mistreatment of a lady and the misfortunes of the other is a beautifully composed, well-worded, heart-rending piece of literature; but on the other hand, this is all unbelievable. It depicts Sarah as a cruel, jealous, short tempered, ill mannered and a mean-spirited woman; which is unbecoming to a lady for whom God had done so great miracles, and who remained extremely faithful towards her husband during all the years of his troublesome migratory journeys. It also depicts Abraham to be unjustly neglectful to his responsibilities towards his firstborn son and the mother of this son, playing in the hands of the stepmother of this boy. Thus there remains no doubt that this is unbelievable and a fabrication of some redactor. Being the noble 'life partner' (an eastern version of 'wife', as the marriage was considered as a life long bondage there) of the patriarch Abraham, Sarah must have been a generous and kind-hearted lady. Having been established that the story is quite incredible, it can be safely concluded that Ishmā'el was not an outcast due to the jealousy of his stepmother. It was rather the design of the Lord to plant a center and a mission of monotheism in the heart of Arabia. At the same time it was a trial of the devotion of Abraham and a sort of trial and training for Hagar and Ishmā'el to inculcate in them the trust and faith in God. God consoled Abraham that He shall not leave the child and his mother uncared-for or let them perish in the wilderness. Rather, as 'Allen P. Ross' puts it in '*The Bible Knowledge Com.*', (Illinois: Victor Books, 1985), p. 63:

God assured Abraham that Ishmael would have a future because he too was Abraham's offspring (vv. 11-13).

10. *The New Jerome Bible Com.* here observes (p. 24):

The peaceful playing of the two boys stirs in Sarah deep feelings of anxiety about her own son's inheritance, since both boys are sons of Abraham. (...), she wants Isaac alone to be the heir of the grand promises.

It is unbelievable that Sarah may be so malicious, envious, unjust, and selfish.

11. *The Nelson Study Bible* has noted on p. 43:

But even in that culture it was reprehensible to send Ishmael away. When a surrogate wife had borne a son to one's husband, that mother and child could not be dismissed even if the first wife subsequently gave birth to a son. This partly explains Abraham's reluctance to do what Sarah demanded.

B. Vawter has also expressed similar observations in '*A New Catholic Com. on Holy Scripture*', p. 193:

Sarai did not have the right to send Hagar away, since Ishmael was Abraham's heir.

It further observes on p.195:

However, for a jealous mother, it sufficed to see her son together with the slave-girl's on a position of equality for her to demand the expulsion of Hagar and her child. If the situation presupposed is that which seems to underlie ch 16, then Sarah did not have the right to drive Hagar away; see on 16:1-6. As contrary to established social custom.

How can one believe that a pious lady of Sarah's calibre and the life partner of the great prophet, Abraham, could have committed so heinous an offence! Should anybody take it as a fact or a fable?

12. *The New Jerome Biblical Com.*, has genuinely felt:

To Abraham, the natural father of Ishma'el, Sarah's ultimatum causes great pain. (p.24).

A pious and Godfearing lady cannot injure her husband's feelings in this manner. It again weakens the credibility of the incident.

13. It means that God appreciates the natural affectionate grievance of Abraham towards his son Ishmā'el, and consoles him that there is no reason to be worried. When you are doing it under My command, you should rest assured that I will not forsake him to get perished.

It also shows that Abraham loved his 'firstborn' and the 'only son' very much.

14. It shows that Abraham had all the natural and due concern and regard towards Hagar. Then how could he have put her at the mercy of her ruthless rival?

15. *LXX, Vulgate, Samaritan Pentateuch, and Syriac Bible* record the word 'great' before the word 'nation', which has been omitted here. It is one of the examples of the intentional alterations of the redactors of the Bible. *New Jerome Bible Com.* Records:

    Besides, from Ishmael 'a great (LXX, Vg, Sam, Syr) people' will come forth. (p.24).

    The wording of the *New Jerusalem Bible* is:

    But the slave-girl's son I shall also make into a great nation, for he too is your child. (p.40).

    Some of the other translations of the Bible have also inserted the word 'great' with the word 'nation', e.g., *The Wycliffe Bible Com., CEV, Knox, New Jerusalem Bible, NEB, NAB, Collegeville Bible Com.*, etc. The omission of 'great' by some redactors is to be noted.

16. The following sentences of the Bible be carefully noted:

    (...) for in Isaac shall thy seed be called. And also of the son of the bondwoman will I make a [great] nation, because he is thy seed.

    What do the words 'for in Isaac shall thy seed be called' signify?

    What the difference is between this and the next sentence, i.e.

    And also of the son of the bondwoman will I make a [great] nation, because he is thy seed.

    If someone says that it is only Isaac in whom Abraham's seed is to be called and not in Ishmā'el, then it can be asked whether Ishmā'el was not a legitimate seed of Abraham. How can two similar sentences like these signify different meanings?

17. The Hebrew word for this 'bottle' is 'chemeth' which means 'a skin', as translated by *New Jerusalem Bible* etc. *Strong's Concise Heb. Bible Dic.* (entry 2573, p.41) says: 'a skin *bottle*'. While explaining the word 'bottle', *Smith's Dic. of Bible* (p. 95) writes:

    The Arabs keep their water, milk and other liquids in leathern bottles. These are made of goatskins. When the animal is killed they cut off its feet and its head, and draw it in this manner out of the skin without opening its belly.

18. Some of the other Translations:
    (i) and took bread and a skin of water, and gave it to Hagar, putting it on her shoulder, along with the child–RSV Catholic edn., 16;
    (ii) gave bread and a skin bag of water. He put the child on her back–CCB, 72;
    (iii) took some bread and a skin of water and, giving them to Hagar, put the child on her shoulder–*New Jeru. Bible*, 40;
    (iv) and took bread and a skin of water, and gave it to Hagar, putting it on her shoulder, along with the child, –NOAB, 26;
    (v) took some bread and a skin of water, and gave them to Hagar. He placed them over her shoulder, together with the child,—The Torah (A new trans. of the Holy Scriptures according to the Masoretic text, Philadelphia: 1967), p. 34.

    How could it be that poor Hagar could carry the load of a bag of bread, a water-skin full of water, and, in addition to it, a boy of seventeen (If the statement of the Bible, that this incident took place after the weaning feast of Isaac, be taken as true, Ishmā'el would have been seventeen at that time)! And how could it be that Abraham, that pious, God-fearing, hospitable, and kind-hearted old patriarch and prophet, became so cruel towards his own second wife and the mother of his firstborn son! And how could it be that the son, a young man of seventeen years' age, instead of extending a helping hand to his kind mother, added insult to her injuries; and plunged onto her shoulder! Isn't it all a scandal for character assassination of the pious and noble personalities of Sarah, Abraham, and Ishmā'el? Just incredible! A footnote of *The New American Bible* (Thomas Nelson Publishers, Nashville, 1987, p. 20) on these verses would show how freely the corrections (or corruptions) and interpolations had been made in the text of the Bible by its redactors to make it agreeable to their whims:

    Placing the child on her back: the phrase is translated from an emended form of the Hebrew text. In the current faulty Hebrew text, Abraham put the bread and the waterskin on Hagar's back, while her son apparently walked beside her. This reading *seems to be a scribal attempt at harmonizing the present passage with the data of the Priestly source,* [stress added] in which Ishmael would have been at least fourteen years old when Isaac was born; (...). But in the present Elohist story Ishmael is obviously a little boy, not much older than Isaac.

19. It is quite unnatural that Abraham would have 'cast out' his beloved son, Ishmā'el, and his mother, Hagar, so helplessly to wander in the wilderness on the orders of his wife, Sarah, the rival of Hagar. He was rather supposed to maintain justice between his wives, being the herald of justice and clemency from the Lord. Noble Sarah could also not have been so cruel as to ask his husband to perform such an inhumane act. In fact it was under the command of God that Abraham had accordingly planted a 'would be' center of monotheism in the heart of Arabia. And it was predetermined that Ishmā'el should be brought up independently in an open and destitute atmosphere to observe of himself the protections and provisions of God: that may inculcate in him the will to surrender himself before God, even if He requires him to offer himself for sacrifice. Since Abraham had done all this under the command of God, and, of course, with His Blessings, he had not to worry about the future of the lad and his mother. God consoled Abraham that He shall not leave the child and his mother uncared-for or let them perish in the wilderness. Rather, as Allen P. Ross puts it in *The Bible Knowledge Com.*, p. 63:

    God assured Abraham that Ishmael would have a future because he too was Abraham's offspring (vv. 11-13).

    Abraham had earlier unhesitatingly plunged himself into the pyre (that otherwise was tantamount to suicide, which is not permissible in any religion or code of life) and had abandoned his homeland for his divine cause unflinchingly; and had observed great wonders of God therein. So he should not have been worried about the future of his beloved 'only son' and his mother when he was doing it under the unequivocal command of his Lord. It figures this part of the story as nothing more than a fable.

20. i.e. bewildering, dreadful, desolate, barren, and mountainous land around Beer-sheba (the Well of Seven).

21. Had Ishmā'el been a grown up youth of 16 or 17 years, how Hagar could have 'cast the child under one of the shrubs'. It makes it decisively clear that the event of settling Ishmā'el and Hagar at Beersheba took place in the childhood of Ishmā'el and the story of the weaning feast and the alleged jealousy of Sarah has no ground.

22. It means that Ishmā'el was not left alone and 'uncared-for'. If his father had left him there, and that too under the command of God, God Himself was very much there as his Protector and Sustainer.

23. It might not have been the angel of God, but God Himself who called to Hagar. It is a sort of alteration made by the redactors of the Bible. *A New Catholic Com. on Holy Scripture*, p.193, has pointed out:

    Here and in 9f reference is made to the 'angel of Yahweh', while in 13 the Person who speaks to Hagar is identified with Yahweh himself. By some this is explained by assuming that in the most primitive form of the story the speaker was Yahweh himself, and only later out of reverence the word 'angel' was inserted in some places (...). However, it is doubtful in these ancient times whether the Israelites thought of the 'angel of Yahweh' as personage distinct from Yahweh himself. The 'angel' (malak), lit. 'messenger' was rather Yahweh himself made manifest to man.

    Eugene H. Maly has also observed in the *Jerome Bible Com.*, (p. 22):

    The versions have the correct reading, as in the CCD [Confraternity of Christian Doctrine Trans. of the Bible]. 'God heard' is a play on the child's name (cf. 16:11), but, to avoid the anthropomorphism, E. has 'the angel of God' speak to Hagar.

    It shows that it was God Himself who addressed Hagar, but the redactor, out of his personal estimate of Hagar or some other considerations, changed it to 'angel of Yahweh'.

24. How lucky this Hagar is as to be addressed directly by God Himself [but according to this corrupted version 'by the angel of the Lord'] out of heaven!

25. Doesn't it reveal the great love and concern of the Lord for Hagar? Is this exile a curse or a blessing for noble Hagar?

26. For God Himself is there to protect you from all kinds of danger. He is aware of all of your needs, conditions, and impending hardships: and He would provide you and your son everything you require.

27. It again reveals the love and concern of the Lord towards Ishmā'el.

28. Had Ishmā'el been a grown up youth of 16 or 17 years, how Hagar could have lifted him up and held him in her hand! It shows that the event of settling Ishmā'el and Hagar at Beersheba took place in

the childhood of Ishmā'el and the story of the weaning feast and the alleged jealousy of God-fearing and noble Sarah has no ground.

29. Had Ishmā'el been a young man of 16 or 17 years, it should have been he, not the old lady—his mother Hagar—who should have done all these pieces of work. It too helps the reader to ascertain the age of Ishmā'el at the time of his being settled at the wilderness of Beersheba and Pārān. It has also some bearing upon the credibility of this part of the story.

30. God repeatedly shows His concern for Ishmā'el. How could this boy have been perished and why need Abraham worry about him when God was with him all the time to protect and rear him up (which fact He Himself asserts in unequivocal terms)!

31. The '*Paran*' mentioned here is the name of Makkah. It has been discussed in detail by the writer of this book somewhere else (but not in the present book). These verses show that Ishmā'el would have been a suckling baby or about to be weaned when he was sent away to Paran or Beer-sheba, otherwise Hagar could not have 'put the child on her shoulder' or 'lifted up the lad, and held him in her hand' or 'cast the child under one of the shrubs'. It renders the so-called weaning feast of Isaac as a baseless fabrication. As a result of it:

    (a) Isaac could not have been there that Ishmā'el could have allegedly mocked his younger brother. It is clearly recorded in the Bible that Ishmā'el was a child of such a young age that his mother could lift him up. Therefore the question of the presence of Isaac at that place does not arise. Isaac was not even born by that time. He was born when Ishmā'el had already attained the age of fourteen years.

    (b) The noble Sarah stands exonerated from all the blames of jealousy, cruelty, and brutality.

32. Gen. 21:8-21 KJV.

33. *New Jerusalem Bible* (21:41) has inserted here footnote 'a', as an introductory remark:

    At this point the three traditions are fused together: vv. 1a, 2a, 7 follow on from 18:15 and are Yahwistic; vv. 2b, 5 follow on from 17:21 and are priestly; vv. 1b, 6 are Elohist.

    Pauline A. Viviano, in *The Collegeville Bible Com.*, 59 explains:

    All three sources are found in this account of the birth of Isaac.

34. *The Collegeville Bible Com.*, 60 asserts:

    The Elohist narrative of Isaac's birth (vv. 8-21) is a duplicate of the story of expulsion of Hagar and Ishmael found in the Yehwistic version in chapter 16.

35. *The Collegeville Bible Com.*, 60.

36. In English '*desolate*' means '*sad and without people, comfort, hope, or friends, etc.*' In the Bible the original Hebrew word for it is **'badad'**, which means '*alone, desolate, only, solitary*' (*Strong's Heb Dic.*, Entry 910, p.19).

37. Isa. 27:10 KJV.

38. *Enc. Biblica*, 1:1076,7.

39. *The Interpreter's Bible Dic.*, 5:946.

40. *The Interpreter's Bible Dic.*, 4:844.

41. William Smith, *A Dic. of Bible* (1988), 143.

42. *Harper's Bible Dic.*, (1994), 1133.

43. *Beersheba* is a compound Hebrew word. Beer means ; *a well*'; and Sheba means '*seven*' or '*oath*'. In Hebrew script **Beer Sheba** is written as: 'ùJ Jà̃'

44. 'ùJ Jà̃': i.e. '*be-ayr sheh-bah*'; (See *Strong's Dic. of the Heb. Bible.*, entry 884, p. 18.).

45. *Enc. Biblica* (1:518) writes: 'i.e., "well of seven" '. *Strong's Dic. of the Heb. Bible.*, (entry 884; 18) explains:

    'ùJ Jà̃' **Beer Sheba.** *be-ayr' sheh-bah*; from 875 and 7651 (in the sense of 7650); 'ấầø' *be-ayr*; from 874; a *pit*; espec. a *well.*'

    Entry 7651, p.112 reads as:

    'ùJ' **shib`ah** *shib-aw`*; from 7650 a prim. cardinal number; *seven* ,(as the sacred *full* one); also (adv.) *seven times*; by impl. a *week;* seven-fold, seventh.'

46. Covenant means: 'the agreement between God and the Israelites' (*Oxf. Eng. Ref. Dic.*, 330).

47. *A Concise Dic. of The Heb. Bible* (entry 875, p.18) explains:

    'Jà̃' *be-ayr*; from 874; a *pit*; espec. a *well.*

    Entry 874, p.18 is:

'Jà̃' **ba`ar**, *baw-ar*; a prim. Root; to dig.

Entry 7650, p.112 reads as:

'ùJ' **shaba** *shaw-bah*; a prim. Root; to *seven* oneself, i.e. *swear* (as if by repeating a declaration seven times): —¾ adjure, charge (by an oath, with an oath), take an oath.

The Enc. Biblica (1:518) explains:

It is taken as meaning 'well of the oath'. One of the Simeonite towns in the southern territory of Judah (Josh. 19.2), on the border of the cultivated land, came to be regarded, for the greater part of history, as the remotest point of Canaan in that direction; whence the phrase 'from Dan to Beersheba'.

It explains in footnote 1 to the same page:

The Hebrew word 'to swear' means literally 'to come under the influence of seven things.'

Gen. 21:31-2, *RSV Catholic Trans.*, p.16:

Therefore that place was called Beer-sheba; because there both of them swore an oath. So they made a covenant at Beer-sheba.

48. *Hastings Dic. of Bible, (*Revised one vol. Edn., 1963), 94.

49.J. Hastings, *A Dic. of Bible*, 1:265.

50. John L. McKenzie, *Dic. of Bible* (1984), 87.

51. See Hastings *Dic. of Bible*, (Revised one vol. 1963 ed.), 375.

52. *Harper's Bible Dic*., 101.

53. F. F. Bruce, *Places Abraham Knew* (London: ECIVZNJ, Scripture Union, 130 City Road, 1984), 53,55,56.

54. J. Hastings, *A Dic. of the Bible*, 1:265.

55. John L. McKenzie, *Dic. of the Bible*, 86 asserts:

The name is literally 'well of seven'.

The Interpreter's Dic. of Bible, 1:375 (col. 2) explains:

It is the 'well of seven,' (...); but in [Gen. 21] vs 31 it is apparently the 'well of the oath.'

7th Day Adventist Bible Dic., ed. Siegfried H. Horn, 131 has noted:

Heb. 'Be'er Sheba', 'well of seven', or 'well of an oath'.

56. *The Interpreter's Bible* 1:639 has explained:

    'Where he is' is an allusion to the site of the 'well' mentioned in vs. 19, a sacred spot among the Ishmaelites.

    And every knowledgeable person knows that it is the 'Well of Zamzam' which is the 'sacred spot among the Ishmaelites.'

57. Gibb, H. A. R. and J. H. Kramer, *Shorter Enc. of Islam*, (Karachi: South Asian Publishers, 1981), 508.

58. *A Lion Handbook: the World's Religions* (Herts, England: The Lion Publishing, 1984), 319,20.

59. How content and composed she is at Abraham's reply and what befitting response of the family of the great patriarch!

60. Dr. Muḥammad Muḥsin Khān, *Trans. of the Meanings of* Ṣaḥīḥ al-Bukhārī *Arb-Eng* (Riyādh: Dārussalām, S. A., PO Box 22743, 1997), 4:351-53.

61. Gen. 26:26-33, *New English Bible*.

Appendix-II

The Text of the Bible

And Some Types of Corruption in It

The Bible is initially divided into two major parts: (i) the Old Testament (OT) and (ii) the New Testament (NT). The NT relates to Jesus Christ and his Apostles. It was originally written in the Greek language, whereas Jesus had delivered his message in the Aramaic language, but it was never written in this language. It consists of 27 books. First four books are the Gospels according to Matthew, Mark, Luke, and John. The next is 'The Acts of Apostles.' Then there are 21 Epistles (letters) letters ascribed to Apostles, 13 of which are considered to have been written by Paul. The last book is 'Revelation' of John.

The OT consists of 39 books.[1] It was mainly written in the Hebrew language with the exception of some chapters of Daniel and Ezra etc.[2] . First five books: Genesis, Exodus, Leviticus, Numbers, and Deuteronomy; are called 'Pentateuch' (five volumes) or 'Torah' (the Law or instruction). They were attributed to Moses who belonged to *ca.* 14-13th centuries BC. But no portion of the Pentateuch had been committed to writing until *ca.* 4 centuries after him, except perhaps 'the Song of Deborah'.

THE TEXT OF THE OT AND SOME TYPES OF CORRUPTION IN IT

Some excerpts are being quoted below from some authorities to afford the reader a first hand knowledge. *Encyclopaedia Britannica*, under the article 'Bible', explains that the books of the Bible are younger by almost 1,000 years than its earliest text, and, during this gap, owing to various causes, a larger number of corruptions were indisputably introduced into the Hebrew text:

> The form in which the Hebrew text of the OT is presented in most manuscripts and printed editions is that of the Masoretic text, the date of which is usually placed somewhere between the 6th and 8th centuries AD. It is probable that the present text became fixed as early as the 2nd century AD [i.e. *ca.* one thousand four hundred years after Moses]. But even this early date leaves a long interval between the original autographs of the OT writers and the present text. Since the fixing of the Masoretic text [the 2nd century AD] the task of preserving and transmitting the sacred books has been carried out with the greatest care and fidelity, with the result that the text has undergone practically no change of real importance; *but before that date [the 2nd century AD], owing to various causes, a larger number of corruptions indisputably were introduced into the Hebrew text. (...). Originally the text consisted only of consonants, since the Hebrew language had an alphabet without vowels. It is also likely that in the earliest texts the words and sentences were not divided* [stress added]. The evolution of the Masoretic text was an attempt to make up for both these deficiencies. It supplied vowels by adding marks to the consonantal text [it is called 'vocalization' or 'application of diacritical marks to the text'. For further study of the theme, please see this author's book '*Muḥammad Foretold in the Bible by Name*, App. II'], and it divided the words and sentences. For many centuries it was believed that these vowel points formed part of the original text; some theologians argued that the points were inspired by the Holy Spirit. But subsequently research has proved beyond doubt that they [i.e. the vowel points] are younger by almost 1,000 years than the text itself.[3]

The same *Encyclopedia* asserts that the credibility of even the Massoretic text is not above board and it is obvious that the text has been tampered with in some places:

> On the basis of a variety of evidence it is possible to show that the Masoretic text is not a completely reliable index to the readings of the autographs of the OT. Even a superficial

> comparison between its readings and the Septuagint[4] translation discloses many passages in which the translators of the OT into Greek ascribed different vowels to the consonantal text or divided the words differently from the way they are now divided in the Hebrew text. In other passages they simply had another text before them. Considering that the Septuagint translation antedates the Masoretes by so long a span, we are forced to admit that the Hebrew text underlying it sometimes comes closer to the original reading of a particular passage than does the Masoretic. Other evidence, too, renders an uncritical accep-tance of Masoretic readings impossible; *it is obvious that the text has been tampered with in some places* [stress added].[5]

According to this article of the *Enc. Britannica* the case of the Septuagint (LXX) is also very disappointing. Some of its texts are confused:

> What complicates the task is, among other things, the sorry state of the Septuagint text itself. Parts of it are well attested and may form the basis for judgements about the Hebrew, but other parts are so confused textually that in some instances scholars are inclined to posit two or more translations. After all, without a reliable text of the translation, the translation cannot very well be used to emend the text of the original. What is more, a study of the Septuagint also reveals many passages in which the translators purposely paraphrased the text or changed its meaning when the original was either embarrassing to them or unclear; for example, certain concrete terms in Hebrew are translated into abstract terms in Greek to avoid the charge of [6]anthropomorphism.[7]

The *Enc. Britannica* indicates that the *Dead Sea Scrolls* provide the evidence of the existence of several textual traditions even in Hebrew:

> They [The *Dead Sea Scrolls*] make clear the existence of several textual traditions even in Hebrew; they have therefore made important contributions to the textual criticism of the OT, but they have not solved its fundamental problem. Barring [except for; unless there be]

a major discovery of manuscript materials, this problem is probably insoluble, and the best that can be achieved is an approximation of the text of the OT.[8]

To sum up the theme, its main features are given below. Attempt has been made to remain as close to the writer's words as possible:

1. Probably the present text became fixed [canonized] in the 2nd century AD [*ca.* 1400 years after Moses].
2. Before the 2nd century AD, a number of corruptions indisputably were introduced into the Hebrew text.
3. The original text consisted only of consonants, without vocalization or vowel/diacritical signs, which was a large source of confusion.
4. The words and sentences were not divided in the earlier texts.
5. Even a superficial comparison between the Heb. Masoretic text and its Greek translation (Septuagint or the LXX) discloses that in many passages of the LXX the words are differently divided from the present Hebrew text.
6. As the texts have obviously been tampered with in some places, the task of arriving at a reliable text is very complicated.
7. The sorry state of the Septuagint text itself also complicates the task.
8. The translators of the LXX purposely paraphrased the text or changed its meaning when the original was either embarrassing to them or unclear.
9. The *Dead Sea Scrolls* make clear the existence of several textual traditions even in Hebrew.
10. The best that can be achieved is an approximation of the text of the OT (and not the exactness).

The 15th edn. (AD 1974) of the *Encyclopaedia Britannica* has afforded a 104-page article on 'Biblical Lit.'. Nahum M. Sarna, Golding Professor of Biblical Studies, Brandseis Univ., Waltham, Massachusetts, has explained this theme in his article under the sub-heading 'Textual Criticism: Manuscript Problems.' Some of the relevant passages are reproduced hereunder. He asserts that the vowel signs were introduced to the Bible text between the 7th, 9th centuries CE:

> The text of the Hebrew printed Bible consists of consonants, vowel signs, and cantillation (musical or tonal) marks. The two latter components are the product of the school of Masoretes (Traditionalists) that flourished in Tiberias (in Palestine) between the 7th and 9th centuries CE. The history of the bare consonantal text stretches back into hoary [very old] antiquity and can be only partially traced. (….); there is much evidence for the existence of a period when more than one Hebrew text-form of a given book was current. In fact, both the variety of witnesses and the degree of textual divergence between them increase in proportion to their antiquity.[9]

According to the writer of this article of the *Britannica*, the biblical text must have endured a long period of oral transmission before its committal to writing:

> In the case of some biblical literature, there exists the real possibility, though it cannot be proven, that it must have endured a long period of oral transmission before its committal to writing. In the interval, the material might well have undergone abridgement, amplification, and alteration at the hands of transmitters so that not only would the original have been transformed, but the process of transmission would have engendered [would have been the cause of] more than one recension from the very beginning of its written, literary career. (….), the possibility of inadvertent and deliberate change, something that effects all manuscript copying, was always present.

The evidence that such, indeed, took place is rich and varied. First there are numerous divergences between the many passages duplicated within the Hebrew Bible itself–e.g. the parallels between Samuel-Kings and Chronicles. (…). There are also rabbinic traditions about the text-critical activities of the scribes (*soferim*) in Second

Temple times. These tell of divergent readings in Temple scrolls of the Pentateuch, of official 'book-correctors' in Jerusalem, of textual emendations on the part of, and of the utilization of sigla (signs or abbreviations) for marking suspect readings and disarranged verses. The Samaritan Pentateuch and the pre-Masoretic versions of the OT made directly from the Hebrew originals are all replete with divergences from current Masoretic Bibles. Finally, the scrolls from the Judaean desert, especially those from the caves of Qumran, have provided, at least, illustrations of many of the scribal processes by which deviant texts came into being. The variants and their respective causes may be classified as follows: aurally conditioned, visual in origin, exegetical, and deliberate.[10]

According to *Enc. Britannica* the 'Problems resulting from Aural Conditioning', 'Problems Visual in Origin', 'Exegetical Problems', and 'Deliberate Changes' are as follows:

1. **Aural Conditioning** would result from a mishearing of similar sounding consonants when a text is dictated to the copyist. Negative particle *lo*', for example, could be confused with the prepositional *lo*, 'to him,' or guttural *ḥet* with spirant *kaf* so that *aḥ* 'brother' might be written for *akh* 'surely.'

2. **Problems Visual in Origin.** The confusion of graphically similar letters, whether in paleo-Hebrew or Aramaic script, is another cause for variations. Thus, the prepositions *bet* (in) and *kaf* (like) are interchanged in the Masoretic and Dead Sea Scroll [DSS] texts of Isaiah.

   (i) ***The Order of Letters also might be Inverted.*** Such ***'Metathesis'***, as it is called, appears in Psalms, in which *qirbam* (their inward thoughts) stands for *qibram* (their grave).

   (ii) ***Dittography***, or the inadvertent duplication of one or more letters or words, also occurs, as, for example, in the DSS text of Isaiah and in the Masoretic text of Ezekiel.

(iii) ***Haplography***, or the accidental omission of a letter or word that occurs twice in close proximity, can be found, for example, in the DSS text of Isaiah.

(iv) ***Homoeoteleuton*** occurs when two separate phrases or lines have identical endings and the copyist's eye slips from one to the other and omits the intervening words. A comparison of the Masoretic text I Samuel, chapter 14 verse 41, with the Septuagint and the Vulgate versions clearly identifies such an aberration.

3. **Exegetical problems**. This third category does not involve any consonantal alteration but results solely from the different possibilities inherent in the consonantal spelling. Thus the lack of vowel signs may permit the word *DBR* to be read as a verb *DiBeR* ('he spoke,' as in the Masoretic text of Hosea) or as a noun *DeBaR* ('the word of,' as in the Septuagint). The absence of word dividers could lead to different divisions of the consonants. Thus, *BBQRYM* in Amos could be understood as either *BaBeQaRYM* ('with oxen,' as in the Masoretic text) or as *BaBaQaR YaM* (the sea with an ox). The incorrect solution by later copyists of abbreviations is another source of error. That such occurred is proved by a comparison of the Hebrew text with the Septuagint version in, for example, II Samuel, chapter 1 verse 12; Ezekiel, chapter 12 verse 23; and Amos, chapter 3 verse 9.

4. Deliberate Changes. Apart from mechanical alterations of a text, many variants must have been consciously introduced by scribes, some by way of glossing—i.e. the insertion of a more common word to explain a rare one—and others by explanatory comments incorporated into the text. Furthermore, a scribe who had before him two manuscripts of a single work containing variant readings, and unable to decide between them, might incorporate both readings into his scroll and thus create a '***conflate text***'.[11]

After pointing out the forms of corruption in the text of the OT, Prof. Nahum M. Sarna describes the difficulties in the reconstruction of the original text:

The situation so far described poses two major scholarly problems. The first involves the history of the Hebrew text, the second deals with attempts to reconstruct its 'original' form.

As to when and how a single text type gained hegemony and then displaced all others, it is clear that the early and widespread public reading of the scriptures in the synagogues of Palestine, Alexandria, and Babylon was bound to lead to a heightened sensitivity of the idea of a 'correct' text and to give prestige to the particular text form selected for reading. Also, the natural conservatism of ritual would tend to perpetuate the form of such a text. The *letter of Aristeas*, a document derived from the middle of the 2nd century BCE that describes the origin of the Septuagint, recognizes the distinction between carelessly copied scrolls of the Pentateuch and an authoritative Temple scroll in the hands of the high priest in Jerusalem. The rabbinic traditions about the textual criticism of Temple-based scribes actually reflect a movement towards the final stabilization of the text in the Second Temple period. (...).

In regard to an attempt to recover the original text of a biblical passage–especially an unintelligible one–in the light of variants among different versions and manuscripts [MSS] and known causes of corruption, it should be understood that all reconstruction must necessarily be conjectural and perforce tentative because of the irretrievable loss of the original edition. But not all textual difficulties need presuppose underlying mutilation (...). Furthermore, each version, indeed each biblical book within it, has its own history, and the translation techniques and stylistic characteristics must be examined and taken into account. (...). None of this means that a Hebrew MS, an ancient version, or a conjectural emendation cannot yield a reading superior to that in the received Hebrew text. It does mean, however, that these tools have to be employed with great caution and proper methodology.

Texts and manuscripts. *Sources of the Septuagint*. A Greek translation of the OT, known as the Septuagint [LXX] because there allegedly were 70 or 72 translators, six from each of the 12 tribes of Israel, and designated LXX, is a composite of the work of many translators laboring for well over 100 years. It was made directly from

Hebrew originals that frequently differed considerably from the present Masoretic text. Apart from other limitations attendant upon the use of a translation for such purposes, the identification of the parent text used by the Greek translators is still an unsettled question.[12]

In view of the important nature of the above quotations their salient features are being afforded hereunder as recapitulation to make the concept clear. Attempt has been made to remain as close to the writer's words as possible:

1. Vowel signs were introduced into the Hebrew Bible by Masoretes between the 7th and 9th centuries CE [AD]. They did not exist before it.
2. More than one Hebrew Text-forms of the books of the Bible existed for a long time.
3. Some Bible books must have endured a long period of oral transmission before their committal to writing.
4. Between its oral transmission and committal to writing the material might well have undergone *abridgement*, *amplification*, and *alteration* at the hands of the transmitters.
5. The possibility of inadvertent and deliberate change was always present. The variants and their respective causes may be classified as follows: (a) *Aurally conditioned*; (b) *Visual in origin*; (c) *Exegetical*; and (d) *Deliberate*.
6. Problems resulting from *aural conditioning* occurred due to mishearing of similar sounding consonants when a text was dictated to a copyist.
7. *Problems visual in origin*: (a) The confusion of graphically similar letters, e.g. '*B*' and '*K*', which respectively mean '*in*' and '*like*'; (b) *Metathesis*, i.e. inversion in the order of letters in a word, e.g. '*qibram*' [their grave] was changed as '*qirbam*' [their inward thoughts]; (c) *Dittography*, i.e. Duplication of one or more letters or words; (d) *Haplography*, i.e. Omission of a letter or word that occurs twice in close proximity; (e) *Homoeoteleuton*, which occurs

when two separate phrases or lines have identical endings and the copyist's eye slips from one to the other and omits the intervening words.

8. *Exegetical Problems*: (a) due to different possibilities inherent in the consonantal spelling in the absence of the vowel signs; (b) the incorrect solution of the abbreviations by the later copyists.
9. *Deliberate Changes*: Glosses and explanatory comments consciously introduced by the scribes and subsequently incorporated in the text.
10. In regard to an attempt to recover the original text of a biblical passage–especially an unintelligible one–in the light of variants among different versions and MSS and known causes of corruption, it should be understood that all reconstruction must necessarily be conjectural and perforce tentative because of the irretrievable loss of the original edition.

The *Cambridge History of the Bible* is a reliable reference book and an excellent source of knowledge. It has dealt with the theme in a number of articles. Some excerpts from only one of them, 'The Old Testament Text', written by Shemaryahu Talmon, Professor of Bible, The Hebrew University of Jerusalem are afforded below:

Any account of the development of the text prior to c. 300 BC, i.e. in the Persian period, not to mention the periods of the Babylonian exile or the first Temple, must perforce rely upon conjecture and, at best, upon deductions and analogies derived from later literature and later manuscripts. (….).

The *absence of vowels meant that many a Hebrew consonant group could be differently pronounced* [stress added], and from this resulted the fact that a variety of meanings could be attached to one and the same word in the original. When ultimately vowels were introduced into the Hebrew text of the Bible, these pronunciation variants sometimes became the basis of *variae lectiones*.[13]

The lack of any system of interpunctuation in written Hebrew at that time was another factor which gave rise to different interpretations of many passages. These diverging interpretations may also in the end turn up as variants in versions which are based on fully interpunctuated manuscripts.[14]

The learned writer of the same article asserts that 'In fact not one single verse of this ancient literature has come to us in an original MS, written by a biblical author or by a contemporary of his, or even by a scribe who lived immediately after the time of the author.' He asserts:

> There is probably no other extant text, ancient or modern, which is witnessed to by so many diverse types of sources, and the history of which is so difficult to elucidate as that of the text of the OT. The task of the scholar who endeavors to trace the antecedents of the text as we know it today is further complicated by the fact that he is concerned with sacred literature, every word of which is considered to be divinely inspired and therefore infallible. However, *having been handed down by human agents for more than two millennia, the text of the scriptures suffered from the shortcomings of man. It becomes faulty to a greater or less degree and even at times distorted. It must therefore be subjected to scholarly critical analysis like any other ancient literary document* [stress added].

The OT books were handed down, as has been said, not only in their original Hebrew or, in some passages, Aramaic tongue, but also in a variety of translations into Semitic or non-Semitic languages. All these textual traditions, as we know them today, differ from one another. What is more, even the witnesses to one tradition, in the original language or in a translation, often diverge from one another. As a result, the scholar who takes a synoptic view of all the sources at his disposal is confronted with a plethora of *variae lectiones* in the extant versions of the OT books. This fact obviously does not become apparent in the common editions of the OT, in Hebrew or in translation, which are in every-day use. However, *it should be borne in mind that the printed editions represent the end of a long chain of textual development and of editorial activities which were aimed at unifying the sacred texts. These late editions can in no way be taken to exhibit faithfully the autographs of the biblical authors.*

In fact not one single verse of this ancient literature has come to us in an original MS, written by a biblical author or by a contemporary of his, or even by a scribe who lived immediately after the time of the author. Even the very earliest manuscripts at our disposal, in Hebrew or in any translation language, are removed by hundreds of years from the date of origin of the literature recorded in them [stress added].

Even a cursory perusal of the sources available immediately reveals that *not one tradition and not one MS is without fault. Each and every one patently exhibits errors which crept into it during the long period of its transmission in the oral stage, when written by hand, and even, though to a lesser degree, when handed down in the form of printed books*. [stress added][15]

In spite of all his above findings the writer of the article has stressed that these errors and textual divergences between the versions materially effect the intrinsic message only in relatively few instances. It would, therefore, be quite reasonable not to underestimate this valuable and unique source of human history, knowledge, and divine guidance. He asserts:

> It should, however, be stressed that these errors and textual divergences between the versions materially effect the intrinsic message only in relatively few instances. Nevertheless this may occur. Some examples of variants significant from a theological or ideo-historical angle may in fact be found. In most instances the differences are of a linguistic or grammatical nature, which resulted either from the unpremeditated impact of the linguistic peculiarities of successive generations of copyists, or from their intentional attempts to adjust the wording of scripture to changing concepts of linguistic and stylist norms.[16]

The writer of the same article has admitted that the older the biblical MSS be, the wider is the over-all range of textual divergence between them. He states:

> The above remarks do not, however, absolve us from accounting for the fact that the further back the textual tradition of the OT is followed, i.e. the older the biblical MSS perused, and the more

> ancient the records which come to the knowledge of scholars, the wider is the over-all range of textual divergence between them. The existing variants, therefore, cannot be simply explained as having arisen solely from the cumulative effect of imperfect copying and recopying of the text over many centuries. The very earliest biblical MSS known–and in this respect the biblical scrolls from Qumran are of decisive importance–exhibit practically all types of variants found in later witnesses.[17]

According to the learned writer of the article, Prof. Shemaryahu Talmon, it is almost impossible to trace back the original text of some book of the OT:

> Even if by retracing the steps of textual development we may be able to arrive at the *Ur-text*[18] of this version or that, the question still remains open whether we shall ever be able to recover the *ipsissima verba*[19] of a biblical author.[20]

Prof. Shemaryahu Talmon points out that originally oral variations may ultimately turn up as textual variants. He further states that by the early third century BC, the written transmission of biblical literature had completely replaced the oral tradition:

> It should, however, be pointed out that originally oral variations may ultimately turn up as textual variants between duplicate texts within the OT. Such instances are found in two versions of one and the same Psalm embedded in a book of the Former Prophets and Psalms (e.g. 2 Sam. 22 = Ps. 18), in Chronicles and Psalms (e.g. 1 Chron. 16:8-36 = Ps. 105:1-15; 96:1-13; 106:1, 47-8), or in the Book of Psalms itself (e.g. Ps. 31:2-4b = 71:1-3; 60:7-14 = 108:8-14). Again, we meet with two or even three presentations of a piece of biblical literature in parallel passages in the Former and Latter Prophets (2 Kin. 18:13-20:19 = Isa. 36:1-38:22 = 2 Chr. 32:1-20; 2 Kings 25:1-22 = Jer. 39:1-10 = 52:4-27; 2 Kings 25:27-30 = Jer. 52:31-4). To some extent also quotations from an earlier book in a later one may exhibit textual variants. However, in these cases literary license and a possible tendency towards intentional variation or rephrasing on the part of the writer who is borrowing may lie at the root of the present

> divergences. (...). The definite shift of emphasis from oral to written transmission of the biblical books would thus have become clearly apparent during the period of Return, i.e. at the end of the sixth and in the fifth century BC, in what, from a wider historical viewpoint, may be termed the Persian period. (....) at this stage [i.e. the early third century BC], the written transmission of biblical literature finally and, to all intents and purposes, completely replaced oral tradition.[21]

The writer of the article under study, Prof. Shemaryahu Talmon, asserts that while translating the Hebrew text of the OT neither proper care had been observed nor authorized supervision:

> At first, the translation of the scriptures into Aramaic was most probably sporadic and undirected. (...). Lacking authorised supervision, the resulting translation often assumed the form of a somewhat free paraphrase of the original, rather than of an accurate rendering into the translator's language. But even when a word-by-word translation was attempted, divergence from the Hebrew *Vorlage*[22] was inevitable. Translation from one language into another always produces inaccuracies since there is no exact correspondence between the vocabulary and the syntax of the two, even if they belong to the same language family. Moreover, the probably divergent first renderings of the Hebrew scriptures into Aramaic were based on originals which may well have differed among themselves to a smaller or larger degree, for reasons set out above.

The same considerations apply with additional force to the translation of the OT books into Greek, a non-Semitic language. This translation was required, for reasons similar to those mentioned above, by Jews living within the sphere of Hellenistic culture, whether in Ptolemaic Egypt, where the Jewish community of Alexandria was the focal point, or in Palestine. Tradition maintains that in this case official non-Jewish agents also showed interest in rendering the OT into Greek, and instigated a properly supervised scholarly translation. This tradition will be further discussed subsequently. The Pseudepigraphic letter of Aristeas credits King Ptolemy II Philadelphus (285-246 BC) with having inaugurated the translation of the Pentateuch into Greek by seventy sages. As a result of their concerted effort, the Septuagint, commonly designated LXX, was in the Pentateuch less open to the controlled impact of translators' idiosyncrasies[23] . It contains indeed fewer deviations from the Hebrew text here than in the renderings of the other books. But it is still open to discussion that this reputedly official undertaking is to be considered the first attempt at translating the OT or parts of it into Greek and to have provided the impetus to further ventures of the same kind, or whether it should rather be viewed as an event which crowned a long series of previous diffuse attempts with a standardised version. (...). The ensuing embarrassing textual diversity of the versions of the sacred books soon called for the application of the methods of textual analysis and textual criticism to remedy this deficiency. As stated above, the ground for this new approach had been laid by the conjunction of scholarly norms borrowed from the Greeks with the care for the accurate transmission of the inspired literature which had been developed within Judaism.[24]

The worthy writer asserts that deviations of the Samaritan. Hebrew text from the Massoretic text were estimated at about six thousand:

> The Samaritan text [the Samaritan Hebrew Pentateuch was rediscovered by Pietro della Valle in 1616] was made available to scholars shortly afterwards when Morinus first printed it in 1632 alongside the other versions in the Paris Polyglot. *Its many deviations from the Massoretic text, later estimated at about six thousand, were soon observed* [stress added]. It was further established that approximately one third [i.e. about two thousand] of these *variae lectiones* could be traced also in the LXX. This concurrence enhanced the doubts which had been raised concerning the veracity of the Massoretic text. It was maintained that, having been revised by the rabbis after the destruction of the Temple, in the first half of the second century A.D., it did not represent the *ipsissima verba*[25] of the divinely inspired message, but a faulty text, resulting from *incuria librariorum* or from wilful malicious tampering with it on the part of the Jews. (...). The rich crop of individual variants which were recorded

> in the apparatus of these works at first sight appeared to disprove the compactness and stability of the Hebrew text. However, closer scrutiny more and more strengthened the conviction that almost all of them can and should be classified as intentional or unintentional secondary scribal alterations. (....), the Greek tradition was deemed especially valuable for the purpose of purging the OT of anti-Christ falsifications which allegedly had been introduced into the Massoretic text by the rabbis.[26]

The writer has also elucidated the impact of the discovery of the Dead Sea Scrolls, which are the oldest extant MSS of the Bible, on the credibility of the text of the OT. He asserts that the Hebrew scrolls from Qumran prove beyond doubt the actual existence of variant readings in the biblical books of the Hellenistic or Roman periods. He concludes that the very notion of an exclusive *textus receptus* had not yet taken root at Qumran:

> This (the First Isaiah Scroll, IQIs[a]), like many other MSS from Qumran, precedes the oldest extant MSS of any part of the OT in the Hebrew Massoretic tradition by more than a millennium, and those in Greek or any other translation by several centuries. (...). [p.183] Because of their diversity, the kaleidoscope of the textual traditions exhibited in them, their concurrence here with one, here with another of the known versions, or again in other cases their exclusive textual individuality, the biblical MSS found at Qumran, in their totality, present in a nutshell, as it were, the intricate and variegated problems of the Hebrew text and versions. (....) [pp. 184ff].
>
> The coexistence of diverse text types in the numerically, geographically and temporally restricted Covenanters' community, the fact that some or most of the conflicting MSS had very probably been copied in the Qumran scriptorium and that no obvious attempts at the suppression of divergent MSS or of individual variants can be discovered in that voluminous literature, proves beyond doubt that the very notion of an exclusive *textus receptus* had not yet taken root at Qumran. (p.185)

We have no reason to doubt that this 'liberal' attitude towards divergent textual traditions of the OT prevailed also in 'normative'

Jewish circles of the second and first centuries B.C. According to rabbinic testimony, even the model codices that were kept in the Temple precincts–the *ʿazārāh*–not only exhibited divergent readings, but represented conflicting text-types. [p.185] (...). The difference consists in the fact that in the end the Temple codices were collated, probably in the first century A.D. and, what is more important, that rabbinic Judaism ultimately established a model text and strove to banish deviant MSS from circulation. [p.185,86] (...). However, even the latest MSS from Qumran which provide evidence of the local history of the text in the crucial period, the last decades before the destruction of the Temple, do not give the slightest indication that even an incipient *textus receptus* emerged there, or that the very notion of a model recension was ever conceived by the Covenanters.[27]

The writer says that mostly the textual variations involved are of the simplest and most common types:

> In a majority of cases the textual variations involved are of the simplest and most common types: interchange of graphically similar letters or auricularly close consonants; haplography or dittography; continuous writing of separate words or division of one word into two; *plene*[28] or defective spelling (as in the cases adduced above); metathesis; differences of vocalisation, sometimes entailing a change of verb conjugations.[29]

He observes that the deliberate alterations into the text of scripture for various reasons of style and dogma have been incorporated in both: the MSS of Qumran and the Jewish MSS alike. He further says that the development of biblical text-transmission may be considered prototypes of phenomena that emerge concurrently and subsequently in the text-history of the OT in Jewish and Christian tradition:

> (....), the deliberate insertion of textual alterations into scripture for various reasons of style and dogma, and uncontrolled infiltration of haphazard changes due to linguistic peculiarities of copyist or to their characteristic concepts and ideas, which may be observed in the wider transmission of the text, have their

counterparts in the 'Qumran Bible' [p.190] (...). We thus encounter in the Qumran writings development of biblical text-transmission which may be considered prototypes of phenomena that emerge concurrently and subsequently in the text-history of the OT in Jewish and Christian tradition, albeit in less concentrated form, and at different grades of variations.[30]

It is important to note that the worthy writer admits the actual existence of variant readings in the biblical books:

The Hebrew scrolls from Qumran prove beyond doubt the actual existence of variant readings in the biblical books of the Hellenistic or Roman periods which until their discovery had been beyond the scope of textual research proper.[31]

To conclude and sum up the observations of Prof. Shemaryahu Talmon, Professor of Bible, the Hebrew University of Jerusalem, they are presented as under:

1. Any account of the development of the text prior to c. 300 B.C. may be based on mere conjecture.
2. The absence of vowels meant that many Hebrew consonant groups could be differently pronounced and, consequently, a variety of meanings and interpretations could be attached to one and the same word in the original. When vowels were introduced into the Hebrew text of the Bible, they sometimes became the basis of *variae lectiones.*
3. Having been handed down by human agents for more than two millennia, the text of the Scriptures suffere from the shortcomings of man. It becomes faulty to a greater or less degree and even at times distorted.
4. In fact not one single verse has come to us in an original MS, written by a biblical author or by a contemporary of his, or even by a scribe who lived immediately after the time of the author.
5. Even a cursory perusal of the sources reveals that not one tradition or MS is without fault. Each and every one patently exhibits errors which crept into it during the long period of

its transmission in the oral stage, when written by hand, and to a lesser degree, when handed down in the form of printed books.

6. These errors and textual divergences effect the intrinsic message only in relatively few instances.
7. The older the biblical MSS be, the wider is the over-all range of textual divergence between them.
8. It is almost impossible to trace back the original text of some book of the OT.
9. Originally oral variations may ultimately turn up as textual variants.
10. While translating the Hebrew text of the OT neither proper care had been observed nor authorised supervision.
11. Deviations of the Samaritan Hebrew text from the Massoretic text were estimated at about six thousand.
12. The Hebrew scrolls from Qumran prove beyond doubt the actual existence of variant readings in the biblical books of the Hellenistic or Roman periods.
13. Textual variations involved are of the simplest and most common types: interchange of graphically similar letters or auricularly close consonants; haplography or dittography; continuous writing of separate words or division of one word into two; *plene* or defective spelling; metathesis; differences of vocalisation.

Peake's Commentary on the Bible is a renowned and reliable work. One of its 'Introductory Articles to the OT' is 'Canon and Text of the OT', written by B. J. Roberts. The writer observes that 'the text transmission of the LXX was far from strict':

From the very outset, and certainly from a very early time in the Christian era, the text transmission of the LXX was far from strict: indeed from the early 3rd cent. A.D. we have a comment by Origen, the first scholar, in our sense of the word, in the history of Christendom, that *the MSS showed the greatest divergence, due both to scribal errors and, what is worse, to revision of the text and additions and omissions of 'whatever seems right' to the revisers* [stress added]. (...), the Church in various areas adopted different recensions of the LXX, which further added to the chaos. After the Edict of Milan in A.D. 313 and the consequent acceptance of Christianity by Constantine as an empire religion, there was an attempt to secure for the OT, just as for the NT, a semi-standardisation of the text; but one need only look at the Greek Codices of the Greek Bible which were produced as a result of the Edict, to realise that there was very little consistency used in the production of such a text, and still less success in establishing the textual [32] minutiae.[33]

Jerome[34] was commissioned by the then Pope to produce a Latin rendering of the whole of the Bible. He accomplished his work, Vulgate, in the late 4th and early 5th cent. AD. B. J. Roberts observes in the same article:

> (...), he [Jerome] stressed that, in translating , 'if we follow the syllables we lose the understanding', and there are innumerable instances of departure from the Hebrew Text to accommodate Christian dogma and interpretation.[35]

The same writer says that in the Vulgate there are numerous scribal errors as well as textual divergences from the LXX and other MSS:

> Firstly, the Isa. A[36] document, which contains the whole of Isa. apart from a few minor lacunae due to wear and tear of the MS. It was the first biblical MS of the scrolls to be published, and even now it is by far the best known. The average person who reads about the Dead Sea Scrolls—and his number is legion[37]—is reassured by the authorities that the scroll agrees to a remarkable degree with the text of the standard Hebrew Bible, and there is no need to dispute this verdict, at least as far as the average reader is concerned. But textual criticism is a detailed study, and from this standpoint it is quite misleading to emphasise this very great measure of agreement. Apart from scribal errors which are numerous, the following divergences stand out: (*a*) the scroll, especially in the second half, presents a

> widely divergent orthography and grammar from that of the classical text; (*b*) there are numerous divergent readings, some of which correspond to known alternatives, e.g. in the LXX and in the *K^e^re* and *K^e^thibh* variants, whereas others were previously unknown; (*c*) in some instances the proper names agree not with the form they have in the common Isa. text but with that in later books, e.g. Chr. That is, the text in MS A [1QIs^{a}] might be regarded as a recension[38], approximating to the classical form, but by no means identical with it.[39]

It is remarkable to note that one of the reasons of errors and misunderstandings in the biblical texts was the absence of any kind of vocalization system in the Hebrew script. It was only after the advent and under the influence of Islām that it was introduced in the Bible texts, as the writer asserts:

> Some time in the 7th cent., probably under the indirect influence of Islam and of developments in the Syriac language, a rough and ready beginning was made to vocalise the consonantal text by the addition of vowel signs.[40]

The text of the Bible was changed both (a) due to deliberate alterations by the scribes and (b) due to accidental/involuntary errors.

As regards the first type, i.e. *deliberate alterations*, glosses were added and consequently some enthusiastical commentators dismissed some phrases from the text taking them as glosses. The scribes have amended and omitted the text. Then there are the late (Tiberian) Massoretes who confused the meaning of a passage because they had failed to understand it. The writer asserts:

> Long before the text assumed its present form it was modified for reasons known to us and unknown. Glosses were added, explanatory, pious, habit (e.g. the adding of the words 'of the covenant' to 'ark' in many places), and others. Unfortunately, some commentaries in the past have shown an undue enthusiasm for this class of textual corruption, and any phrase in the text which might contradict a preconceived theory was apt to be dismissed as a gloss: on the other hand it is generally recognised that, e.g. the book of Ezek. contains numerous instances of the

glossator's work. Other early interferences were made by scribes who expunged the names of foreign deities and substituted for them the word *bosheth* ('shame'), e.g. Mephibosheth for Meribaal.

From the period which followed the fixing of the consonantal text we have Rabbinic evidence of textual criticism. *Tikkune ha-Soph^e^rim* (emendations of the scribes), mentioned in Rabbinic commentaries, refer to attempts to avoid anthropomorphisms in the text by a change of suffix, in as many as eighteen passages. '*Itture ha-Soph^e^rim* (omissions of the scribes) refer to grammatical points. *Soph^e^rin* are marginal notes inserted in the Massoroth to indicate that the form is 'unexpected' and should probably be replaced by another word. *N^e^kuddoth (puncta extra-ordinaria)* are dots placed over words in ten passages in the Pentateuch which were queried by Massoretes on textual or exegetical grounds, and the fact that they are frequently mentioned in the Mishnah and other Rabbinic writings shows that they were commonly acknowledged. Again the retention of *K^e^re* and *K^e^thubh* variants shows Massoretic concern for textual criticism.

There are other places where scribes can be held responsible for textual corruption [stress added]. There are innumerable instances where a vocalisation is queried on the basis of an LXX reading, and it lies to hand to suggest that if any case is to be made for a 'recension' in the Massoretic text, it is in the interpretation given to it by the Massoretes responsible for the Tiberian vocalisation. On the other hand, *it is sometimes thought these late Massoretes confused the meaning of a passage because they had failed to understand it and consequently pointed it wrongly* [stress added].[41]

As regards the second type, i.e. *involuntary scribal errors*, the writer asserts that there has been the confusion of similar letters, haplography, dittography, homoeoteleu-ton, etc. He says:

> The possibility of *involuntary scribal errors* is well demonstrated by the very carelessly written Qumran Scroll 1QIs[a], and in a recent introduction to the study, *The Text of the OT*, by E. Wurthwein (Eng. Tr. P. R. Ackroyd, 1957), very good use is made of the MS to demonstrate the types and classes of error in the

Hebrew MT [Massoretic Text]. The only caveat which might be entered is that 1QIs[a] is not a Massoretic MS nor does it belong to Judaism but rather to a sect, and perhaps it is not fair to the Massoretes to put them to this undeserved disrepute. A better source would be the fragments from the Cairo Geniza, where the same types of error occur, but the incidence is not nearly so common.

There have been useful manuals of textual corruption published–one in English by J. Kennedy (ed. by N. Levison), *An Aid to the Textual Amendment of the OT* (1928). It discusses such errors as confusion of similar letters, in both the archaic and Aramaic scripts, e.g. *Beth* and *Kaph*, *Daleth* and *Resh*; inversion of letters; haplography (writing a letter once where it should be repeated, or omission of a word which is similar to the adjacent word); dittography (the reverse of the previous error); homoeoteleuton (where phrases and even passages have been omitted from between two similar words or even endings of words). How such omissions could have taken place in such official texts as the prototype of the present *Biblia Hebraica* and all the MSS supporting it defies explanation, because the Rabbis were strict in the matter of checking and correcting standard MSS, but it is a fact that they exist. For instance in I Sam. 14:41 a lengthy passage has disappeared by homoeoteleuton with the word 'Israel', which occurs immediately before the beginning of the lost passage and which ends the passage.

Other assumed errors or sources of error are disputed among scholars. It is sometimes thought that abbreviations, particularly in the divine names, coupled with the wrong division of words constitute a possible error. That such abbreviations occur in the Geniza fragments is demonstrable, but it is still open to argue that they did not occur in more official MSS. Another debatable point is whether or not MSS were copied by dictation. This could have been a common source of corruption and would account for the numerous variations between similarly sounding gutturals; but, again, there is scepticism among scholars on the possibility.

The final note, however, in any discussion of textual errors must be one of caution. The prestige of the Massoretic scribal activity, increasingly recognised of recent years, makes the *a priori*[42] likelihood of errors less than was previously believed. Increased study of Hebrew philology and semantics, and better acquaintance with cognate languages show that departure from the accepted text is frequently hazardous, and fresh information, particularly from the Dead Sea Scrolls and the Cairo Geniza, makes the history of the text not only more interesting but enhances its standing as a text-form, the early standardisation of which made it unique among all textual transmissions.[43]

Almost similar views have been expressed by the Dummelow's Commentary in its introductory articles in a different way:

> For many centuries no vowel signs were used at all, and the consonants were written without any spaces between words. The scribes who copied were undoubtedly very careful, but sometimes the same consonant was written twice. Sometimes, of two consonants of the same form one was omitted; or a word might occur twice in one verse, and the scribe going on to the second as he copied the first would omit the intervening words. About the third century A.D. certain consonants began to be used to express unchangeably long vowels. This was called *scriptio plena*, i.e. full writing. About the middle of the sixth century when the Jews were much scattered, the danger arose that the proper pronunciation of Hebrew would be lost. A set of scribes called Masoretes, i.e. Traditionalists, introduced a complete system of points to indicate the vowels as traditionally pronounced.[44]

Encyclopedia Americana has afforded 73 pages (p.647 to 719) for Bible and its related themes under different topics by different writers. The topic of its 4th article is 'Textual Criticism of the OT' which is written by J. Philip Hyatt, Vanderbilt University. The author of the article has also pointed out similar forms of corruptions in the text of the Bible and has asserted, 'These features of the original languages of the OT (Old Testament) have helped to make errors possible in the transmission of its text.':

> The purpose of textual criticism is to reconstruct the original text of the OT. It frequently is called *lower criticism,* to distinguish

it from *higher criticism*, which deals with questions of authorship, date, source analysis, historical background, and the like.

This type of criticism is not peculiar to Biblical studies. It must be practiced on any piece of literature that we wish to study seriously and that has not come down to us in a copy made by the author's own hand. There is a textual criticism, for example, of the plays of Shakespeare. The peculiarities of OT textual criticism arise from the nature of the Hebrew language and the history of the OT text.

The OT is written in Hebrew, with the exception of the following passages, which are in the closely related Aramaic language: Ezra 4:8 to 6:18; 7:12-26; Daniel 2:4b to 7:28; and Jeremiah 10:11, and a few isolated words or expressions in Genesis. In ancient times these languages were written with consonants only, the pronunciation of vowels being preserved only by oral tradition. In time some of the vowels were indicated by the use of certain consonant letters (called *matres lectionis*), and eventually all vowels were marked by these or by vowel points. Certain of the letters of Hebrew and Aramaic are similar, either in appearance or in sound. For example, in the square script that came into use about 200 B.C. the following pairs of letters are very similar in appearance and may easily be confused: D and R, B and K, H and CH, T and CH. Certain letters may be readily confused in sound; there are two K-sounds, three S-sounds, and two T-sounds. In ancient times the words often were not divided in manuscripts, and verses were not separated as they are now. These features of the original languages of the OT have helped to make errors possible in the transmission of its text.[45]

The same writer, J. Philip Hyatt, traces the History of the text as follows:

The books of the OT were written between 1000 and 100 BC., and the canon was closed toward the end on the 1st Christian century. Not a single book has come down to the present in its original, autograph form. The earliest manuscripts are those generally known as the Dead Sea Scrolls, which were found in the caves of Wadi Qumran and Wadi Murabbaat and elsewhere in the desert region of Palestine near the Dead Sea. Complete scrolls or fragments have been found of all books of the OT except Esther. Many are from the 1st and 2nd centuries B.C. These manuscripts contain several difficult kinds of Hebrew text. Some are like the Greek Septuagint or the Samaritan Pentateuch, while others are very similar to the Masoretic text, which is discussed below.

(...). It is probable, therefore, that a 'proto- Masoretic' text was established by the year 100 A.D. This was the result of a process extending over two or three centuries, climaxed by needs that were felt in Judaism as the result of the rise of Christianity and the capture of Jerusalem by the Romans in 70 A.D. Rabbi Akiba may have been the leader in the final stage of this process.

For four centuries after Akiba the textual scholars were the *Sopherim*, the Scribes. While they were concerned mainly with the correct copying of the text, they were students of it as well. In various ways they sought to point out difficulties in the text: by the 'extraordinary points' placed above words in fifteen passages, which point out passages that are doubtful in one respect or another; by the eighteen 'emendation of the Scribes' (*tiqqune ha-sophrim*), most of which attempt to avoid blasphemy against God; and by the *Sebirin*, which point out 'unexpected' forms. The Scribes made subdivisions in the text that eventually became chapters and verses.

It was not until the time of the Masoretes that a really standard text was established. The Masoretes were biblical scholars who lived in the period between the 6th and 10th centuries A.D. The word *Masorete* means 'one who hands down the tradition.' These scholars were not scientific critics of the text but men who sought to preserve the best traditions regarding the reading of the text. There were several Masoretic schools, both in Palestine and Babylonia. The Masoretes sought to fix a standard, authoritative text on the basis of the MSS available to them, and to provide the text with the notations that would be of aid in its study. One of the most important of their activity was to provide the text with complete vowel points. They also provided it with elaborate symbols to aid in the correct reading of the text, partly the equivalent of modern punctuation marks. They furnished in some cases indications of variant readings in two families of MSS (the so-called *kethib-Qere*).[46]

Under the sub heading 'Reconstruction of the Original Hebrew Text' the writer, J. Philip Hyatt, explains the types of corruption of the biblical text:

> It should be obvious from this history of the text that a period of a thousand years or more elapsed between the completion of the latest book of the OT and most of the MSS on which modern study is based. During this time the text was repeatedly copied and recopied by hand. When one thinks of the errors that may arise even with the use of modern typewriters and composing machines, it is not difficult to realize why errors arose in this repeated copying by hand. Errors could arise from failure to read a text properly, failure to hear correctly when manuscripts were written from dictation, fatigue, failure to understand what one was writing, and even sheer carelessness. Sometimes material originally written in the margin was incorporated in the text.

It can be proved that errors have slipped into the text by comparison of parts of the Hebrew Bible that give the same material in two places: for example, II Samuel 22 and Psalm 18; or Psalm 14 and Psalm 53; or Isaiah 36 to 39 and II Kings 18:13 to 20:19. More extensive comparison may be made of the material in I-II Chronicles that has been adapted from I-II Samuel and I-II Kings. Small or large differences suggest that one form or the other [or none of them] may be original.

Errors also are obvious to the modern scholar in passages that do not make sense, even when read by one who has a thorough knowledge of Hebrew. The purpose of textual criticism, therefore, is to remove as many errors as possible from the present text and thereby to recover the original text.

A comparison of the available Hebrew MSS helps only a little in recovery of the original text of the OT. Careful studies have shown that the Masoretic MSS that have come down to us contain few significant variants. Those that occur are largely differences in orthography or vocalization (and possibly dialects) and seldom give differences in meaning. The task of the OT textual critic is therefore different from that of the NT textual critic, who must rely largely upon careful comparison of early Greek MSS.

The complete Isaiah scroll among the Dead Sea Scrolls (known as IQIsa) is one of the earliest and best-known pre-Masoretic MSS. While it very often agrees with the Masoretic text, it offers in a few places readings that appear to be superior to the readings of that text. For example, the Masoretic text of Isaiah 3:24 may be translated as follows:

> Instead of sweet spices there will be rottenness,
> And instead of a girdle, a rope;
>
> Instead of well-set hair, baldness,
> And instead of a robe, a girdling of sack-cloth;
> Branding instead of beauty.

The last line of this verse presents two difficulties: it reverses the order of the words in the four preceding lines, and it assumes a meaning for the common Hebrew word *ki*, here translated 'branding,' that it has nowhere else in the Bible. The Dead Sea Scroll of Isaiah contains an additional word to the last line, which makes it possible to render it as follows:

> For instead of beauty (there will be) shame.
>
> In a few instances the Dead Sea Scroll of Isaiah supports the reading of the Septuagint or another ancient version. (Consult the marginal notes to Isaiah in the Revised Standard Version of the Bible, where these readings often are cited.)[47]

The writer observes that the original text of the OT was altered in very ancient times, before the earliest known MSS and versions:

> In a small number of cases the original text of the OT was altered in very ancient times, before the earliest known MSS and versions, for example, in II Samuel the word *Baal* (the name of a non-Hebrew deity) in personal names has been replaced by the word *bosheth*, which means 'shame.' In Chronicles, however, the original forms have been retained. For example, the name of Saul's son is given as *ish-bosheth* in II Samuel 2:8, but as *Esh*

Baal in I Chronicles 8:33. It is certain that his original name was not one that meant 'man of shame,' but rather 'man of Baal.'[48]

The writer asserts that sometimes the textual critic must resort to emendation of the received Hebrew text; but his purpose should be to recover the actual text rather than to improve what was written by the ancient author:

> Recovery of the original text often requires more than comparison of ancient Hebrew MSS and comparison of parts of the OT. The textual critic sometimes must resort to emendation of the received Hebrew text. The purpose of an emendation never should be to 'improve' what was written by an ancient author but simply to recover what he actually wrote. OT scholars in the latter part of the 19th century and the first quarter of the 20th very often emended the Hebrew text and frequently seemed to have little respect for the Masoretic text. Scholars now have greater respect for that text and resort to emendation only as a last resort. This heightened respect has come in part from the discovery of the Dead Sea Scrolls, in part from increased knowledge of the history of the text and the recovery of the relatively early MSS, and in part from careful study of the Semitic languages that are cognate [that have the same origin] with Hebrew.

Thus the primary concern of the scholar should be to understand and interpret the Masoretic text; if he cannot do that, he may resort to emendation.[49]

The writer has classified the task of emendation in the following three categories:

> Emendations of the Hebrew text may be classified as follows:
>
> Those that rest on the evidence of an ancient version, such as the Septuagint;
>
> Those that are based on conjecture without versional support; and
>
> Emendations that involve both conjecture and occasional evidence.[50]

As regards the emendations based on the evidence of an ancient version, such as the Septuagint, the writer writes:

> Several of the ancient versions of the OT were produced before the time of the Masoretes. The most important are the Greek Septuagint, the Aramaic Targums, the Syriac Peshitta, and the Latin Vulgate of St. Jerome. These versions sometimes differ in detail from the Hebrew Bible. It is possible, therefore, that in some instances they represent the original text and the Masoretic text does not.

It is frequently very difficult to decide whether one of these versions or the Masoretic text represents the original reading. It is rash to assume that in every case of difference the Septuagint or another version is more original only because it is older than our Masoretic MSS. The scholar must very carefully consider every individual case of variation. For example, in comparing the Septuagint with the Hebrew text, the scholar must exercise great care. He must realize that the various translators of the Septuagint differed in their competence and in care they took in their work. Sometimes they paraphrased rather than translated literally; sometimes they misunderstood a verse or passage. Corruptions have taken place in the MSS of the Septuagint itself, as in the Hebrew text. Nevertheless, even when these and other possibilities have been considered, the Septuagint and other ancient versions sometimes do give sound aid in restoring the original Hebrew.[51]

The writer has afforded here 'an example' that 'will illustrate their use in textual emendation'. He explains:

> In I Samuel 14:41 a long clause obviously has dropped out of the Masoretic text but has been preserved in the Septuagint and the Vulgate. In the following translation, the words in italics are omitted in the Hebrew:

And Saul said to the Lord, God of Israel, '*Why hast thou not answered thy servant today? If the guilt be in me or Jonathan my son, O Lord God of Israel, give Urim; but if the guilt be in thy people Israel* give Thummim [a perfect lot].' Jonathan and Saul were taken, and the people escaped.

It is clear that this longer form of the verse is necessary to the sense, and it is easy to see why the Hebrew scribe made the omission. His eye skipped from the word 'Israel' near the beginning of the verse to the same word near the end, and he unconsciously omitted all the intervening words. This type of error is known as *homoeoteleuton*. The same error sometimes is made by typists today.

Another kind of error may be illustrated from Psalm 49:11. The first half of the verse in Hebrew may be translated literally: 'Their inwardness (*qirbam*) is their home for ever, their dwellingplaces to all generations.' This is nonsense, which is not adequately relieved by the King James Version: 'Their inward thought is, *that* their house *shall continue* for ever, *and* their dwellingplaces to all generations,' the words in italics not being in the Hebrew at all but inserted in order to attempt to make sense of the verse. Yet, when one turns to the Septuagint, Peshitta, and Targum, one finds that the verse should be read: 'their graves (*qibram*); are their homes forever, their dwellingplaces to all generations.' The scribal error was simply that of transposing B and R, so that what was originally written as *qibram* eventually became *qirbam*.

A few suggested emendations of the Masoretic text have been confirmed by the discovery of the Dead Sea Scrolls of Isaiah. For example, the Masoretic text of Isaiah 49:24, 25 reads as follows:

Can prey be seized from the mighty,
or the captives of a *righteous man* be rescued?

For thus says the Lord:

Even the captives of the mighty shall be seized,
and the prey of the tyrant be rescued;

For I will contend with those who contend with you,
and your children I will save.

In the second line the italicized term seems strangely out of place. It breeds the poetic parallelism, and one expects on the basis of the reading of the fifth line a word such as 'tyrant'. That is just the word that is presupposed by the Septuagint, Peshitta, and the Vulgate, and the Hebrew word for 'tyrant' occurs in the Dead Sea

Scroll. The error probably arose from the fact that in the Hebrew square script the word ^{c}*aris* (tyrant) and *saddiq* (righteous man) are very similar in appearance.[52]

As regards the emendations that are based wholly on conjecture the writer of the article explains:

> Emendations that are based wholly on conjecture must be the last resort of the textual critic, yet they are sometimes necessary and sound. They may be suggested out of a knowledge of the types of errors that scribes can make, the forms of the Hebrew letters, and common sense as to the meaning of a passage. One very simple emendation that has commended itself to most modern scholars may be found in Amos 6:12. The first half of the verse reads in Hebrew: 'Do horses run on the rock? Does one plow with oxen?' the first rhetorical question implies the answer 'no,' but the second implies 'yes.' One naturally expects in the light of the context that both questions imply the same answer. The King James Version attempts to resolve difficulty by translating, 'Will one plow there with oxen,' but 'there' is not in the Hebrew. A simple solution gives a suitable rendering. The Hebrew word *bab*^{e}*qarim,* 'with oxen' can be divided into two Hebrew words, *b*^{e}*baqar yam*, 'with oxen the sea.' We thus translate the emended text: 'does one plow the sea with oxen?' The difficulty arose from the fact that in ancient times manuscripts did not always separate words, or in some cases words were wrongly separated.[53]

As regards the emendations that are exercised partly on the basis of ancient versions and partly by conjecture, the writer elucidates as follows:

> Sometimes the text may be emended partly on the basis of ancient versions and partly by conjecture. A good example is Proverbs 25:27. Translated literally, the Hebrew seems to say: 'It is not good for one to eat much honey; and searching out their glory is glory.' The meaning of this is far from apparent. One may attempt to restore the original text by comparing the Septuagint and Targum and adopting their reading at the end of the verse, and

then conjecturing that the first word (in Hebrew) of the second half of the verse is the same as the first word in the Proverbs 25:17. One then gets the proverbial saying: 'It is not good for one to eat much honey; so be sparing of complimentary words.'[54]

However, it is heartening to note that the learned writer has, ultimately, acknowledged the worth and credibility of the biblical literature to some extent. He has observed:

> Textual criticism has made great progress in the attempt to restore the original text of the OT. Much remains to be done, but on the whole the original text of the OT is as well known as that of any other book that has survived from antiquity and probably better known than most.[55]

The *Dummelow's Commentary* asserts that the Mosaic authorship regarding the Pentateuch is not genuine:

> The traditional view was that Moses was the author of the five books which bear his name in our Bibles; and until comparatively recent times this belief was accepted without question or inquiry regarding its grounds. A thorough study of these books, however, has led many to the conclusion that this view of their authorship does not fit in with the facts, and that another view is necessitated by the evidence which the books themselves present.[56]

The *Dummelow's Commentary* expresses the view that the Pentateuch was anonymously written and it is not fair to ascribe it to Moses in its present form:

> It must also be noted that as a whole the five books are anonymously written, and that there is no passage in the OT which claims Moses as their author. The 'Law of Moses' indeed is frequently spoken of, and it is unquestionable that Israelitish law did originate with him; but this expression is not evidence that Moses was the writer of the Pentateuch as we have it, or that the laws which it contains represent throughout his unmodified legislation. (....).
>
> On close examination, however, it must be admitted that the Pentateuch reveals many features inconsistent with the traditional

view that in its present form it is the work of Moses. For instance it may be safely granted that Moses did not write the account of his own death in Dt 34. (...). In Gn 14:14 and Dt 34 mention is made of Dan; but the territory did not receive that name till it was conquered by the Danites, long after the death of Moses (Josh 19:47 Jg 18:29). (....).

A careful examination has led many scholars to the conviction that the writings of Moses formed only the rough material or part of the material, and that in its present form it is not the work of one man, but a compilation made from previously existing documents. In this connexion it must be remembered that editing and compiling is a recognised mode of authorship in OT history. Just as St. Luke tells us (Lk 1:1) that before our Four Gospels were written, there were many earlier accounts of our Lord's life already in existence, so the OT writers tell us of similar accounts already written of the facts which they record. And not only so, but they distinctly indicate that they used these earlier accounts in composing their own books. It is most interesting to find embedded in the existing books fragments of the old literature of ancient Israel, as geologists find the fragments of the lost animal life of early ages embedded in the rocks of to-day. See, for example, 'the book of the Wars of Jehovah' (Nu 21:14), 'the book of Jesher' (2S 1:18) 'the book of Gad and Nathan' (1Ch 29:29), 'the book of Shemaiah and Iddo' (2Ch 12:15). Here we have evidence of the existence of sources of information to which editors and compilers of later days had access. We find also several ancient poems incorporated in the sacred text, eg. Gn 4:23f, Ex 15, 17:16, Nu 21:17,18, 27f, Jg 5, etc., and it is probable there were other early writings available besides those which can now be traced. *There is thus nothing strange in the suggestion that the books of the Pentateuch were based on preexisting materials* [sress added].[57]

Hereunder the *Dummelow's Commentary* affords the main grounds of the conviction that the Pentateuch is not the original work of one man, but a compilation of the previously existing documents:

> Composition. The following are the main grounds of the conviction that the Pentateuch is not the original work of one man, but a compilation of the previously existing documents.

(1) In the historical parts we find duplicate accounts of same event, which do not always agree in detail. Sometimes the two accounts are set down side by side; sometimes they are fused together more or less completely; but in many instances no attempt has been made either to remove or to reconcile their differences. Thus two distinct and independent accounts of the Creation are given, one in Gn 1-2:4, the other in Gn 2:4-25. Two accounts of the flood may be detected on a careful reading of Gn 6-9. Again we find two sets of instructions for the observance of the Passover in Ex 12, one in vv. 1-13, the other in vv. 21-27. We may also instance the contrasts between such passages as Gn 27:1-45 and 27:46-28:9, where Rebekah is actuated by one motive in the former and by quite another in the latter; Gn 28:19 and 35:9-15, where the name is given to Bethel in very different circumstances; Gn 35:10 and 32:28. Compare also Ex 3:1-6:1 with 6:2-7:13, where the latter section takes no account of the former, but begins the story of the mission to Pharaoh anew, as if 3:1-6:1 had never been written.

(2) Similarly in the legislative portions of these books we find apparent contradictions, and these not in minor or insignificant details, but in fundamental enactments; and the only way in which we can solve the problem thus presented is by understanding that in these books (especially Exodus to Deuteronomy) we have the records of laws laid down at various periods of the national history, and dealing with radically different conditions of life. In Ex 20-23, e.g., we have a set of laws which are evidently suited to the circumstances of an agricultural and pastoral community scattered over a considerable tract of country with their flocks and herds. This legislation is of a very simple and practical nature, based on the fundamental principles of truth and righteousness, and having reference to a primitive state of society. (....).

In the book of Deuteronomy we find a more advanced type of legislation, applying evidently to different circum-stances. Many injunctions, indeed, are repeated, but many others are changed. The principles are the same as in the older legislation, but the rules are largely modified. (....).

Again, in the book of Leviticus, with parts of Exodus and Numbers, we find another type of legislation, founded still on the same Mosaic principles, but more elaborate, more priestly, more rigid than that of Ex 20-23 or that of Deuteronomy. (...).

(3) Different parts of the Pentateuch exhibit marked differences of vocabulary and literary style. Many of these differences, especially of vocabulary, can only be appreciated by those acquainted with Hebrew; but any one can see that the book of Deuteronomy is written in a much more rhetorical style than, say, the book of Leviticus, and can appreciate its lofty and inspiring eloquence. Again, in one set of passages, of which Gn 1-2:4 is a type, the Almighty is called God (Hebrew *Elohim*), while in another set, of which Gn 2:4-26 is an example, He is designated Lord (Hebrew *Jehovah*); and there are many other points of difference which are most satisfactorily explained by the theory that the writer of the Pentateuch, as we have it, made use of and incorporated into his work documents originally separated.

Following up the clue given by these differences, scholars have endeavored to disentangle the separate documents from which it is suggested that the Pentateuch was compiled, and we shall now give a brief outline of the results of their investigations.[58]

The writer has also tried to trace the various sources of the material contained in the books of the Pentateuch:

Sources.

(a) There is first what we may call the Primitive source (itself resting upon older written authorities), usually denoted by the symbol JE. (...). It [Primitive or JE source] begins at Gn 2:4, and may be said to supply all the more detailed and picturesque narratives in Genesis, and Exodus, part of Numbers, and the first twelve chapters of Joshua. (...). It makes use of the term 'Jehovah' for God from the very outset of its narrative. Plausible attempts have been made to analyze it into two components, J and E; but for these reference must be made to larger works. (....).

It seems probable that the older written authorities underlying this Primitive or Prophetic narrative were drawn up not later than 750 B.C., and perhaps even a century earlier; (...).

(b) There is, secondly, the Priestly document (usually designated P). This work is so called because it regards the history of Israel from the Priestly point of view, (...).

This Priestly document avoids all anthropomorphic representations of God, and in this respect is in striking contrast to the Primitive writing JE, which represents God as thinking and acting like a man: (...). A feature of its references to God is that it makes use of the name Elohim (God) for God almost exclusively (...). The writer of this document evidently belonged to the priestly class; his aim was entirely a religious one; (...). The Priestly document thus exhibits signs of the discipline and purification which the nation experienced in the exile and is appropriately dated at the close of that event.

(c) The third document underlying the Pentateuch is the book of Deuteronomy, usually cited as D, and identified in its main parts with the Law-book discovered in the Temple by Hilkiah in the eighteenth year of King Josiah, 621 B.C. (...).

It is supposed that these three documents — the Primitive writing, the Priestly writing, and the book of Deuteronomy — were welded together somewhat in this way. The first attempts to write a history of Israel probably originated in the schools of the prophets in the ninth century B.C.: and in the Primitive writing JE we have the finished result. About the same time as JE was composed, the Second Legislation (D) was set down in writing and made public as recorded in 2K 22. This was afterwards combined with the earlier writing, which gave it a historical background. Then during, or immediately after the exile, the ritual law was drawn up in accordance with the priestly traditions, and given an appropriate setting in a historical framework, the result being the Priestly writing (P). Finally a later historian, taking these as his authorities, wove them together into a complete whole, connecting them by notes and explanations, where these were necessary; not putting the history in his own words or presenting it from his own standpoint as a modern historian would do, but piecing together the sections of the sources which referred to the same events, and thus preserving not only the history, but the very words in which it had reached him, for all coming generations. In this writer's work we have the Pentateuch of the OT Scriptures.[59]

Dr. Geddes MacGregor, Dean of the Graduate School of Religion and Prof. of Philosophical Theology in the Univ. of S. California has afforded, inter alia, another type of corruption in his esteemed book *The Bible in the Making.* It would be pertinent to give an excerpt from it as well:

> For all the care that scribes often devoted to their task, a great many errors inevitably crept in. Deviations occur even among the most reliable of the ancient Greek manuscripts.

Before the invention of printing, the difficulty of reproducing the Bible did not consist solely in the labor of copying by hand. Parchment was scarce, so that contractions were very freely used. Sometimes a valuable manuscript, such as the Codex Ephraemi, a fifth-century Bible now in the Bibliotheqe Nationale, Paris, was treated so that, the writings have been erased by scraping and pumicing[60] , the pages might be used over again for making another book. The lower writing was not usually quite obliterated, however, though it was extremely difficult to decipher it until chemical means were found to revive what had been rubbed out. Such a book, with one set of writing superimposed upon another, is called a *palimpsest*. Again, MSS were often corrected by later copyist who scraped out with a knife what seemed to them incorrect, and modern scholars know that in many cases it was the corrector, not the MS, that was at fault. Sometimes a note would be made in the margin which a subsequent copyist would take to be part of the text. The hazards of inaccuracy in copying out the Bible by hand in the circumstances that prevailed in those days were so great that it is indeed astonishing that a text has been preserved which, despite technical problems it presents to the learned, may be taken as generally not straying very far from the sense of the original.[61]

Recapitulation summaries have been afforded for some of the early parts of this article. They cover almost all of the important points. Thereafter, it was not deemed necessary to provide them again. It was also not considered proper to quote more authorities. All the important themes have been elucidated. Moreover, almost all of the real and unbiased authorities unanimously endorse these themes. It can safely be concluded on the basis of the above evidence that the text of the OT of the Bible, *verbatim et literatim*, cannot be taken as free from corruption and alteration. However, the real message can be collected from it, using the critical and analytical apparatus. It may be noted that these types of corruption crept into the text of the Bible in spite of all the humanly possible care that had been sincerely afforded by the early scholars of the Bible. Dr. Geddes MacGregor has noted some measures taken towards the faultless transmission of the Bible texts. He writes:

> (…). With the fall of the Temple at Jerusalem in that year [A.D. 70], the ritual worship with its animal sacrifices was at end, and the dispersed Jews had nothing to take with them on their wanderings but their Bibles. To the copying out of these they devoted immense care. The regulations for making a copy of the Scriptures are set forth in the Talmud (the great post-Biblical collection of Jewish law and legend) and show how scrupulously careful the scribes had to be. The scroll of the Law for use in a synagogue had to be fastened, for instance, with strings made from the skin of 'clean' animals. The length of each column was prescribed: not more than sixty nor fewer than forty-eight lines were permitted. Lines had to be drawn before the writing was done, and if a scribe inadvertently wrote more than three words without first lining his copy, the whole thing was rendered worthless. He had to see that the space of a thread lay between each two consecutive letters that he wrote, and he was not allowed to write even a single letter from memory, without first looking at the approved text from which he was making the copy. He had to see that he never began the sacred name of God with a pen newly dipped in ink, lest he spatter this. The ink had to be black, made exactly according to a carefully delineated prescription. Throughout the whole of his work,

> the scribe was required to sit in full Jewish dress, and he was forbidden to speak to anyone, (...). Any copies that did not entirely conform to the exacting standard had to be destroyed. What chiefly accounts for the absence of early Hebrew MSS, however, is the fact that as soon as any scroll became worn out it had to be put in a special room called Geniza, adjoining the synagogue, the contents of which room were periodically cleared out and destroyed. The Jews had no interest in preserving tattered old copies of the Scriptures for the sake of their antiquity: what they wanted were accurate copies, and so long as accuracy of current copies was ensured by the rigid regulations, old ones could be discarded.[62]

It would be interesting to note that the Bible itself bears witness that corruption has been exercised in its text 'by the lying pen of the scribes', as stated by the Prophet Jeremiah:

> How can you say, '(...) we have Yahweh's Law?' Look how it has been falsified by the lying pen of the scribes![63]

The students of the Bible know that almost all of its books had been written long after the death of the prophets to whom they are attributed. The later compilers had no instruments to verify the credentials and credibility of those prophets. Jeremiah asserts that there had been some adulterers making false prophecies and statements 'of their own delusions' without receiving anything from God:

> For the country is full of adulterers; yes, because of a curse, the country is in mourning and the pasturage in the desert has dried up; they are prompt to do wrong, make no effort to do right. (...). For I shall bring disaster on them, when the year of punishing them comes, Yahweh declares. (...). But in the Prophets of Jerusalem I have seen something horrible: adultery, persistent lying, (...). Yahweh Sabaoth[64] says this, 'Do not listen to what those prophets prophesy to you; they are deluding you, they retail visions of their own, and not what comes from Yahweh's mouth. (...).' (...). I did not speak to them, yet they prophesied! (...). I have heard what the prophets say who make their lying prophecies in my name. 'I have had a dream,' they say, 'I have

had a dream!' How long are there to be those among the prophets who prophesy lies and are in fact prophets of their own delusions?[65]

It can thus be concluded that the text of the OT had to suffer many types of setbacks due to a lot of reasons and in a number of manners as detailed above. As such all possible analytical and critical measures should be adopted to ascertain the validity and intent of its text. But, at the same time, withal its shortcomings, it has preserved a lot of theological, historical, and prophetic substance in it and is not to be discarded outright.

THE TEXT OF THE NT AND SOME TYPES OF CORRUPTION IN IT

In this section 'Some Types of Corruption in The Text of the NT' are being discussed in the first place. The study of the 'Text of the NT' will be undertaken after it.

SOME TYPES OF CORRUPTION IN THE TEXT OF THE NT

Like the OT text there exist various types of corruption in the NT text as well. The scholarly book named *The Text of the NT* 66 deals exclusively with this theme. The heading of Chapter VII of the book is 'The Causes of Error in the Transmission of the Text of the NT'. It would be very pertinent to undertake a study of its themes. The learned writer has divided them into two sub-headings:

(I) Unintentional Changes

(II) Intentional Changes.

In the following paragraphs both these types of changes shall be described under separate sections.

I. Unintentional Changes:

1. Errors Arising from Faulty Eyesight:

(a) The scribe who was afflicted with astigmatism[67] found it difficult to distinguish between Greek letters which resemble one another, particularly when previous copyist had not written with care. Thus in the uncial[68] script the sigma, the epsilon, the theta, and the omicron were sometimes confused, etc.[69]

(b) When two lines in the exemplar from which a scribe was making a copy happened to end with the same word or words, or even sometimes with the same syllable, his eye might wander from the first to the second, accidentally omitting the whole passage lying between them.[70] Thus is to be explained the curious reading at John xvii, 15 in Codex Vaticanus, which lacks the words which are enclosed in square brackets: 'I do not pray that thou shouldst take them from the [world but that thou shouldst keep them from the] evil one.' (...). Many other examples of omission, called haplography[71], occur in a wide variety of MSS. (...). Sometimes the eye of the scribe picked up the same word or group of words a second time and as a result copied twice what should have appeared only once (this kind of error is called dittography).[72]

2. Errors Arising from Faulty Hearing :

When scribes made copies from dictation, or even when a solitary scribe in his own cell pronounced to himself the words which he was transcribing, confusion would sometimes arise over words having the same pronunciation as others, but differing in spelling (as the English words 'there' and 'their' or 'grate' and 'great').[73]

3. Errors of the Mind:

The category of errors of the mind includes those variations which seem to have arisen while the copyist was holding a clause or sequence of letters in his (somewhat treacherous) memory between the glance at the MS to be copied and the writing down of what he saw there. In this way one must account for the origin of a multitude of changes involving the substitution of synonyms, variation in the order of words, and the transposition of letters. (….).[74]

4. Errors of Judgement:

Words and notes standing in the margin of the older copy were occasionally incorporated into the text of the new MS. Since the margin was used for glosses (that is, synonyms of hard words in the text) as well as corrections, it must have often been most perplexing to a scribe to decide what to do with a marginal note. It was easiest to solve his doubt by putting the note into the text which he was copying. Thus it is probable that what was originally a marginal comment explaining the moving of the water in the pool at Bethesda (John v.7) was incorporated into the text of John v. 3b-4 (see the KJV for the addition). Again, it is altogether likely that the clause in later MSS at Rom. viii. 1, 'who walk not according to the flesh but according to the spirit', was originally an explanatory note (perhaps derived from vs. 4) defining 'those who are in Christ Jesus'. (...). Other errors originated, not because of the exercise of faulty judgement, but from the lack of judgement altogether.[75]

II. Intentional Changes

Odd though it may seem, scribes who thought were more dangerous than those who wished merely to be faithful in copying what lay before them. Many of the alterations which may be classified as intentional were no doubt introduced in good faith by copyists who believed that they were correcting an error or infelicity of language which had previously crept into the sacred text and needed to be rectified. A later scribe might even re-introduce an erroneous reading that had been previously corrected.[76]

1. Changes Involving Spelling and Grammar:

The Book of Revelation, with its frequent Semitisms and solecism[77], afforded many temptations to style-conscious scribes. [The writer has given here some concrete examples of the Greek language to elaborate the theme].[78]

2. Harmonistic Corrections:

Some harmonistic alterations originated unintentionally; others were made quite deliberately. Since monks usually knew by heart extensive portions of the Scriptures, the temptation to harmonize discordant parallels or quotations would be strong in proportion to the degree of the copyist's familiarity with other parts of the Bible. The words which belong in John xix. 20, 'It was written in Hebrew, in Latin, and in Greek', have been introduced into the text of many

MSS at Luke xxiii. 38. (...). Frequently OT quotations are enlarged from the OT context, or are made to conform more closely to the Septuagint wording. For example, the clause in the King James Version at Matt. xv. 8, '[this people] draweth nigh unto me with their mouth'–a clause which is not found in the earlier MSS of Matthew– was introduced into later MSS by conscientious scribes who compared the quotation with the fuller form in the Septuagint of Isa. xxix.13. [There are other examples in it as well to elaborate the point].[79]

3. Addition of Natural Complements and Similar Adjuncts:

The work of copyist in the amplifying and rounding off of phrases is apparent in many passages. Not a few scribes supposed that something was lacking in the statement in Matt. ix. 13, 'For I came not to call the righteous, but sinners', and added the words 'unto repentance' (from Luke v. 32). So, too, many a copyist found it hard to let 'the chief priests' pass without adding 'the scribes' (e.g. Matt. xxvii. 3), or 'scribes' without 'Pharisees' (e.g. Matt. xxvii. 41); or to copy out the phrase, 'your Father who sees you in secret will reward you' (Matt. vi. 4, 6), without adding the word 'openly'. (...). A good example of a growing text is found in Gal. vi. 17, where the earliest form of the text is that preserved in [the writer has given here some reference] 'I bear on my body the marks of Jesus'. Pious scribes could not resist the temptation to embroider the simple and unadorned [the writer has given here the actual Greek word] with various additions.[80]

4. Clearing up Historical and Geographical Difficulties:

In earlier MSS of Mark i.2 the composite quotation from Malachi (iii.1) and from Isaiah (xl. 3) is introduced by the formula, 'As it is written in Isaiah the prophet'. Later scribes sensing that this involves a difficulty, replaced [the writer has given here the Greek words] with the general statement [the writer has given here the actual Greek words]. Since the quotation which Matthew (xxvii.9) attributes to the prophet Jeremiah actually comes from Zechariah (xi. 12f.), it is not surprising that some scribes sought to mend the error, either by substituting the correct name or by omitting the name altogether. A few scribes attempted to harmonize the Johannine account of the chronology of passion with that in Mark by changing 'sixth hour' of John xix. 14 to 'third hour' (which appears in Mark xv. 25). At John i. 28 Origen altered ...to ... in order to remove what he regarded a geographical difficulty, and this reading is extant today in MSS [?] and many others, including those which lie behind the KJV. The statement in Mark viii. 31, that 'the Son of man must suffer many things ... and be killed and after three days (?) rise again', seems to involve a chronological difficulty, and some copyists changed the phrase to the more familiar expression, 'on the third day' (?).

The author of the Epistle to the Hebrews places the golden altar of incense in the Holy of Holies (Heb. ix. 4), which is contrary to the OT description of the Tabernacle (Exod. xxx. 1-6). The scribe of codex Vaticanus and the translator of the Ethiopic version correct the account by transferring the words to ix. 2, where the furniture of the Holy Place is itemized.[81]

5. Conflation[82] of Reading:

What would a conscientious scribe do when he found that the same passage was given differently in two or more MSS which he had before him? Rather than make a choice between them and copy only one of the two variant readings (with the attendant possibility of omitting the genuine reading), most scribes incorporated both readings in the new copy which they were transcribing. This produced what is called a conflation of readings, and is characteristic of the later, Byzantine type of text. For example, in some early MSS the Gospel according to Luke closes with the statement that the disciples 'were continually in the temple blessing God', while others read 'were continually in the temple praising God'. Rather than discriminate between the two, later scribes decided that it was safest to put the two together, and so they invented the reading 'were continually in the temple praising and blessing God'.

In the early MSS at Mark xiii. 11 Jesus counsels his followers not to be 'anxious beforehand' (...). Other MSS of Mark read 'do not practice beforehand' (...), which is the expression used also in the Lucan parallel (xxi. 14). Rather than choose between these two verbs, a good many copyists of Mark gave their readers the benefit of both. In Acts xx. 28 the two earlier readings, 'church of God' and 'church of the Lord', are conflated in later MSS, producing 'the church of the Lord and God'.[83]

6. Alterations because of Doctrinal Considerations:

The number of deliberate alterations made in the interest of doctrine is difficult to assess. Irenaeus, Clement of Alexandria, Tertullian, Eusebius, and many other Church Fathers accused the heretics of corrupting the Scriptures in order to have support for their special views. In the mid-second century Marcion expunged his copies of the Gospel according to Luke of all references to the Jewish background of Jesus. Tatian's Harmony of the Gospels contains several textual alterations which lent support to ascetic or encratite[84] views.

Even within the pale of the Church one party often accused another of altering the text of the Scriptures. Ambrosiaster, the fourth-century Roman commentator on the Pauline Epistles, believed that where the Greek manuscripts differed on any important point from the Latin manuscripts which he was accustomed to use, the Greeks 'with their presumptuous frivolity' had smuggled in the corrupt reading. In revising the Old Latin text of the Gospels, St. Jerome was apprehensive lest he be censured for making even slight alterations in the interest of accuracy–a fear that events proved to be well founded!

The manuscripts of the New Testament preserve traces of two kinds of dogmatic alterations: those which involve the elimination or alteration of what was regarded as doctrinally unacceptable or inconvenient, and those which introduce into the Scriptures 'proof' for a favourite theological tenet or practice.

In transcribing the prologue to the Third Gospel, the scribes of several Old Latin manuscripts as well as the Gothic[85] version obviously thought that the Evangelist should have referred to divine approval of his decision to compose a Gospel, and so to Luke's statements (i.3), 'It seemed good to me . . . to write an orderly account . . .', they added after 'me' the words 'and to the Holy Spirit'. The addition imitates the text of Acts xv. 28, which reads, 'For it has seemed good to the Holy Spirit and to us . . .'.

The inconsistency between Jesus' declaration in John vii. 8, 'I am not going up to the feast, for my time has not yet fully come', and the statement two verses later, 'But after his brothers had gone up to the feast, then he also went up, not publicly but in private' (a discrepancy which Porphyry seized upon to accuse Jesus of 'inconstantia ac mutatio'), led some scribes to change ... ('I am *not yet* going up ...'). Jesus' statement, 'But of that day and hour no one knows, not even the angels of heaven, nor the Son, but the Father only' (Matt. xxiv. 36 and Mark xiii. 32), was unacceptable to scribes *who could not reconcile Jesus' ignorance with his divinity, and who saved the situation by simply omitting the phrase* οὐδὲ ὁ υἱός [stress added].

In Luke ii there are several references to Joseph and Mary which, in the ordinary text, doubtless appeared to some persons in the early Church to require rephrasing in order to safeguard the virgin birth of Jesus. In ii. 41 and 43 instead of the words 'his parents' some manuscripts read 'Joseph and Mary'. In ii. 33 and 48 certain witnesses alter the reference to Jesus' father either by substituting the name Joseph (as in vs. 33) or by omitting it altogether (as in vs. 48). [86]

THE TEXT OF THE NT

A brief account of the second part of the topic has been afforded so far. The first part of the topic 'The text of the New Testament' is being dealt with hereunder.

The New Testament of the Bible contains 'twenty-seven' different writings.[87] The arrangement of the book is as follows:

> You may also have noticed that the New Testament writings are arranged in groups. The four Gospels [(1) Matthew; (2) Mark; (3) Luke; and (4) John] are grouped together at the beginning. That meant separating the gospel written by Luke from Acts, which he considered to be the second part of the work he had begun in the gospel. Then we have fourteen letters that were either written by Paul or were attributed to his authorship. The last, Hebrews, does not really belong in the group, since it does

not claim any connection with the Pauline tradition. The others, whether by Paul or by disciples writing in Paul's name, are divided into two groups, each in descending order of length. The first group comprises letters addressed to churches. The second comprises those addressed to individuals. Then we have a group of seven letters that were attributed to other apostolic figures: James, Peter, John and Jude. Finally, Revelation, a prophetic vision of the end of this world with the great victory of Jesus and his 'holy ones,' brings the collection to its close.[88]

Jesus Christ neither himself wrote or compiled any of the Gospels nor he asked his disciples to do so. Geddes MacGregor reports, '*Since Jesus, like other famous teachers in the ancient world, left no writings* [stress added].'[89] The apostles as well preached the gospel by word of mouth. Rev J. Kudasiewicz[90] asserts:

> Hence, the faith of community, and not the Jesus of history, gave rise to the Gospels. (...). All the evangelists testify that Jesus preached the Gospel but did not write down his words and deeds; nor did he command his disciples to write but to proclaim (Mt 10:7,27; 24:14; 28:19). In carrying out Jesus' mandate the apostles preached the Good News by word of mouth. Thus a pre-literary period preceded the writing down of Gospels during which the words and deeds of Jesus were passed on orally by the tradition of the early Church.[91]

And during this period it was 'adapted to the various needs of community' by the apostles:

> In the course of that oral transmission those words had been explained by the apostles and adapted to the various needs of the community which received them with faith.[92]

The committal to writing of even the first Gospel commenced after more than a quarter century from the death of Jesus:

> More than a quarter century transpired from the death of Jesus to the composition of the first Gospel, during which time the Gospel message was transmitted orally.[93]

The needs of the community had a great influence on the evangelists' work of redaction. Each one of them had his determined purpose and also his own addressees whose problems and needs he took into account:

> The evangelists-redactors adapted themselves to the different situations of the churches for which their works were intended. They not only wrote down and composed the words and deeds of Jesus into certain literary wholes but also explained them, taking into account the state of the churches. Thus interpretation and adaptation had their place at this stage. The needs of the community had a great influence on the evangelists' work of redaction. Each one of them had his determined purpose and also his own addressees whose problems and needs he took into account. The needs of the churches inspired the work of redaction, affecting the work in its minutest details; because of that, the particular Gospels came to differ with each other in a marked way.[94]

There are three different and independent sources for the Gospels and their reader does not have a direct approach to the events, words and deeds of Jesus:

> There are in a certain sense three sources for the Gospels: Jesus, the apostles, and the early Church as well as the evangelists-redactors. All these had their own original personality, their own tendencies and designs which left their mark on the works to whose development they contributed.

It follows from the history of the formation of the Gospels that a contemporary reader of the Gospels does not have an immediate approach to the events, words and deeds of Jesus; between him and those facts there is an early community and the evangelists-redactors. (....). The Jesus-event was interpreted in the light of faith, both by that community as well as by the evangelists-redactors. Therefore, it can be said that there exist two 'hermeneutic instances' between the Jesus-event and the reader. The words and deeds of Jesus had been reread anew in the light of the Pasch [Pass over] and were deepened by reference to the Old Testament and to the needs of particular church communities.[95]

The evangelists did not intend to set forth the Jesus-event in the form of naked facts; they intended to interpret them theologically. Their chief task was to impress the viewpoint of salvation:

> From the genesis of the Gospels it follows that they contain in themselves an historical element: the words and deeds of Jesus from Nazareth. But this element was not set forth in the form of naked facts, or as a chronicle or official record but was interpreted theologically. (...). In the mystery of Jesus Christ what eye could not see nor ear hear was revealed to the believing readers: the salvation dimension of his activity. (...). They did not want to write the human history of Jesus but salvation history; they narrated the deeds of Jesus from the viewpoint of salvation.[96]

The transmission of historical events was not the only purpose of the evangelists:

> The transmission of historical events, however, was not their only and most important purpose. Historians of the Ancient East, especially the biblical ones, understood historical truth differently from contemporary Western historians. The Western historian is especially sensitive to the facts and events of the past; he pays less attention to the meaning of those facts. For him, therefore, the ideal of truth is the chronicle, the documentary film, the recorded word. (...). But the Eastern historian was sensitive to the meaning that was contained in the events: the religious, ethical and educational sense. Since he was so taken up with the meaning of history, he attached lesser importance to the facts themselves.

Such an understanding of history affected their historical writing. They wrote and composed so as to draw the most meanings from the historical events. Thus they often omitted that which would have been for a journalistic historian most important. At other times they selected those facts that would express the intended truth. Finally, in narrating historical facts they emphasized different things: they abbreviated some events and condensed them, while they amplified others in order to better clarify the meaning. Today that way of writing history is considered faulty; but in those times that was the way the writing of history was practiced. Since the evangelists lived and wrote in that environment, that was the way they understood their task, as they put the words and deeds of Jesus on record.[97]

The evangelists included only those episodes and quotations that were suitable for their intended purpose:

> The evangelists did not want to write a biography of Jesus according to our standards. That is why we do not find in their works a complete history of Jesus from Nazareth. They only narrated those episodes and quoted only those words that were suitable for achieving their intended purpose. The words that St. John said about himself can be referred to all: 'There were many other signs that Jesus worked.... but they are not recorded in this book. These are recorded so that you may believe that Jesus is the Christ...' (Jn 20:30).[98]

According to Rev. J. Kudasiewicz the traditional Catholic assertion about the Gospels is unacceptable. He says:

> Research on the genesis of the Gospels and the analysis of the work of the evangelists-redactors have led us to the same conclusion... The four Gospels are not biographies of Jesus. The traditional Catholic assertion, according to which the evangelists are historians photographing in a way the reality to which they were witnesses cr about which they found out from immediate witnesses, is unacceptable. Such a view of the Gospels is one-sided.[99]

As to the sources of the Synoptic Gospels Rev. J. Kudasiewicz asserts:

> At present the most accepted hypothesis among Protestant and Catholic scholars is the so-called two-sources theory. In the present state of research it is the best documented. This hypothesis can be sketched in the following way. The Gospel of Mark was the oldest of all the Gospels; it was the source for Matthew and Luke. The last two have another common source, symbolized by Q from the German *Quelle* or 'source' which included mainly the sayings of Jesus, although not exclusively.

Hence it is called the 'source for the sayings of the Lord.' Matthew and Luke drew on these two sources. Aside from that, however, each evangelist had his own exclusive sources, either written or preserved by oral tradition.

The first assumption of this hypothesis is the primacy of Mark with reference to Matthew. An analysis confirms that. (...). It seems then that the primitive character of Mark is justified. (...).

The second source for Matthew and Luke was the collection of the sayings of the Lord, Q. In comparing Matthew with Luke it is noticeable that they have much material in common, especially the sermons of Jesus which are partially in agreement and partially different. It cannot be that Matthew is dependent on Luke or vice versa. There are a number of reasons for that. (...). Both evangelists, however, profited from the common source [Q] in different ways. Matthew placed the words of Jesus in great masterly discourses but Luke spread them out throughout his whole work, thereby preserving their structure and even their context. Because of this it is possible with some probability to reconstruct the source Q.[100]

It would be interesting to note some information about the compilation of the source 'Q' at this point:

> Who is the author of that source? When did it arise? What was its first form like and its theology? Because of penetrating research a reply to the questions can be attempted. The authors of Q were the first disciples of Jesus who regarded their mission as a continuation of the teaching of the Master. Palestine was the place where this source originated, and where after the death and resurrection of Jesus the first Judeo-Christian communities developed. These were characterized by a prophetic-apocalyptic enthusiasm because they lived in an atmosphere of expectation of the end of the world and of the universal judgement. That impressed itself on the form and content of the sayings which had a clearly Palestinian, Judaic and apocalyptic color. The source Q did not arise suddenly but was the result of a very long evolutionary process. It was recorded in writing earlier than the Gospel of Matthew. Hence it cannot be identified with that Gospel. The source was edited in Greek.[101]

Some of the specific features of the source 'Q' are also being afforded hereunder:

> There is an absence of passion and resurrection narratives in Q. (...). In the light of Q, Jesus of Nazareth is not only one of the many prophets but the eschatological prophet, the prophet of the last times, the Son of Man on earth. It is precisely that which distinguishes him from all the preceding prophets, giving him special authority. The favorite title of Jesus in Q is 'Son of Man' who was shown in glory (Mk 11:3; Lk 13:35) as the eschatological Judge (Lk 6:46). Jesus as the Son of Man and Judge is the court of last resort which decides the fate of all humanity (Lk 11:30; 12:40; 17:24; 26:30). Although Q does not contain narratives about the passion of Jesus, still it preserves the words of Jesus about an earthly and humiliated Son of Man (Mt 8:20; 11:6, 19). As we can see, the theology of Q has a primitive and limited character; it is shaded by Judaism and eschatology. It required a revision and deepening of perspective; the individual evangelist-redactor achieved that.[102]

Geddes MacGregor has also dealt with the theme under the chapter 'How the NT took shape'. He asserts that the Gospels were written after the death of St. Paul:

> It was only after Paul's death that the Gospels as we know them were written. (...). The most commonly accepted view is that Mark was written at Rome about the time of the Fall of Jerusalem in A.D. 70; Matthew at Antioch ten years later; and Luke and Acts ten years later still. It is a pity that Luke and Acts are not placed together in the New Testament, since they were written by the same author, (...). The case of John is a special one.[103]

As regards the Gospel of John, he says:

> Some, for very complex reasons, were disposed to treat his Gospel as belonging to a very late date (perhaps the middle of the second century) and therefore very far removed indeed from the lifetime of any eye-witness. (...). It is quite probable that the Gospel according to St John, substantially in the form in which we now have it, was written before the end of the first century,

and there is considerable evidence in support of it, (...), and it may well have reached its present form before A. D. 100.[104]

As to the last book of the NT, Revelation, it was written about A.D. 95. G. MacGregor says:

> The Christians of the first three centuries often suffered very cruel persecution, not least, in the first century, under the Emperor Nero and the Emperor Domitian. The book called Revelation or the Apocalypse reflects this, being written probably about A.D. 95, towards the end of Domitian's reign. Its author is called John. Whoever he was, he was certainly not the author of the Gospel bearing the name, for the style of the two books is entirely different. The author of Revelation wrote Greek with very marked Hebraisms, and he must have been a man of very different temper and outlook from the one who wrote the Gospel.[105]

The books of the NT had mostly been written by A.D. 120, but they had not been collected by that date in their present form:

> Though the books now in the New Testament were mostly written by A.D. 120 [An exception is II Peter, which is probably to be dated between A.D. 150 and 175 (footnote by G. MacGregor)], they had by no means been collected by that date in their present form, nor had they acquired anything like their present status among Christians.[106]

In most of the Western churches the list of the authoritative books of the NT was adopted by the end of 2nd century AD:

> Towards the end of the second century A.D. most of the Churches in the West, notably the one at Rome, had accepted a list of books as authoritative, were calling them the New Testament, and were reading them liturgically along with Septuagint or Greek Version of the Old Testament. The body of writing that was thus recognized consisted of the four Gospels, the Acts, and thirteen letters of Paul. Other books, notably Revelation, the Epistle to the Hebrews, II Peter, II and III John, and Jude, were regarded as less authoritative. (...). In the Eastern Church (...). The great Alexandrian scholar Origen (c. 185 - c. 254), who probably knew more about the technicalities of the subject than anyone else in

his day, drew up a list of books that he considered to be generally accepted by all Christians, and a list of those which, though acknowledged in some places, had no such universal status. In the first of these two lists he put the four Gospels, fourteen letters which he attributed to St. Paul–one of these was Hebrews, now known to be certainly not Paul's letter–the Acts, I Peter, I John, and Revelation. In the second list he placed James, II Peter, II and III John, Jude, Barnabas, and the Shepherd. Origen himself was disposed to acknowledge both lists, which, taken together, give us exactly what is now contained in the New Testament, plus Barnabas and the Shepherd. Eusebius of Caesarea, another great scholar of the early Church, born about A.D. 260, preferred to omit both Barnabas and the Shepherd, so his list was similar to the one in our modern editions of the NT. But Revelation, long felt to be a very doubtful book for inclusion, was only squeezed in. Indeed in the Eastern Church in the Middle Ages it was more often omitted from than included in manuscripts of the NT.

Though the Western or Latin view of what ought to be the contents of the NT had been substantially formulated and expressed by A.D. 200 there was no such fixed or universal opinion on the subject in the Eastern Church. Among the Eastern or Greek Fathers in the fourth century there was considerable difference of opinion. For instance, the lists of Athanasius, John Chrysostom, and Gregory of Nazianzus–all highly influential men in the history of Christian Church–differed greatly. That of Athanasius was most like the list of books we recognize today as canonical; but it was the list of Gregory of Nazianzus that won widest acceptance in the East. His list included the four Gospels, the Acts, fourteen letters attributed to Paul, and seven other letters; it excluded Revelation.

It was about this time that St Jerome undertook his translation of the Bible into Latin, in the 'Vulgate' that was to have an enormous influence on Christianity in the West. (...). Though he knew well that the Epistle to the Hebrews enjoyed less favour in the Western Church than it did among Christians in the East, he decided to include it and ascribe it to St Paul, though he took care to acknowledge that this was not according to Western custom. He also included Revelation.

Even in the West slight departures from Jerome's list were not unknown; but on the whole it may be said that he finally determined for Western Christians what books the NT would contain.

Books had been made according to the modern format (that is, in bound pages, as in the book you are now reading) from at least the first century A.D. A book in this form was known as a codex. (...). But these codices were rare and the change from scroll to codex form was very gradual. It is interesting to note that Western Christians appear to have been very progressive, favouring the codex form in its earlier days. 'From the second century, when ninety-seven per cent of the non-Christian Biblical papyri were in the roll form, we now have eight Christian Biblical papyri, and all of these are in the form of the codex. [107]

To sum up the section on the 'TEXT OF THE NT (NEW TESTAMENT) AND SOME TYPES OF CORRUPTION IN IT', hereunder are the salient features of it:

1. As to the types of corruption, almost all the points noted in the section regarding the OT are equally applicable and relevant to the NT, which can be seen in that section.
2. The NT of the Bible contains 'twenty-seven' different writings starting with four Gospels.
3. Jesus preached the Gospel but did not write down his words and deeds; nor did he command his disciples to record them in writing. The apostles preached by word of mouth and the words and deeds of Jesus were passed on orally.
4. In the course of that oral transmission those words had been explained by the apostles and adapted [changed] to the various needs of the community.
5. The committal to writing of even the first Gospel commenced after more than a quarter century from the death of Jesus.
6. The needs of the community had a great influence on the evangelists' work of redaction. Each one of them had his

determined purpose and also his own addressees whose problems and needs he took into account.

7. There are three different and independent sources for the Gospels: (a) Jesus, (b) the apostles, and (c) the early church as well as the evangelist/redactors. Their reader has no direct approach to the events, words and deeds of Jesus, because there is an early community and the evangelists-redactors between him and these facts.
8. The evangelists did not intend to set forth the Jesus-event in the form of naked facts; they intended to interpret them theologically. Their chief task was to impress the viewpoint of salvation.
9. Since the Eastern historian was so taken up with the meaning of history, he attached less importance to the facts themselves. The evangelists-redactors abbreviated some events and condensed them. They amplified others to clarify the meaning better. Today that way of writing history is considered faulty.
10. The evangelists narrated only those episodes and quoted only those words that were suitable for achieving their intended purpose.
11. The traditional Catholic assertion, according to which the evangelists are historians photographing in a way the reality to which they were witnesses or about which they found out from immediate witnesses, is unacceptable. Such a view of the Gospels is one-sided.
12. At present the most accepted hypothesis among Protestant and Catholic scholars is the so-called two-sources theory. The Gospel of Mark was the oldest of all the Gospels; it was the source for Matthew and Luke. The last two have another common source, symbolized by 'Q'. Matthew and Luke drew on these two sources. In addition to it each evangelist had his own exclusive sources, either written or preserved by oral tradition. It is probable to reconstruct the source 'Q'.

13. The authors of 'Q' were the first disciples of Jesus who regarded their mission as a continuation of the teaching of the Master. Palestine was the place where this 'source' originated. It was the result of a very long evolutionary process. It was recorded in writing before the Gospel of Matthew. It was edited in Greek.
14. There is an absence of passion and resurrection narratives in 'Q'. In the light of 'Q', Jesus of Nazareth is not only one of the many prophets but the prophet of the last times. The favorite title of Jesus in 'Q' is the 'Son of Man'. As we can see, the theology of 'Q' has a primitive and limited character. It required a revision and deepening of perspective; the individual evangelist-redactor achieved that.
15. Mark was written at Rome about the time of the Fall of Jerusalem in AD 70; Matthew at Antioch ten years later; and Luke and Acts ten years later still. The case of John is a special one.
16. Gospel according to St John was written before the end of the first century, and it may well have reached its present form before AD 100.
17. The last book of the NT, Revelation, was written *ca.* AD 95.
18. The books of the NT had mostly been written by AD 120 (except II Peter, which is probably to be dated between A.D. 150 and 175), but they had not been collected by that date in their present form.
19. in most of the Western churches the list of the authoritative books of the NT was adopted by the end of 2nd century AD. In the Eastern church Origen (c. 185-c. 254) prepared two lists and Eusebius (b. 260) prepared the list of books of the NT similar to the present one.

The section of the OT was concluded with the following passage, which is equally true in respect of the NT with some modifications that have been duly incorporated in it:

It can thus be safely concluded that the text of the NT had to suffer many types of setbacks due to a number of reasons as detailed above. As such all possible analytical and critical measures should be adopted to ascertain the validity and intent of its text. But, at the same time, withal its shortcomings, it has preserved a lot of theological, historical, and prophetic substance in it and is not to be discarded outright.

References

1. The Catholic OT consists of 46 books, having 7 additional books called 'Apocrypha' (plural of 'apocryphon'). Apocrypha is a Greek word meaning 'hidden'. They are the books for which divine authorship is falsely claimed. They are generally included in the Catholic Bibles; but not in the Protestant Bibles.
2. Ezra 4:8 to 6:18; 7:12-26; Daniel 2:4b to 7:28; and Jer. 10:11.
3. *Encyclopaedia Britannica* (University of Chicago, n.d.), 3:577.
4. 'Septuagint' means seventy, commonly written as 'LXX'. It was the Greek translation of the OT of the Bible, made by almost 70 or 72 scholars in Alexandria during the third and second centuries BC.
5. *Enc. Britannica* (University of Chicago, n.d.,) 3:577.
6. Anthropomorphism: 'attributing of human shape or characteristics to a god etc.' (*Webster's New World College Dic.*, 1997; p. 1245).
7. *Encyclopaedia Britannica* (University of Chicago, n.d.), 3:577.
8. *Encyclopaedia Britannica* (University of Chicago, n.d.), 3:577.
9. *Encyclopaedia Britannica*, 15th edn., 1989, 3:759.
10. *Encyclopaedia Britannica* 15th edn., 1989, 3:759.
11. *Encyclopaedia Britannica* 15th edn., 1989, 3:759-60.
12. *Encyclopaedia Britannica*, 15th edn., 1989, 3:760.
13. *variae lectiones*, i. e., 'various readings'.
14. 'The Old Testament Text', written by Shemaryahu Talmon, Professor of Bible, The Hebrew University of Jerusalem, in *The Cambridge History of the Bible* (1970), 1:159-60.
15. *The Cambridge History of the Bible*, 1:161-2.
16. *The Cambridge History of the Bible*, 1:162.

17. *The Cambridge History of the Bible*, 1:162.
18. *Ur-text*, i.e. 'the earliest version of a text, from which extant texts are deemed to be derived'.
19. *Ipsissima verba*, i.e. 'the very word'.
20. *The Cambridge History of the Bible*, 1:163-4.
21. *The Cambridge History of the Bible*, 1:164-5.
22. *Vorlage* means: 'An original version of a MS from which a copy is produced'.
23. *Idiosyncrasies* means: 'An unusual habit or way of behaving; an unusual or unexpected feature'.
24. *The Cambridge History of the Bible*, 1:167-8.
25. *Ipsissima verba* means: 'the very word'.
26. *The Cambridge History of the Bible*, 1:170,71,74.
27. *The Cambridge History of the Bible*, 1:183-86.
28. *Plene* means: 'pertaining to a system of full orthographic notations in Heb, whereby vowel sounds are indicated by certain vocalic signs'.
29. *The Cambridge History of the Bible*, 1:188.
30. *The Cambridge History of the Bible*, 1:190.
31. *The Cambridge History of the Bible*, 1:190-92.
32. *minutiae* [plural] means: 'very small and exact but unimportant details'.
33. *Peake's Commentary on the Bible*, 75.
34. Jerome (ca.342-420): Born at Strido near Aquileia. He studied at Rome, where he was baptized, and then travelled in Gaul before devoting himself to an ascetic life with friends at aquileia. About 374 he set out for Palestine. (...), and in 386 finally settled at Bethlehem, where he ruled a newly-founded men's monastery and devoted the rest of his life to study. (...). His greatest achievement was his translation of most of the Bible into Latin [Vulgate] from the original tongues, to which he had been orig. prompted by Damasus. (F.L.Cross, *The Oxford Dic. of Christian Church*, 1974, 731)
35. *Peake's Commentary on the Bible*, 76.

36. 'At present only two MSS of Isa. from cave 1 have appeared in facsimile: A (1QIsa), in *The Dead Sea Scrolls of St Mark's Monastery*, vol. I, *The Isaiah Manuscript and the Habakkuk Commentry*, ed. M. Burrows (1950), and B (1QIsb), in *The Dead Sea Scrolls of the Hebrew University*, ed. E. L. Sukenik (1955), with further fragments from the same scroll in *Discoveries in the Judaean Desert I, Qumran Cave I*, ed. D. Barthelemy and J. T. Mililk (1955), section 8, Plate XII. They are designated here as texts A and B respectively.' (*Peake's Com., 76*)
37. *legion* means: 'Numerous, very many'.
38. *Recension* means: 'A critical revision of a text; a text established by critical revision; a review'.
39. *Peake's Commentary on the Bible*, 77.
40. *Peake's Commentary on the Bible*, 78.
41. *Peake's Commentary on the Bible,* 79.
42. *a priori*, means: 'denoting knowledge gained independently of experience.'
43. *Peake's Commentary on the Bible*, 79.
44. *A Commentary on the Holy Bible*, ed. J. R. Dummelow, xiv.
45. 'Textual Criticism of the OT' by J. Philip Hyatt of the Vanderbilt University, in *Enc. Americana*, Grolier Inc, 1984, 3:658.
46. *The Encyclopaedia Americana*, (1984), 3:658.
47. *The Encyclopaedia Americana*, (1984), 3:659-70.
48. *The Encyclopaedia Americana*, 3:660-1.
49. *The Encyclopaedia Americana* (1984), 3:661.
50. *The Encyclopaedia Americana*, 3:661.
51. *The Encyclopaedia Americana* (1984), 3:661.
52. *The Encyclopaedia Americana* (1984), 3:661-2.
53. *The Encyclopaedia Americana*, 3:662.
54. *The Encyclopaedia Americana* (1984), 3:662.
55. *The Encyclopaedia Americana* (1984), 3:659-662.
56. *Dummelow Com. on Holy Bible* (1956), xxiv.
57. *Dummelow's Commentary on Holy Bible*, xxvf.
58. *Dummelow's Commentary on Holy Bible*, xxvif.

59. *Dummelow's Com.. on Holy Bible*, xxvii-xxix.
60. *Pumicing*, i.e. 'rubbing one's skin to clean it or make it soft'.
61. Geddes MacGregor, *The Bible in the Making* (1961), 9-10.
62. *Bible in the Making*, 8-9.
63. Jer 8:8 *The New Jerusalem Bible*, 1311.
64. *Sabaoth* is a Greek word meaning 'hosts' (*NIV Compact Dic. of Bible*, 514).
65. Jer 23:10-26 *New Jerusalem Bible*, 1335-36.
66. Bruce M. Metzger, *The Text of the New Testament, Its Transmission, Corruption, and Restoration* (Oxford: at the Clarendon Press, 1964).
67. *Astigmatism* means: 'A defect in an eye, lens or mirror by which rays from a single point are not focused at a single point'.
68. *Uncial*, i.e. 'written in majuscule (large letters) writing with rounded unjoined letters found in manuscripts of the 4th-8th century, from which modern capitals are derived'.
69. Bruce M. Metzger, *The Text of the NT* (1964), 186-7.
70. It is called *Homoeoteleuton* as already explained above (p. 179).
71. *Haplography* is 'the inadvertent writing once what should have been written twice' (*the Chambers Dic.*, p. 762).
72. *The Text of the NT* (1964), 189-90.
73. *The Text of the NT* (1964), 190.
74. *The Text of the NT* (1964), 192-3.
75. *The Text of the NT, Its Transmission, Corruption, and Restoration* (1964), 194.
76. *The Text of the NT, Its Transmission, Corruption, and Restoration* (1964), 195.
77. *solecism* means: 'a breach of syntax; any absurdity, impropriety, or incongruity'.
78. *The Text of the NT* (1964), 196-7.
79. *The Text of the NT* (1964), 197-8.
80. *The Text of the NT* (1964), 198.
81. *The Text of the NT* (1964), 199f.

82. *Conflation*: 'combining (e.g. two different versions of a text)'.
83. *The Text of the NT* (1964), 200.
84. *encratite* means: 'one of a heretical sect in the early church who abstained from marriage, and from meat and wine' (*The Chambers Dic.*, 1995, p. 553).
85. *Gothic*, i.e. 'of or pertaining to the Goths (people of a Germanic tribe which invaded the Eastern and Western Empires between the 3rd and the 5th centuries and founded kingdoms in Italy, France, and Spain) or their language; designating the style of handwriting used in Western Europe from the 13th century, and the typefaces derived from it'. (*The New Shorter Oxford English Dic.* (1993), 1:1121).
86. 6 *The Text of the NT* (1964), 201ff.
87. Rheme Perkins, *New Testament Introduction* (Bombay: St. Paul Publications, Bundra, Bombay, 1992), 13.
88. Rheme Perkins, *NT Introduction* (1992), 13f.
89. Geddes MacGregor, *The Bible in the Making* (1961), 35.
90. Some excerpts are being noted from his book *The Synoptic Gospels Today* in the following lines of the text. Being a devout Christian scholar, Rev. Joseph Kudasiewicz has undertaken pure research to prove the authenticity of the Gospels. He is a specialist in the field of synoptical Gospels, their historical, literary, and theological dimensions. But, at the same time, he has affirmed that the actual or naked words and events have not been recorded in the Gospels of necessity. The writer of the present paper feels himself privileged of having read such a scholarly piece of research and pays sincere tributes to the worthy author. It is to be recommended that this masterly work be gone through to understand the theme.
91. Rev. Joseph Kudasiewicz, *The Synoptic Gospels Today* (Metro Manila: ST PAULS, 1203, Philippines, 1997), 3.
92. *The Synoptic Gospels Today* (1997), 3.
93. *The Synoptic Gospels Today* (1997), 5.
94. *The Synoptic Gospels Today* (1997), 50.

95. *The Synoptic Gospels Today* (1997), 51-2.
96. *The Synoptic Gospels Today* (1997), 52-3.
97. *The Synoptic Gospels Today* (1997), 53-4.
98. *The Synoptic Gospels Today* (1997), 54.
99. *The Synoptic Gospels Today* (1997), 57.
100. *The Synoptic Gospels Today* (1997), 63-4.
101. *The Synoptic Gospels Today* (1997), 64-5.
102. *The Synoptic Gospels Today* (1997), 66-7.
103. *The Bible in the Making*, 37.
104. *The Bible in the Making*, 37-8.
105. *The Bible in the Making*, 38-9.
106. *The Bible in the Making*, 39.
107. *The Bible in the Making*, 40-42.

Appendix-III

The Status of The Book of Chronicles

The book of Chronicles, although now included in the canon of the Bible, has been regarded as less authentic by the authorities and as such its assigning the name of 'Moriah' to the site of the Solomon's Temple carries no weight. W. H. Bennett confirms this in the Jewish Enc:

> Chronicles (from its position in many manuscripts [MSS], etc., after Nehemiah) only obtained its place in the canon by an afterthought.[1]

He states that it was not included in some Christian lists of canonical books: 'The omission[2] of Chronicles from some Christian lists of canonical books is probably accidental.'[3] As to its date of composing, he asserts:

> It is part of a larger work, Chronicles-Ezra-Nehemiah, composed in the Greek period between the death of Alexander (B.C. 323) and the revolt of the Maccabees (B.C. 167).' (...). Chronicles-Ezra-Nehemiah must be later than the times of Ezra and Nehemiah (458-432). In style and language the book belongs to the latest period of Biblical Hebrew. The descendants of Zerubbabel (I Chron. iii. 24) are given, in Masoretic text, to the sixth generation (about B.C. 350); in the LXX, Syriac, and Vulgate, to the eleventh generation after Zerubbabel (about B.C. 200) [which shows that it was written or added after BC 200]. The list of high priests in Neh. xii. 10, 11, extends to Jeddua

(c.330). These lists might, indeed, have been made up to date after the book was completed; but other considerations point conclusively to the Greek period; e.g., in Ezra vi. 22, Darius is called 'the king of Assyria.' On the other hand, the use of the book in the Ecclesiasticus (Sirach) referred to above, the absence of any trace of the Maccabean struggle, and the use of the LXX, Chronicles by Eupolemus (c. B.C. 150; see Swete, l.c. p. 24), point to a date not later than B.C. 200. Hence Chronicles is usually assigned to the period B.C. 300-250.[4]

Dr. Emil G. Hirach, Prof. of Rabbinical Literature and Philosophy, Univ. of Chicago, asserts in the Jewish Enc. that its historical accuracy was doubted by the Talmudic authorities and that the Chronicler exercised 'great freedom' in ascribing names (to persons or places):

On the whole, Chronicles was regarded with suspicion; its historical accuracy was doubted by the Talmudic authorities, (…). The names were treated with great freedom;[5]

The 7th-Day Adventist Bible Com. observes that while narrating the construction of the Temple the Chronicler has exercised full liberty in adding or omitting the details to suit his designs:

Certain items concerning the building of the Temple have been omitted, others are presented more briefly, others are given in the same wording as Kings, while others are entirely new.[6]

H. Bennett, Prof. of Hebrew at Norfolk, England, asserts in the Jewish Enc. that interpolations of various kinds were freely exercised in it. In addition to the liberties that were freely enjoyed by the author during its compilation, interpolations and additions have been made even after it had been 'substantially completed' by some later scholars:

(…) and perhaps additions were made to the book after it was substantially complete. In dealing with matter not found in other books it is difficult to distinguish between matter which the chronicler found in his source, matter which he added himself, and later additions, as all the authors concerned wrote in the same spirit and style; (….). Where Chronicles contradicts Samuel-Kings, preference must be given to the older work, except where

> the text of the latter is clearly corrupt[7]. With the same exception, it may be assumed that sections of the primitive 'Chronicles' [some older book on the annals of history of the concerned period other than the book of Chronicles of the Bible, which the Chronicler used as a source] are much more accurately preserved in Samuel-Kings than in Chronicles. (...) The consistent exaggeration of numbers on the part of the chronicler shows us that from a historical point of view his unsupported statements must be received with caution. (...). What they prove is that he did not possess that sense of historical exactitude which we now demand from the historian.[8]

J. E. Goldingay, Registrar and Lecturer in OT, St. John College, Nottingham, makes similar observations in his article on 'Chronicles, book of' in *New Bible Dic.* II Ed:

> Like most OT books, however, Chronicles is of anonymous authorship, and no conclusions are possible as to who wrote it. (...), he did wish to bring a specific message from God applied to the people of his own day, and it is this that leads him to his extensive working of his text, omitting what was now irrelevant, adding material that was now newly relevant, changing what was now misleading, and so on. Chronicles has been regarded as poorer history than Samuel-Kings, (...). Some of its alterations to Samuel-Kings raise historical problems: (...) textual corruption or misunderstanding has often been suspected. (...) — here the author perhaps resembles an artist painting the figures of the past in the dress of his own age [anachronism]. Such characteristics have led to the questioning of the extra material Chronicles includes which does not appear in Samuel-Kings. (...), and the main narratives, as we have noted, are substantially derived from Samuel-Kings.[9]

J. L. McKenzie has also recorded in his *Dic. of Bible* that the Chronicler, instead of history, was interested in his three self-framed purposes, one of which was 'the primacy of the temple and the cult':

It may be summed up by saying that the Chronicler intended to write not what happened, but what ought to have happened; (...).

This ideal is specified by three theological principles which he represents as governing events: (...), and the primacy of the temple and the cult. (...). The third principle appears in the space and importance which the Chronicler gives to the temple and its cult and personnel, (...). It is necessary to see the Chronicler's purpose.[10]

Rev. J. Mulcahy, Professor of Sacred Scripture, Holy Ghost College, Kimmage, Dublin has interestingly analyzed the themes and purposes of the Chronicler in '*A New Catholic Commentary on Holy Scripture*' and has exposed his 'credentials' in the following words:

The claim of Jerusalem to be the only place where legitimate worship of Yahweh is possible is the second principal element in the Chronicler's theme. (....). In the neutral passages (...) there seems to be no reason to doubt the strictly historical character of the narrative. In the other passages, however, we should be doing an injustice to him, were we to judge him merely as an historian. Since, for him, history is a handmaid of theology, it is the theological understanding that is important for him, not the naked historical fact. If he clothes this naked fact with somewhat imaginary adornments, we must accept this as his method of teaching theology and not reproach him for the lack of an historical exactness which a comparison between his text and that of Sm-Kgs shows that he never intended. On other matters, which were not affected by the Chronicler's special point of view and purposes, historical value is recognized in his traditions.[11]

H. Pfeiffer has undertaken a fairly detailed analytical study of the book of Chronicles in his article on it in the *Interpreter's Dic. of Bible*. Some excerpts from his article will help the reader in making some genuine opinion:

The Chronicler not only teaches the proper faith in God, after the manner of the Priestly Code, by such graphic fictitious stories, (...). To raise the low morale at such times, the Chronicler exaggerated the splendor of the Jewish kingdom in the past, (...). In glorifying Judaism and the Jews through the centuries beyond all possibilities, the Chronicler necessarily rewrote the history from David to Cyrus; he freely omitted from his sources, added to them, modified them, being blissfully unaware of anachronisms[12] and impossibilities. (...). In general the Chronicler modified our canonical sources with complete freedom to suit his ideas. (...), and modified what did not agree with his religious views or his notions of the facts of history. (...). Elsewhere the Chronicler rewrote the narration of Samuel and Kings in order to express his own views, which often differed from those of his sources; (...). These examples suffice to illustrate the various methods by which the Chronicler rewrote, edited, shortened, expanded, and arbitrarily changed the passages in Samuel and Kings which suited his purposes, omitting the rest, (...); in the other half the Chronicler, unless he had access to other sources unknown to us was able to display his vivid imagination by composing freely, without any guidance. (...). A date ca 250 B.C. or a little earlier is far more probable than 400-350 B.C.,[13]

Almost every scholar who worked on the book of Chronicles, has expressed similar views about it. They can be summed up as below:

1. Originally, the 'Chronicles' was not deemed fit to be included in the canon of the OT. It was included in the canon at some later stage.
2. It was omitted from some Christian lists of canonical books.
3. 'Like most OT books, Chronicles is of anonymous authorship, and no conclusions are possible as to who wrote it.', as stated by New *Bible Dic.*
4. According to the *Jewish Enc.* 'Chronicles is usually assigned to the period BC 300-250.'
5. Being written about seven centuries after the incident by some anonymous author, it is clear that the writer was not an eye-witness of the incident.
6. As recorded by the *Jewish Enc.* 'On the whole, Chronicles was regarded with suspicion; its historical accuracy was doubted by the Talmudic authorities.'
7. The Chronicler has retold the 'history' already recorded by the book of Samuel, Book of Kings, etc. But according to

New Bible Dic. 'Chronicles has been regarded as poorer history than Samuel-Kings,'

8. The Chronicler was working for some self framed purposes or principles, for which, as the *Interpreter's Dic. of Bible* puts it, he: '*necessarily rewrote the history from David to Cyrus; he freely omitted from his sources, added to them, modified them, being blissfully unaware of anachronisms and impossibilities. (...). In general the Chronicler modified our canonical sources with complete freedom to suit his ideas. (...), and modified what did not agree with his religious views or his notions of the facts of history.*'; and '*In glorifying Judaism and the Jews through the centuries beyond all possibilities, (...). Elsewhere the Chronicler rewrote the narration of Samuel and Kings in order to express his own views, which often differed from those of his sources; (...) These examples suffice to illustrate the various methods by which the Chronicler rewrote, edited, shortened, expanded, and arbitrarily changed the passages in Samuel and Kings which suited his purposes, omitting the rest.*' [stress added]
9. One of his self-framed purposes was, in the words of McKenzie: 'the primacy of the temple'; and 'It is necessary to see the Chronicler's purpose'.
10. It was in view of his this self-framed purpose that he tried to glorify and sanctify the 'Solomon's Temple', and forged to locate Moriah at the site of Abraham's offering of his only son for sacrifice.

References

1. *The Jewish Enc.*, 4:60.
2. Had this 'omission' been only from one list, even then it could not have been declared outright 'accidental' without assigning any justification; but the omission here is from 'some Christian lists [the plurality of the lists is esp. to be noted] of canonical books' and, its omission from so important a document as the list of canonical books cannot so generously and heedlessly be declared as 'accidental '.
3. *The Jewish Enc.*, 4:60.

4. *The Jewish Enc.*, 4:60-1.
5. *The Jewish Enc.*, 4:60.
6. *The 7th-Day Adventist Bible Com.*, 3:118.
7. 'latter' here clearly refers to 'Samuel-Kings', which shows that even 'Samuel-Kings' is not safe from 'corruption' according to the writer of this article of the *Jewish Enc.*
8. *The Jewish Enc.*, 4:62-3.
9. *New Bible Dic.*, 2nd edn., 187-8.
10. *J. L. McKenzie's Dic. of Bible*, 131-2.
11. Rev. Reginald C. Fuller, *A New Catholic Commentary on Holy Scripture*, revised and updated 1975 edn., (Hong Kong: Thomas Nelson Ltd., 1981), 353, 55-6.
12. 'Anachronisms' means: 'mistake of time, by which some thing is put in wrong period; some thing out-of-date'.
13. *The Interpreter's Dic. of Bible*, 1:574-80.

Appendix-IV

A Brief Account of the History of The Solomon's Temple (Chapter X)

There had been no building of a 'Temple' amongst the Israelites before King Solomon. Actually there was no place for a fixed building of a temple in the nomadic life of the people. The 'Tabernacle' (a tent of specific dimensions) served as the 'Temple' and the 'Ark of the Covenant'[1] was placed therein. The lack of a shrine of Yahweh became disagreeable when David (*ca.* 1010-970 BC) had consolidated his power and built a permanent palace for himself. The King said, 'I dwell in a house of cedar, but the ark of God dwells in a tent' (2 Sa. 7:2). He collected materials, gathered treasure and bought the threshing floor of Araunah the Jebusite as the site (1 Ch. 22: 8; 2 Sa. 24: 18-25).[2] His son, Solomon (who reigned *ca.* 970-930 BC over the United Monarchy of Israel) began the actual construction in his 4th year, and the Temple was completed 7 years later (*ca.* 960 BC; but, according to Smith's BD, p. 679, *ca.* 1005 BC, which is quite improbable). Its treasures were emptied by the kings of Judah several times to pay tribute or to buy alliances (2 K 12:18; 16:8; 18:15). Josiah (king of Judah *ca.* 640-609 BC) ordered the repair of the Temple. The high priest, Hilkiah, discovered the book of law during the repairs commissioned by Josiah (*ca.* 622 BC). There is general agreement that it was the original form of the book of Deuteronomy of the Pentateuch (Torah). Josiah undertook the religious reforms that were based on the 'Torah' discovered in the Temple by Hilkiah (2 K 22: 8ff). The Temple of Solomon was destroyed and the Israelites of Jerusalem were taken as exiles by the Babylonian emperor, Nebuchadnezzar, in 587-6 BC at the time of his conquest of Jerusalem. The Solomon's Temple had not been there on earth for the next almost seventy years. Cyrus of Persia defeated the Babylonian regent prince Belshazzar in 539 BC and the Babylonian empire came to an end for good. Cyrus was a just and kind ruler. He freed and permitted the Israelites to go back to and settle in Jerusalem. He allowed them to rebuild their 'Temple' and promised to provide them proper help for the purpose. The construction started in 537 BC. 7th Day BD explains:

But the builders encountered so much opposition from enemies in their homeland that the work soon came to a virtual stop and remained interrupted until the reign of Darius 1. In the 2nd year of his reign the prophets Haggai and Zechariah encouraged Zerubbabel, the governor, and Joshua, the high priest, to make another effort to rebuild the Temple. They responded, and with the enthusiastic support of the whole nation and the good will of the Persian officials and of the king himself, the new Temple, usually referred to as the Second Temple [or the Temple of Zerubbabel], was completed, along with its auxiliary structures, in the period of 4½ years, from 520 to 515 B.C. (Ezr. 3:8 to 4:5; 4:24 to 6:15). (...). Antiochus IV Epiphanes desecrated the Temple in 168 B.C. by erecting an altar dedicated to Jupiter Olympius in the Temple court and sacrificing swine on it. He stole the sacred furniture from the holy place and removed all Temple treasures (Jos. *Ant.* xii 5, 4; 1 Macc 1:21-23). However, the Temple was repaired, refurnished, and rededicated in 165 B.C., after the Maccabean forces took Jerusalem (1 Mac 4:43-59) (...). When Pompey conquered Jerusalem in 63 B.C. the Temple was spared any damage, but it was later pillaged by Crassus [in 54 BC]. It may have suffered some further damage in the conquest of Jerusalem by Herod in 37 B.C. (...). When Herod announced his intention of rebuilding a new Temple [commonly called 'Temple of Herod'], the Jews feared he would tear down the old one and then fail to rebuild it. Consequently, Herod devised a method of reconstruction by which the old was demolished only as the new construction progressed; it appeared at the different stages as if he were doing nothing but repairing the older structures, while in reality a completely new complex of buildings was erected without interrupting the services. He first rebuilt the Temple proper. This work was begun in 20/19 B.C. and lasted 18 months. He had all building material finished to size before it was brought to the Temple area, and employed only priests to work on the inner Temple structure. After that was finished, most of the outer buildings, including the cloisters, were completed during the next 8 years, but the work of decoration and embellishment went on until the procuratorship of Albinus (A.D. 62-64), immediately before the outbreak of the Jewish war. Since building activities were still going on during Christ's ministry, it is understandable that the Jews said the Temple had been in building for 46 years (Jn 2:20). (...). The whole Temple with all its buildings was destroyed by fire during the capture of Jerusalem by the forces of Titus in A.D. 70. (...). Although the Temple built by Herod the Great was actually a new structure, the Jews always referred to it as still the Second Temple, considering his work no more than a repair and remodeling. Because of the Jews' hatred for him, the orthodox Jewish writings, like the Mishnah, which gives detailed descriptions of this Temple, never mention the name of its builder. (...). The old Temple area was enlarged to twice its former size, including also the palace grounds of Solomon's time. Archeological investigations show that the present Moslem enclosure, the *Haram esh-Sherif*,[3] almost exactly covers Herod's Temple area, and large parts of the present walls rest on foundations or wall stumps of Herod's time. [4]

It may be appreciated here that there had been no building of the Temple for about seven centuries when the Mosque of Omar was built. According to the Jewish Enc.:

The mosque was built over a rock the traditions of which were sacred, probably the site was the same as that of the Temple which Hadrian erected to Jupiter. This in turn was on the site of Herod's Temple.[5]

It is thus clear that for the last two millennia there does not exist any form of the Solomon's Temple on the spot.

References

1. McKenzie (p. 54), with ref. to Ex. 25:10ff, explains the 'Ark' as:

   A small portable box or chest: 3¾ X 2¼ X 2¼ ft, made of acacia wood, overlaid with gold inside and out. On its top were two cherubim facing each other. This is the place where Yahweh meets Israel and reveals His commandments. It contained the two tablets of stone which were thought to go back to the Mosaic period, a vessel of manna and the rod of Aaron. It was carried on the head of the column when the Hebrews traveled through the desert and before the army in battle. After the settlement of the Israelites in Canaan the ark was finally established at Shiloh, [Shiloh was 9 mi NNE of Bethel, in the central mountain range.] It was taken into battle against Philistines, who defeated Israel and captured the ark. It was finally placed in the temple of Solomon.

2. *Smith's DB*, 679 observes:

   The gold and silver alone accumulated by David are at the lowest reckoned to have amounted to between two and three billion dollars.

   Apparently it looks to be improbable. It seems that the lexicographer might have reckoned it from the 'Chronicler', who is known for his exaggerations (see I Chronicles 22:14).

3. It may be noted here that the *Haram esh-Sherif* neither signify the Mosque of 'Umar nor the al-Aqṣā Mosque. It rather means the whole area covered by the Herod's Temple.

4. *7th Day Adventist BD*, p. 1099 ff.

5. *The Jewish Enc.* 12:100.

Appendix-V

A Brief Account of the History of Jerusalem

Ihsanur Rahman Ghauri

Jerusalem is one of the most ancient Canaanite cities. Its meanings have been explained by *International Standard Bible Encyclopedia* as:

> With regard to the meaning of the original name there is no concurrence of opinion. The oldest known form, Ura-sa-lim, has been considered by many to mean either the 'City of Peace' or the 'City of (the god) Salem,' but other interpreters, considering the name as of Hebrew origin, interpret it as the 'possession of peace' or 'foundation of peace.' *It is one of the ironies of history that a city which in all of its long history has seen so little peace and for whose possession such rivers of blood have been shed should have such a possible meaning for its name* (stress added).[1]

It has been recorded as 'Salem' in the Bible (Gen 14:18) which has been identified with Jerusalem in Ps 76:3 and in early Jewish tradition. Modern scholars also endorse this tradition. 'The priest of God Most High', Melchizedek, was the king of Salem when Abraham visited it in nineteenth century BC. As to its antiquity the book *Jerusalem* explains:

> Various pre-historic sites of the Lower Paleolithic[2] period have been found. In the Mesolithic[3] period, which followed, the climate was stabilized in its present form and, due to the prevailing dryness, conditions became much more difficult for

prehistoric man in the Jerusalem area. Only two sites are dated to this period. The agricultural revolution of the Neolithic[4] period enabled man to make progress against the desert: 16 sites are indicated for this period. In the Chalcolithic[5] period, settlement contracted somewhat, probably because of the strong attraction of the Jordan Valley and the Negev, which led to a relative decline of the mountain area.[6]

International Standard Bible Encyclopedia traces its antiquity as follows:

> Pre-Israelite period. — The beginnings of Jerusalem are long before recorded history: at various points in the neighborhood, e.g. at el Bukei'a to the Southwest, and at the northern extremity of the Mount of Olives to the Northeast, were very large settlements of Paleolithic man, long before the dawn of history, as is proved by the enormous quantities of Celts[7] scattered over the surface. It is certain that the city's site itself was occupied many centuries before David, and it is a traditional view that the city called Salem (Genesis 14:18), over which Melchizedek was king, was identical with Jerusalem.[8]

The first certain reference to this city is about 1450 BC, when the name Ur-u-salem occurs in several letters belonging to the Tell el-Amarna Letters correspondence. In 7 of these letters occurs the name Abd Khiba, and it is clear that this man was 'king,' or governor of the city, as the representative of Pharaoh of Egypt. (...). Incidentally we may gather that the place was then a fortified city, guarded partly by mercenary Egyptian troops, and there are reasons for thinking that then ruler of Egypt, Amenhotep IV, had made it a sanctuary of his god Aten — the sun-disc.[9]

It is reported to be 'inhabited as early as 3200 B.C.E.'[10] Pottery from the fourth millennium B.C. has been excavated at Jerusalem.[11] Pottery of Early Bronze (3150-2200 BC) and Middle Bronze Ages (2200-1550 BC) shows that people lived there during the third and early second millenniums. Stewart Henry Perowne, Orientalist, historian, and author, explains:

Excavation has shown that a settlement existed on the site south of the Temple platform, possibly in the Early Bronze Age and certainly by 1800 BC. A massive town wall still survives, just above the spring that determined the location of the ancient settlement.[12]

The walled city of this period was very small, occupying only between eight and nine acres. At the upper end, a little to the N of the spring, there was a sanctuary. The royal palace and cemetery lay below this, and the rest of the hill to its South tip was occupied by the city. Remains of Early Bronze Age wall have been discovered on this part of the hill. In 15th century BC the Hurrians or Horites came into Palestine. One of the writers of Amarna Letters was '*Abd Ḥiba* or *Arti-Ḥepa*, who reigned at Jerusalem in the 14th century BC. A strong masonry rampart which has been excavated on the East slope of Ophel comes from this period.[13] In the early twelfth century BC 'the children of Judah [as well as the children of Simeon (see Judg. 8:3)] fought gainst Jerusalem and took it; they struck it with the edge of the sword [slaughterted its inhabitants] and set the city on fire.'[14] Quoting this verse W. Smith observes:

> In the fifteen centuries which elapsed between this siege and the siege and destruction of the city by Titus, A.D. 70, the city was besieged no fewer than *seventeen times* [stress added]; twice it was razed to the ground, and on two other occasions its walls were levelled. In this respect it stands without a parallel in any city, ancient or modern.[15]

The Jebosites soon recaptured and rebuilt the city.[16]

Defeating the Jebosites, King David captured Jerusalem in about the first quarter of the tenth century BC and made it his capital which was a step of great historical importance. It was neither situated in the area of northern tribes nor in the area of southern tribes. It, therefore, played an important role in the unification of the kingdom. He made it a religious capital of the nation as well by bringing the Ark of Covenant and setting up a tent for it near his palace. After building his own palace, David wanted to build a house for God too, but was not allowed to do so (II Sam.7).[17]

King Solomon built his palace and the Temple. He also built the wall of the city as it had been considerably expanded during his and his father David's reign.

In 922 BC the city was plundered by the Egyptian Pharaoh, Sheshak (Sheshonq I).

About the middle of the 9th century BC it was plundered by the Palestinians and Arabians.

By the reign of Jehoshaphat the city had again largely recovered its importance (cf. 1 Kings 22), but in his son Jehoram's reign (849-842 BC) Judah was invaded and the royal house was pillaged by Philistines and Arabs (2 Chron. 21:16-17).[18]

In 786 BC, during Amaziah's reign (797-767 BC), Jehoash of Israel (798-782 BC) invaded Jerusalem[19] (2 Kings 14:8-9). Judah was defeated in the battle at Beth-shemesh.

(…), and [Jehoash of Israel] brake down the wall of Jerusalem from the gate of Ephraim unto the corner gate, 400 cubits. And he took all the gold and silver, and all the vessels that were found in the house of the Lord, and in the treasures of the king's house, and hostages, and returned to Samaria.[20]

Amaziah's son, Azariah (Uzziah), was the king of Judah during 767-740 BC. He repaired the town-wall and fortified it with towers. His son Ahaz feeling the weakness of his little kingdom, bought with silver and gold the alliance of Tiglath-pileser III, king of Assyria (745-727 BC). He exhibited such a weakness about his faith that he made an altar similar to Tiglath-pileser's for his own ritual in the temple (2 Kings 16:10-12). His reign is darkened by a record of heathen practices, so much so that he made his son pass through the fire as a human sacrifice (2 Kings 16:3-4; compare 2 Chr. 28:3).

In 722 BC, in the reign of Hoshea (731-722 BC), the northern kingdom of Israel came to an end, its capital, Samaria, having been captured by the Assyrian emperor Sargon II, son of Shalmanesser. 27,290 captives were deported from Samaria to Gozan, Harran, Media, Hulah, and Nineveh. Judah was ruled by king Ahaz (732-716 BC) at that time.

King Ahaz of Judah was succeeded by his son Hezekiah (716-686 BC) who undertook some religious reforms. Hezekiah was succeeded by his son, Manasseh (686-642 BC). He reigned Judah for almost half a century and his period was the dark age for the Israelite religion. He introduced idol-worship in the very temple of Solomon. He did not tolerate the religion of Israel. He was made prisoner in 701 BC by the Assyrian king Sennacherib (705-681 BC) who carried him off to Babylon and made Judah his tributary. He returned after some uncertain interval of time to Jerusalem.

In 640 BC Josiah, son of Amon, succeeded his father. He destroyed all relics of idolatry. The Temple was restored. In the course of repairs (in *ca.* 620 BC) Hilkiah the chief priest found the 'book of the law of the Lord'. He was aided by Jeremiah the prophet in spreading through his kingdom the knowledge and worship of Jehovah. He carried out his endeavours to abolish every trace of idolatry and superstition. In 609 BC he was mortally wounded in the battle against Pharaoh Necho in the valley of Esdraelon and died before he could reach Jerusalem.[21]

On the Eastern side the Babylonians captured Nineveh, the capital of Assyrian empire. In 612 BC they also took the suzerainty of Jerusalem from the Assyrians. They brought the Assyrian empire to an end in 609 BC, despoiled Jerusalem and took its king to Babylonia.

During this time Jeremiah (*ca.* 620-580 BC) prophesied for forty-two years (*ca.* 626-584 BC), actively foretelling in streets and courts of Jerusalem the approaching ruin of the city. These messages were received with contempt and anger by the king and court (Jeremiah 36:23).

On 15 March, 597 BC Nebuchadnezzar II took Jerusalem. Jerusalem was despoiled of all its treasures. Many Jews exiled including Jehoiachin and Ezekiel. Nebuchadnezzar nominated Zedekiah as king of Jerusalem. After ten years Zedekiah rebelled against Nebuchadnezzar. Jerusalem was besieged for more than a year until 'famine was sore in the city.' All the men of war 'fled by night by the way of the gate between the two walls, which was by the king's garden,' and the king 'went by the way of the Arabah,' but was overtaken and captured 'in the plains of Jericho.' A terrible punishment followed his faithlessness to Babylon (2 Kings 25:1-7). The city and the temple were despoiled and burnt; the walls of Jerusalem were broken down (2 Kings 25:8f; 2 Chronicles 36:17f). It is probable that the ark was removed also at this time.

In 538 BC Cyrus the Persian captured the Babylonian empire. He allowed the Jews to return to Jerusalem and to rebuild the house of Yahweh (Ezr 1:1f). Over 40,000 Jews (Ezr 1:2-64) under Sheshbazzar, prince of Judah (Ezr 1:8,11), governor of a province, returned, bringing with them the sacred vessels of the temple. The daily sacrifices were renewed and the feasts and fasts restored (Ezr 3:3-7). The foundations of the restored temple were laid (Ezr 3:10; 5:16), but on account of the opposition of the people of the land and the Samaritans, the building was not completed until 20 years later (Ezr 6:15).

In March 516 the building of the Temple was completed and in 515 BC Jerusalem was given the autonomous status and became the capital of the new state of Judea.

In 444 BC Nehemiah built the fortifications and the walls of the city. The rebuilding took 52 days. No doubt the wall was far weaker than that which Nebuchadnezzar destroyed 142 years previously, but it followed the same outline and had the same general structure. As to the history of the next 100 years, *International Standard Bible Enc.* explains:

> For the next 100 years we have scarcely any historical knowledge of Jerusalem. A glimpse is afforded by the papyri of Elephantine where we read of a Jewish community in Upper Egypt petitioning Bagohi, the governor of Judea, for permission to rebuild their own temple to Yahweh in Egypt; incidentally they mention that they had already sent an unsuccessful petition to Johanan the high priest and his colleagues in Jerusalem. In another document we gather that this petition to the Persian governor was granted. These documents must date about 411-407 BC. Later, probably about 350, we have somewhat ambiguous references to the

destruction of Jerusalem and the captivity of numbers of Jews in the time of Artaxerxes (III) Ochus (358-337 BC). With the battle of Issus and Alexander's Palestinian campaign (*ca.* 332 BC), we are upon surer historical ground.[22]

In 333 BC the Greek king Alexander the Great of Macedonia captured the city. After the death of Alexander the Great (323 BC), Palestine suffered much from its position, between the Ptolemies of Egypt and the Seleucids of Antioch. Each became in turn its suzerain, and indeed at one time the tribute appears to have been divided between them. Ptolemy captured Alexanria and made it the capital of the state. In 321 Ptolemy Soter invaded Palestine, and, it is said, captured Jerusalem by a deceitful way, entering the city on the Sabbath as if anxious to offer sacrifice. He carried away many of his Jewish prisoners to Egypt and settled them there. In the struggles between the contending monarchies, although Palestine suffered, the capital itself, on account of its isolated position, remained undisturbed, under the suzerainty of Egypt. In 217 BC, Ptolemy (IV) Philopator, after his victory over Antiochus III at Raphia, visited the temple at Jerusalem and offered sacrifices. He is reported (3 Macc:1) to have entered the 'Holy of Holies.'

Antiochus III the Great (223-187 BC) defeated Ptolemy V in 198 BC as a result of which Palestine went under the control of the Seleucids. The Jews helped him in besieging the Egyptian garrison in the Akra. Jesus ben Sira has given an account of the prosperity of the city about this time (190-180 BC). The Jews had enjoyed considerable prosperity and religious liberty under the Egyptians. But the new Seleucid ruler increased the taxes, and fidelity to the tenets of Judaism came to be regarded as treachery to the Seleucid rule. Antiochus III suffered a defeat by the Romans at Magnesia in 190 BC who took his son Antiochus IV to Rome as hostage. He (Antiochus IV) was released in exchange to Demetrius in 175 BC and was allowed to seize the throne of Syria (175-164 BC). Antiochus IV hastened (170 BC) against Jerusalem with a great army, captured the city, massacred the people and despoiled the temple (1 Macc 1:20-24). Two years later Antiochus, being afraid of Rome in Egypt, appears to have determined that in Jerusalem, at any rate, he would have no sympathizers with Egypt. In 168 BC he sent his chief collector of tribute, who attacked the city with strong force and entered it (1 Macc 1:30). He looted the city, set it on fire and demolished the dwellings and walls. He massacred the men, and many of the women and children he sold as slaves (1 Macc 1:31-35; 2 Macc 5:24). He destroyed the Great Temple of Jerusalem and tried to convert the people of Judea to idolatry. *International Standard Bible Enc.* has observed:

> He (Antiochus IV) sacrificed swine upon the holy altar, and caused the high priest himself — a Greek in all his sympathies — to partake of the impure sacrificial feasts; he tried by barbarous cruelties to suppress the ritual of circumcision. In everything he endeavored, (...), to organize Jerusalem as a Greek city, and to secure his position he built a strong wall, and a great tower for the Akra, and, having furnished it well with armor and victuals[23], he left a strong garrison. But the Syrians had overreached[24] themselves this time, and the reaction against persecution and attempted religious suppression produced the great uprising of the Maccabeans.[25]

In 167 BC Mattathias of Modin, a Jewish priest, defied Antiochus' ban on Judaism and escaped into mountains outside Lydda with his sons and began a revolt. In 165 BC Mattathias died, his sons continued the revolt. Judas Maccabaeus and his brothers retook Jerusalem from the Syrians. They cleansed the Great Temple, reconstructed the altar, restored the temple-services, and destroyed the idols.

Judas defeated three Syrian armies in the open, but he could not expel the garrison in the Akra. In 163 BC a great Syrian army came to the relief of the hard-pressed garrison. Lysias, accompanied by the boy-king himself (Antiochus V), approached the city from the South via Beth-Zur. At Beth-zachariah the Jews were defeated, and Judas' brother Eleazar was slain, and Jerusalem was soon captured. The fort on Mt. Zion which surrounded the sanctuary was surrendered by treaty, but when the king saw its strength he broke his oath and destroyed the fortifications (1 Macc 6:62). But even in this desperate state Judas and his followers were saved. A certain pretender, Philip, raised a rebellion in a distant part of the empire, and Lysias was obliged to patch up a truce with the nationalist Jews more favorable to Judas than before his defeat; the garrison in the Akra remained, however, to remind the Jews that they were not independent. In 161 BC another Syrian general, Nicanor, was sent against Judas, but he was at first won over to friendship and when, later, at the instigation of the Hellenistic party, he was compelled to attack Judas, he did so with hastily raised levies and was defeated at Adasa, a little North of Jerusalem. Judas was, however, not long suffered to celebrate his triumph. A month later Bacchides appeared before Jerusalem, and in April, 161 BC, Judas was slain in battle with him at Berea.[26]

By 152 BC, Judas' brother, Jonathan, was virtual ruler of the land. He gained more than any of his family had ever done. He was appointed high priest and *strategos*, or deputy for the king, in Judea. He repaired the city and restored the temple-fortress. He made the walls higher and built up a great part of the eastern wall. He also made a great mound between the Akra and the city to isolate the Syrian garrison.

Simon succeeded Jonathan. He captured the Akra in 139 BC, destroyed it, and partially levelled the hill on which it stood. In 135 BC his son, John Hyrcanus[27] (King of Judea from 135-104 BC), succeeded him.

The name 'Maccabees' and the 'Maccabean' is generally given to Mattathias and his sons, and the name 'Hasmonean' to their descendants (135-63 BC), when John Hyrcanus became the ruler. In 134 BC John Hyrcanus was besieged in Jerusalem by Antiochus VII Sidetes and John Hyrcanus had to surrender hostages and heavy tributes. McKenzie states in his *Dic. of the Bible*:

> After the death of Antiochus VII in 128 BC Judea was practically independent. John ruled with the title of ethnarch and high priest. He extended Jewish rule over E Palestine and Edom, where he forced the Edomeans to submit to circumcision. He attacked Samaria and destroyed the temple of Samaritans on Mt. Gerizim. The Pharisees, alarmed at his ambitions and the secular character of his rule, broke with Hasmoneans during his reign.

Aristobulus I (105-104 BC), son of John Hyrcanus: He imprisoned his mother, to whom the sovereignty had been bequeathed by the will of John, and imprisoned his brothers except Antigonus, whom he associated with himself in government but later assassinated. Aristobulus assumed the title of king.

Alexander Jannaeus (Jonathan), brother of Aristobulus I (104-76 BC): Salome Alexandra, widow of Aristobulus, released her brothers-in-law from prison and set Jonathan, who preferred to go by his Greek name, upon the throne. Alexander extended the Jewish kingdom, in spite of a number of setbacks, almost to the limits of the ancient kingdom of David. (...). Alexander extended his rule over Philistia (capturing it from Ptolemy Lathyrus of Egypt's Control) and (...) some of the Hellenistic cities. In his expansion northward in Palestine he confronted the Nabatean king Obodath, who held Damascus and halted his advance in that direction. This defeat aroused his adversaries among his own people, who summoned help from the Seleucid king Demetrius III Eukairos. Demetrius invaded Judea and defeated Alexander. The defeat, however, turned the patriotism of the Jews to sympathy with Alexander; Demetrius, thus deprived of support, was forced to withdraw. Alexander revenged himself by having 800 of his Jewish captives and their wives and children executed before their eyes; he himself dined with his concubines, watching the spectacle. Antiochus XII Dionysus, the successor of Demetrius III, invaded Palestine, and Alexander was unable to resist him; but after Antiochus was defeated and killed by the Nabateans, Alexander continued his conquest in E Palestine. (...).

Salome (75-67 BC), widow of Alexander Jannaeus: She appointed Hyrcanus II, the elder son of Alexander, high priest and, recognizing the unchecked ambition of Aristobulus II, the younger son, kept him in private life. After her death the civil war between Hyrcanus and Aristobulus led each brother to seek the assistance of Pompey, then engaged in his eastern conquests. Aristobulus, however, finally refused Roman arbitration; and Pompey attacked and took Jerusalem in 63 BC. He ended the Hasmonean monarchy, detached the territories conquered by earlier Hasmonean rulers, and made Judea part of the province of Syria.[28]

Pompey allowed Hyrcanus to remain high priest, but without the title of 'king.' He reverently left the treasures in the temple untouched; he merely laid a tribute upon the city, and demolished the walls. Aristobulus II was taken to Rome as prisoner, and the city became tributary to the Roman Empire. The greedy Crassus plundered what Pompey had spared in 54 BC.

In 47 BC Antipater was appointed procurator in return for very material services rendered by him to Julius Caesar in Egypt. At the same time Caesar allowed Hyrcanus to rebuild the walls of Jerusalem. Antipater made his eldest son, Phaselus, governor of Jerusalem, and gave Galilee to the care of his younger son, Herod.

Julius Caesar confirmed Hyrcanus in the high priesthood, and gave him civil power as ethnarch, and made Herod's father, Antipater the Idumean, his chief minister, procurator of Judaea. Upon Antipater's assassination, his sons Herod and Phasaelus, with Hyrcanus, resisted Antigonus (Aristobulus' son and Hyrcanus' nephew), who with a Parthian army attacked Jerusalem. Herod escaped.

In 40 BC Herod succeeded his father as procurator of Judea by order of the Roman Senate, but the same year the Parthians under Pacorus and Barzapharnes captured and plundered Jerusalem and re-established Antigonus. Herod, was appointed king of Judea by Antony in 37 BC. He took Jerusalem after a 5 months siege. Antigonus was killed by Antony's command. Herod slew the chiefs of the Asmonaeans, and the whole sanhedrim, and finally, the last of the Asmonaeans, Hyrcanus.

Herod's most magnificent work was to rebuild the temple from its foundations beginning 20 or 19 BC. The construction of the sanctuary was accomplished in 11-10 BC by 1,000 specially trained priests. The court was finished in 9 BC. However, the temple was not considered completed until AD 63 or 64, under Herod Agrippa II and the procurator Albinus. Herod also built four great towers on the old wall. In 4 BC disturbances occurred, and shortly afterward Herod died. He died some months after Christ's birth. Jesus Christ was born somewhere in AD 1-5. *Fausset's Bible Dic.* writes:

At the Passover A.D. 30 our Lord's crucifixion and resurrection took place.[29]

Roman emperor, Caligula[30] ordered his statue to be erected in the temple. The Jews protested against it, and by Agrippa's intercession Caligula agreed to withdraw his order. A famine commenced in A.D. 45 which lasted two years.

Gessius Florus (A.D. 65) tested the Jews' endurance to the last point, desolating whole cities and openly allowing robbers to buy impunity in crime. He tried to get the treasure from the temple, but after plundering the upper city failed. Young Eleazar, son of Ananias, led a party which withheld the regular offerings from the Roman emperor, virtually renouncing allegiance. So the last Roman war began. The insurgents from the temple and lower city set on fire the Asmonaean palace, the high priest's house, and the archives repository, 'the nerves of the city'. They slew the Roman garrison, and burnt Antonia. The high priest and his brother were found slain in the aqueduct.

Cestius Gallus marched on the city, but was obliged to retire from the N. wall of the temple back to Scopus, where he was utterly defeated in November, A.D. 66. C. Gallus' first advance and retreat gave the Christians the opportunity of fleeing as Christ counselled them, 'when ye see Jerusalem compassed with armies, then let them which are in Judea flee to the mountains (Matthew 24:16). Vespasian, until the fall of Gistala, in October or November, A.D. 67, was subduing the northern country. John son of Levi escaped to Jerusalem, and in two years and a half (A.D. 70) Titus began the siege, the Zealots then having overcome the moderate party. The Zealots were in two parties: one under John of Giscala and Eleazar, holding the temple and Antonia, 8,400 men; the other under Simon Burgioras in a tower, holding the upper city, from the Coenaculum to the Latin convent, the lower city in the valley, and the Acre N. of the temple, 10,000 men and 5,000 Idumeans. Strangers and pilgrims swelled the number to 600,000. Josephus says a million perished in the siege, and 40,000 were allowed to depart into the country, besides an immense number sold to the army, part of the '97,000 carried captive during the whole war'. This number is thought an exaggeration.[31]

On 7 September, 70 Jerusalem fell to the Roman general, Titus, son of Vespasian. The Roman troops put the city to fire and destroyed most of the Third Temple. Only the 'Wailing Wall' was left standing. The Romans abolished the Jewish high priesthood and the Sanhedrin.

At that time the city was distracted by internal feuds. Simon held the upper and lower cities; John of Gischala, the temple and Ophel; the Idumeans, introduced by the Zealots, fought only at Walls for themselves. Yet another party, too weak to make its counsels felt, was for peace with Rome, a policy, which, if taken in time, would have found in Titus a spirit of reason and mercy. The miseries of the siege and the destruction of life and property were at least as much the work of the Jews themselves as of their conquerors. On the 15th day of the siege the third wall (Agrippa's) was captured; the second wall was finally taken on the 24th day; on the 72nd day the Antonia fell, and 12 days later the daily sacrifice ceased. On the 105th day the temple and the lower city were burnt, and the last day found the whole city in flames.

The city and temple were wholly burnt and destroyed, excepting the W. wall of the upper city and Herod's three great towers, which were left as memorials of the strength of the defenses. The old and weak were killed, the children under 17 sold as slaves, the rest were sent to the Egyptian mines, the amphitheatres, and Rome. The 10th legion of the Roman army so thoroughly levelled and dug up, that no one visiting Jerusalem would believe it had ever been inhabited. Hadrian completed the fulfillment of Christ's words[32] by razing the ruins still left and drawing a plow over the temple foundations.

For 60 years after its capture silence reigns over Jerusalem. The site continued to be garrisoned, but it was not rebuilt to any extent. In 130 AD it was visited by Hadrian, who found only few buildings standing. Two years later (132-35 AD) occurred the last great rebellion of the Jews in the uprising of Bar-Cochba (son of a star), who was encouraged by the rabbi Akiba. With the suppression of this last effort for freedom by Julius Severus, the remaining traces of Judaism were stamped out, and it is even said that the very site of the temple was plowed up by T. Annius Rufus and an altar of Jupiter was placed upon the temple-site. The Jews were excluded from Jerusalem.

In 138 Hadrian rebuilt the city, giving it the name AElia Capitolina. A statue of horse-ridden Hadrian was placed on the site of the 'Holy of Holies'. Either Hadrian himself, or one of the Antonine emperors, erected a temple of Venus on the north-western hill, where subsequently was built the Church of the Holy Sepulchre. The habit of pilgrimage to the holy sites, which appears to have had its roots far back in the 2nd century, seems to have increasingly flourished in the next two centuries.

International Standard B. Encyclopedia. has recorded:

> In 362 Julian is said to have attempted to rebuild the temple, but the work was interrupted by an explosion. The story is doubtful.[33]

Fausset's BD relates the event as follows:

> In the apostate Julian's reign the Jews at his instigation attempted with great enthusiasm to rebuild the temple; but a whirlwind and earthquake shattered the stones of the former foundation, and a fire from the temple mount consumed their tools. Ammianus Marcellinus (23:1), the emperor's friend, attests the fact. Providence baffled Julian's attempt to falsify Christ's words.[34]

International Standard Bible Encycl. states:

> The site of the temple itself appears to have remained in ruins down to the seventh century.[35]

In AD 614/615 Palestine was conquered by the Persians Chosroes II who destroyed Jerusalem including the church of the Holy Sepulchre and took the 'True Cross' as booty, on which Jesus was believed to have been crucified. He slew thousands of monks and clergy.

About the recapture of Jerusalem by the Romans *International Standard Bible Enc.* states:

In 629 Heracleus, (...), reached Jerusalem in triumph, bearing back the captured fragment of the cross. (...). The triumph of Christendom was but short. Seven years earlier had occurred the historic flight of Mohammed from Mecca (the Hegira), and in 637 the victorious followers of the Prophet appeared in the Holy City. After a short siege, it capitulated, but the khalif [or 'khalifah'?] Omar treated the Christians with generous mercy. The Christian sites were spared, but upon the temple-site, which up to this [time] had apparently been occupied by no important Christian building but was of peculiar sanctity to the Moslems through Mohammed's alleged visions there, a wooden mosque was erected, capable of accommodating 3,000 worshippers.[36]

Fausset's BD asserts:

Caliph Omar (637 A.D.) took the city from the patriarch Sophronius, who said, 'Verily, this is the abomination of desolation spoken of by Daniel the prophet, standing in the holy place. Christians were allowed liberty of worship.[37]

Dr. Ṭāriq al-Suwaydān has recorded the event as follows:

When the patriarch [Sophronius] saw this scene, he was impressed and the grace of Islām seemed to be great. He said to his fellow citizens that no man on earth could withstand this nation. Surrender to them to salvage yourselves. Agreement was written among them. 'Umar granted them peace and security in the city. He guaranteed that their places of worship, their churches, and their holy places shall neither be demolished, nor touched. In this way the holy city witnessed the most merciciful conqueror of its history. It is recorded in the history of the holy land that whenever any conqueror took hold of the land, he completely destroyed it and murdered its inhabitants.[38]

The author further noted:

After this agreement the gates of the holy city were opened for 'Umar bin Khaṭṭāb and he entered it. He began to go around the city. When he reached the Church of the Holy Sepulchre there was the call for Prayer. The Patriarch asked him to offer his prayer there in the Church. 'Umar said to him, 'No; if I offered prayer at this place, the Muslims might take it from you at some later time, saying 'Umar offered his prayer here.' (....).'Umar kept going around in search of al-Aqṣā Mosque but could not find it. He enquired the Patriarch about it. He said, 'Is it that one which is sacred to Jews?' 'Umar replied in positive. He led him to it. He found it in the condition that the Christians had turned it into the place for rubbish and impurities. 'Umar pulled up his sleeves and started sweeping and cleansing the mosque. When the Muslims, the leaders, and the troops saw it, they gathered and started cleansing the Holy Mosque. (...). Then 'Umar took his coat, offered his prayer on it, and left it there. It was the first prayer of the Muslims in the al-Aqṣā Mosque after Prophet Muḥammad (pbuh). (...). Then 'Umar ordered at the spot to start the construction of the al-Aqṣā Mosque after removing the dunghill and garbage. (....).[39]

In *ca.* 640 AD (about two years after the fall of Jerusalem), Mu'āwiya was appointed commander of the army operating in Syria and Palestine. He governed these countries for forty years, first as governor, and later as caliph. Some of the events are being recorded below from the *Encyclopaedia of Islam*:

> During the long rule of Mu'āwiya, the Muslim place of worship on the Temple area, approximately described by Bishop Arculfus in *ca.* 680 must have taken shape. (...) Mu'āwiya built the Muslim sanctuary there "after 'Umar". It stands also to reason that the plan for erection of the Dome of the Rock, which needed immense preparations, was made during the protracted and orderly rule of Mu'āwiya. The inscription in the dome bears the year 72/691-2, but the beginning of 'Abd al-Malik reign (65-86/ 685-705) was extremely turbulent. 'Abd al-Malik had good reasons to make efforts towards the completion of the building, which would show him as the great champion of Islām, but the early years of his caliphate were hardly suited for both conceiving such an enormous undertaking and carrying it out to its very end during a comparatively short period. Contrari-wise Mu'āwiya is known also by his extensive buying and building activities in Mecca, in which he was not followed by later Umayyads. (....).

The real urge for the erection of the Dome of the Rock on the site where it stands and in the form which it has, was religious, in addition, of course, to the natural acculturation of the Arabs to an environment, where magnificent edifices were the eloquent witnesses of a triumphant Church and of great rulers. (....).

The end of Umayyad rule was for Jerusalem (*ca.* 750 AD), (...), a period of great tribulations. In the wake of a rebellion against the last Umayyad Marwān II, the walls of Jerusalem were pulled down and its inhabitants punished. Earthquakes aggravated the situation.[40]

Dr. Ṭāriq al-Suwaydān writes:

> 'Abd al-Malik bin Marwān started the complete construction of the al-Aqṣā Mosque, and made this 'Dome of the Rock' a grand edifice. (...). But 'Abd al-Malik died before the cpompletion of the building. After him his son, al-Walīd completed it.[41]

The Mosque of 'Umar still exists in the S.E. corner of the al-Aqṣā mosque. Sulaymān bin 'Abd al-Malik, while he was still a crown prince, started construction of Ramla[42] as capital city of the province of Filasṭīn.

After the end of the Umayyad period, Jerusalem underwent the reign of 'Abbāsid dynasty for 750-969 AD. In 870 AD patriarch Theodosius praised the Muslims for permitting the Christians to build churches and to live in accordnace with their religion without oppressing them. Jerusalem remained under the control of Fāṭimids, Turkomāns and Saljūks for 969-1099 AD.

The crusaders [laid siege on June 6, and] took Jerusalem in A.D. 1099, July 15th, and it remained in Christian possession 88 years, [until] Saladin retook it in 1187.[43]

Encyclopaedia of Islam has recorded:

> The massacre of the Muslims and the Jews in the town was perpetrated out of military and religious considerations alike. (....). There was a gruesome bloodbath, no doubt. (...). Jerusalem became a Christian city, where no Muslim or Jewish cult was permitted and no non-Christian could take residence permanently. The mosques were turned into churches or used as secular

buildings. The newly-founded kingdom was appropriately called the kingdom of Jerusalem, since the conversion of the Holy City into a Christian sanctuary had been the purpose of its erection. (...). Jerusalem remained closed to Muslims and Jews, but, in the course of time, they were permitted to come there for business and prayer. (...).

After the decisive victory of Ḥaṭṭīn (July 1187), Saladin advanced towards Jerusalem and laid siege on the city. After prolonged negotiations, in which the defenders threatened to kill the Muslim prisoners and all non-combatants, to burn all the valuables and to destroy the buildings on the Ḥaram al-Sharīf, an agreement was reached in November 1187, which permitted the inhabitants to ransom themselves after surrender. Only the Eastern Christians remained, and Jerusalem soon assumed the character of a predominantly Muslim city. (....). The influx of Learned Jews from France attested for the period *ca.* 1210-15 in both literary texts and Geniza letters proves that Ayyūbid rule at that time must have had a reputation of an orderly government able to guarantee the safety of foreigners. (...). The Khwarazmians over-ran Syria and Palestine, took Jerusalem in August 1244 and plundered and murdered in the town, desecrating the Holy Sepulchre and other churches.[44]

At the beginning of the period of Mamlūks (1250-1516), Jerusalem was mostly in ruins and deserted. The Mamlūks undedrtook the rebuiling of the city. In those days the city was the seat of pious Ṣūfis. Jerusalem remained under Ottoman Turks for 1516-1831. *Fausset's Bible Dic.* has summarised it as follows:

> In a dismantled state it was ceded to the Christians by the treaty with the [Roman] emperor Frederick II, in 1219 [or 1229?][45], and has ever since remained in the Mahometans' hands. From the first siege by the children of Judah (Judges 1:8), 1400 B.C. [?], to A D. 1244 Jerusalem underwent 27 sieges, the last being by the Kharesmian hordes who slaughtered the priests and monks. There was the city before David, the second that of Solomon 1000 to 597 B.C., the third city that of Nehemiah which lasted for 300 years. A Grecised city under Herod (the fourth city) succeeded. This city, destroyed by Titus A.D. 70, was followed by a Roman city, the fifth,

which lasted until the Mahometan time, the sixth city. Then followed the Christian city of Godfrey and the Baldwins, the seventh; lastly the eighth, the modern city of 600 years of Moslem rule. The Ottoman Suleiman in 1542 built the present walls. After a brief possession by the [Ibrāhīm] Pasha of Egypt from 1832 to 1840, Jerusalem was restored to the Sultan of Turkey, in whose hands it continues.[46]

By 1865 Jerusalem was connected with the outer world by telegraph. In 1868 the first road between Jerusalem and Jaffa usable by wheeled vehicles was completed. The railway followed in 1892.

On 11 december 1917 the British general Allenby entered Jerusalm. The military government of the British army was replaced by civil administration on 1 July 1920. According to the census of 1931, the population comprised 90,503 persons: Jews were 51,222; Muslims 19,894; Christians 19,335. It became about 150,000 at the beginnig of the World War II. The mayor of the municipal Corporation was always appointed from among the Muslims.[47]

In April 1920 there occurred first bloody clashes among Jews and Muslims in Jerusalem, in which many of them were killed and injured. Al-Ḥājj Amīn al-Ḥusaynī was appointed as Muftī of Jerusalem by the new British High Commissioner Sir Herbert Samuel. In 1921 he was elected head of the Muslim Supreme Council created by the government. He convened a conference of the Muslims in Jerusalem in 1931. Mawlānā Muḥammad ‘Ālī Jawhar was buried in the western portico[48] of the Ḥaram in the same year. The mass immigration of Jewish refugees in 1933 and after caused fighting among Jews and the Arabs.

Nowadays Jerusalem is the capital of the modern state of Israel which was established on May 14, 1948, as a Jewish state on the land that had been given under the control of the British Government by the League of Nations after World War I.

Encyclopaedia Americana has recorded the history of this stage of the history of Jerusalem in a precise manner:

In the 19th century, Jerusalem and the rest of Palestine, then part of the Ottoman Empire, became the focus of international concern. For several centuries European countries had had political and commercial interests in Palestine because of its position at the crossroads to India and the Far East. Several of these countries had attempted to expand their influence there from the 16th century on by extending their protection and patronage over the Christian Holy Places and the Christian subjects of the Ottomans. They also sought certain privileges within the empire. It was such privileges that the Ottomans had granted to the French and the Russians that the British, Austrians, Prussians, and Italians attempted to have set aside in their favor in the 19th century.

The Ottoman Turks were defeated in World War I and evicted from Palestine by the British, to whom the League of Nations awarded the Palestine mandate. The mandate period witnessed an immense struggle between Arab and Jewish nationslist movements for control of Palestine, with Jerusalem as the chief prize and heart of the conflict. (...).

By the end of World War II the British had despaired of unreveling the tangled issue, and it was turned over to United Nations. A UN resolution of November 29, 1947, recommended the partition of the country between Arabs and Jews and the internationalization of Jerusalem. The Palestinian Arabs and the Arab states rejected the plan. The day after its adoption a general attack was launched against the Jews throughout the area. As a result of the ensuing war, Jerusalem was divided by an armistice agreement in 1949 between Jordan and Israel, with the Old (Walled) City and East Jerusalem under Jordanian control and West Jerusalem (the New City) under Israeli rule.

Jordan ruled East Jerusalem for 19 years, until 1967. On June 5, 1967, after war broke out between Israel and Egypt, Jordan's King Hussein opened hostilities in the Jerusalem sector. The Israeli Army conquered and occupied East Jerusalem on June 7, and on June 27 the city was annexed to the state of Israel.[49]

Encyclopaedia of Islam narrates:

> The Peel Royal Commission, sent out in 1936 to investigate the situation, for the first time recommended the creation of an Arab and a Jewish state and the conversion of Jerusalem, together with Bethlehem, into a separate unit remaining under British mandate. But neither this nor any other of the subsequent attempts of the mandatory government to find a solution led to results. On 29 November 1947, the General Assembly of the United Nations adopted Resolution 189 (II) calling for the division of Palestine into two states, but united by economic union. Jerusalem was to be "internationalized".

Immediately after this decision the country was in flames. Jerusalem in particular suffered great losses in life and property even before 15 May 1948, the official end of the British mandate. (….). The ceasefire divided Jerusalem by a line slightly west of the western wall of the old city. (….). On 13 Dec. 1948 the Transjordonian parliament resolved the annexation of the areas of Palestine occupied by the Arab Legion. Israel followed suit by transferring its parliament from Tel Aviv to Jerusalem in Feb. 1949 and proclaiming Jerusalem its capital on 13 Dec. 1949. Both actions were in contradiction of the UN resolution of Nov. 1947, which had foreseen Jerusalem as a *corpus separatum.* The matter came up repeatedly in the UN until 1952, when it was left dormant, until the war of 1967 created an entirely new situation.[50]

Abba Eban had been Israeli minister of foreign affairs. He wrote a richly illustrated article on 'Jerusalem' in the Year Book 1973 of *Merit Students Encyclopedia.* Some excerpts are afforded below from this scholarly work:

Yet none of this would have brought Jerusalem into the war had King Hussein heeded a message from Israeli Prime Minister Levi Eshkol on June 5, 1967. Fighting had broken out with Egypt as a result of President Gamal Abdel Nasser's blockade of the Straits of Tiran [at the mouth of Khalīj 'Aqabah] on May 22 and his intimidatory troop concentrations accompanied by threats to destroy Israel. Eshkol's message, conveyed through the United Nations chief of staff, General Odd Bull, said plainly that if Jordan kept out of the war, Israel would leave every-thing as it was. The reply was an all-out Jordonian assault on western Jerusalem. Indeed, the fighting in Jerusalem was the fiercest of that in any sector–and it took a heavy toll of Israeli lives. On June 5, Israel hastily improvised troop convoys for the Jerusalem front. By June 7 the laconic[51] message of the brigade commander ('The Temple Mount is ours') conveyed the momentous news that Jerusalem was united. It had known many masters. Now, after 19 centuries, its original builders were back again. Soon the barriers were down–the barbed-wire fences, the tank traps, the Mandelbaum Gate, all the symptoms of ghetto-like separation–and Jews, Muslims, and Christians, with multitudes of pilgrims from all over the world, swarmed together, mingling, jostling, sometimes colliding, but always together in a single human destiny. Requests from United Nations organs that they get themselves divided again–back to their respective cages and compartments–evoked their good-humoured derision.[52]

Abba Eban concludes his scholarly article with the following passage:

> Jerusalem's population distribution (218,300 Jews, 62,300 Muslims, and 11,100 Christians) cannot fail to be determinant in its political status. But on a deeper and higher level of history, Jerusalem represents the confluence of many streams of memory and culture. Its sun has risen and set on a multitude of human longings, passions, agonies, and hopes. It is the capital of one nation and yet also the touchstone of the entire human condition.[53]

The 'Chronology of Jerusalem' is being recoded hereunder:

The following chronological table gives a list of the more important incidents that had a direct or indirect bearing on the history of the Jews of **Jerusalem**:

B.C.

1500. Earliest historical mention of **Jerusalem**, found in the El-Amarna tablets.

1048. David takes possession of **Jerusalem** from the Jebusites.

1007. Solomon's Temple completed after seven years' labor.

972. Shishak of Egypt takes the city from Rehoboam.

713. Sennacherib advances toward **Jerusalem**.

700. Hezekiah perfects the water-supply.

586. (Ab 9.) Captured by Nebuzar-adan [Nebuchadnezzer].

516. Rebuilt during reign of Darius.

350. Seized by the Persians [in 529/530 and not in 350].

332. Visited by Alexander the Great?

320 or 305. Seized by Ptolemy Soter.

170. Plundered by Antiochus Epiphanes.

165. Judas Maccabeus recaptures **Jerusalem** and reconsecrates the Temple.

166. Pompey enters **Jerusalem** [It maybe 66 and not 166].

37. Besieged and taken by Herod the Great.

20. Restoration of the Temple begun by Herod the Great.

Note: The first four entries are obviously doubtful.

C.E.

29. (April.) Jesus of Nazareth executed at **Jerusalem**.

70. (Nisan 14.) Siege commenced by Vespasian, lasting 134 days.

70. (Ab 9.) **Jerusalem** destroyed by Titus.

135. Hadrian rebuilds the city.

136. **Jerusalem** called Ælia Capitolina.

362. Restoration of the Temple undertaken by Julian the Apostate.

614. Jews aid the Persian Chosroes II. in attack on **Jerusalem**.

628. Retaken by Heraclius; Jews forbidden to enter the city.

637. Omar puts **Jerusalem** under Moslem power.

688. 'Abd al-Malik builds the Dome of the Rock.

1046. Solomon ben Judah head of the yeshibah at **Jerusalem**.

1077. Seljuk Turks capture **Jerusalem**.

1099. (July 15.) Crusaders put 70,000 infidels to the sword, and found a new Christian kingdom.

1100. "Assize of **Jerusalem**" established by Godfrey of Bouillon.

1140. Judah ha-Levi visits **Jerusalem**.

1173. Benjamin of Tudela visits **Jerusalem**.

1187. (Oct. 2.) Saladin defeats the Franks and takes **Jerusalem**.

1211. Several hundred English and French rabbis settle in **Jerusalem**.

1218. Al-Ḥarizi visits **Jerusalem**.

1267. (Aug. 12.) Naḥmanides visits **Jerusalem**.

1437. Elijah of Ferrara made chief rabbi.

1492. Jews expelled from Spain settle in **Jerusalem**.

1517. Capture by Ottoman Turks.

1580. Naḥmanides synagogue closed by the Moslems, claiming that it had previously been a mosque.

1621. Isaiah Horowitz and a number of his friends settle in **Jerusalem**.

1627. Ibn Farukh, governor of **Jerusalem** and persecutor of the Jews, deposed.

1705. Jews subjected to certain vexatious restrictions in matters of attire.

1798. Napoleon visits Palestine; Jewish community of **Jerusalem** accused of assisting him and its members threatened with death.

1827. First visit of Moses Montefiore.

1838. Edward Robinson commences archeological research in **Jerusalem**.

1840. Crémieux, Montefiore, and Albert Cohn visit **Jerusalem**.

1841. (Nov. 7.) S. M. S. Alexander, convert to Christianity, consecrated first Anglican Bishop of **Jerusalem**.

1854. Albert Cohn establishes many charitable institutions.

1862. (Sept. 5.) Treaty to preserve the Holy Sepulcher signed by Russia, France, and Turkey.

1880. Siloam Inscription discovered.

1892. (Sept. 13) Railway from **Jerusalem** to Jaffa, built by a French company, opened.

1898. (Nov. 1.) William II. of Germany visits **Jerusalem** in state and receives a Jewish deputation.

1900. Abarbanel Library founded.[54]

References

1. *International Standard Bible Encyclopedia*, (Albany, OR USA: Books For The Ages, AGES Software, Version 1.0 © 1997), s.v. 'Jerusalem' by Geerhardus Vos, 6:181.
2. Paleolithic is the 'Old Stone Age: before 10,000 BC.
3. Mesolithic is the Middle Stone Age: 10,000 to 7,500 BC.
4. Neolithic, i.e. 'the latest part of the Stone Age, following the mesolithic period, esp. as characterized by the use of ground or polished stone implements and weapons' (New Shorter Oxf. Dic., 1993).
5. Chalcolithic, i.e. Copper Age: 4,000 to 3,150 BC.
6. Israel Pocvket Library, *Jerusalem* (Keter Books, 1973), 5.
7. It should have been 'celts' and not 'Celts'. 'celts' means 'a stone or metal axe without perforation or grove for hefting (handle)'; whereas 'Celts' were ancient W European people settled in Britain before coming of the Romans. They were fierce fighters and fine horsemen. They were good farmers and used ploughs pulled by oxen.
8. *International Standard Bible Encyclopedia*, 6:227.
9. *International Standard Bible Encyclopedia*, 6:227-28.
10. *Enc. of Judaism* Second (2005) edn., 2:1201.
11. *Interpreter's Dic. of the Bible* (2000), 2:846.
12. *Enc. Britannica: Macropaedia* 15th edn. (1982), s.v. 'Jerusalem' 10:139.
13. *Interpreter's Dic. of the Bible* (2000), 2:846-47.

14. Judges 1:8 NKJV. It shows that even before the construction of the temple, Jerusalem was not a 'City of Peace'.
15. William Smith, *A Dic. of the Bible*, (Michigan: Regency Reference Library, Zondervan Pblg. House, Grand Rapids, 1967), 302.
16. *Interpreter's Dic. of the Bible* (2000), 2:847.
17. See *Interpreter's Dic. of the Bible* (2000), 2:848.
18. *International Standard Bible Encyclopedia*, 6:231.
19. *Encyclopaedia Britannica: Macropaedia* 15th edn. (1982), 10:139.
20. 2 Kings 14:14 KJV.
21. See W. Smith's *Dic. of the Bible*, 1967, s.v. 'Josiah', p.324.
22. *International Standard Bible Encyclopedia*, 6:237.
23. 'Victuals' means 'supplies of food and stores'.
24. 'overreach' means 'fail by trying to achieve more than is possible'.
25. *International Standard Bible Encyclopedia*, 6:239.
26. See *International Standard Bible Encyclopedia*, 6:240f.
27. John Hyrcanus or Johanan (135-104 BC), son of Simon Maccabeus, was the High priest and a prince of the Hasmonean family. He was a wise and just ruler and a skilful warrior.
28. John L. McKenzie, *Dic. of the Bible*, (1984), 340.
29. A. R. Fausset, *Fausset's Bible Dic.*, (AGES Software Albany, OR USA, Version 1.0 © 2000), 2(G-M):434.
30. Caligula (Caesar Augustus) was third emperor of Rome. He was born on Aug. 31, 12 C.E. and was assassinated at Rome on Jan. 24, 41. He formed a strong friendship for the Jewish king Agrippa. He professed belief in his own divinity, and ordered alters to be erected to himself and worship to be paid to him (Jewish Enc. 3:514).
31. Extracted from *Fausset's Bible Dic.*, 2 (G-M):435-36.
32. He beheld the city and wept over it, saying, (...); 'and they shall not leave in thee one stone upon another;' (Luke 19:41,42, 44).
33. *International Standard Bible Encyclopedia*, (1997) 6:247.
34. *Fausset's Bible Dic.*, 2000, 2 (G-M):437-38.
35. *International Standard Bible Encyclopedia*, (1997) 6:248.
36. *International Standard Bible Encyclopedia*, (1997) 6:248, 49.
37. *Fausset's Bible Dic.*, 2000, 2 (G-M):438.
38. Dr. Ṭāriq al-Suwaydān, *Falasṭīne, al-Tārīkh al-Muṣawwar*, (al-Ibdā' al-Fikrī, Kuwait, 2004), 84.

39. *Falasṭīne, al-Tārīkh al-Muṣawwar*, (2004), 85, 86.
40. *The Encyclopaedia of Islam*, New (1986) Edn., s.v. 'al-Ḳuds' by O. Grabar, Harvard Univ., 5:324,25,26.
41. *Falasṭīne, al-Tārīkh al-Muṣawwar*, (2004), 90.
42. 'Ramla' is situated on the coastal plain 40 km/25 miles west-nort-west of Jerusalem. In the reign of al-Walīd, his brother Sulaymān was governor of Filasṭīn. Stimulated by the example of 'Abd al-Malik, the builder of the Qubbat al-Ṣakhrah in Jerusalem (...), Sulaymān founded the town of al-Ramla and made it the seat of the provincial government.
43. *Fausset's Bible Dic.*, 2 (G-M):438.
44. *Encyclopaedia of Islam*, s.v. 'al-Ḳuds', 5:330,31
45. Emperor Frederick II was born in 1194. He was crowned Emperor by the Pope in Rome on 22-11-1220. He set sail from Brindisi, a port of South Italy in the Adriatic Sea, for the Crusades in the Holy Land. Following complex negotiations he obtained Jerusalem, Bethlehem, and Nazareth from Sultan al-Kāmil of Egypt. He crowned himself king of Jerusalem in the Church of the Holy Sepulchre on 18-3-1229. In the meantime papal troops had penetrated into his kingdom of Sicily. Frederick returned at once and reconquered the lost areas. He died on 13 Dec., 1250.
46. *Fausset's Bible Dic.*, 2000, 2 (G-M):438.
47. In 1944, after the death of the Muslim mayor, the Jewish acting mayor demanded to be appointed officially. As a result the council was dissolved and a commission of British officials was appointed.
48. 'Portico' means: 'roof supporterd by columns, esp. one forming an entrance to a large building'.
49. *Encyclopaedia Americana* 1985, s.v. 'Jerusalem' by J. L. Kraemer, 16: 26f.
50. *The Encyclopaedia of Islam*, 5:337.
51. 'laconic' means: 'terse; using few words'.
52. *Merit Students Encyclopedia*, Year Book 1973, s.v. 'Jerusalem' by Abba Eban, the then Israeli minister of foreign affairs (p. 55).
53. *Merit Students Encyclopedia*, Year Book 1973, p. 55.
54. The *Jewish Encyclopaedia* 7:146,48:

Sources Consulted
(for 'Hist. of Jerusalem')

Encyclopaedias, etc.

Compton's Enc. Chicago: Compton's Learning Co., 1989, s.v. 'jerusalem' (12:99-102).

Enc. Americana. Connecticut: Grolier Incorpora-ted, 1986, s.v. 'Jerusalem', by J. L. Kraemer, Tel Aviv University, 16:26-32.

Enc. of Islam, New (1986) edn., s.v. 'al-Ḳuds' by O. Grabar, Harvard Univ.

Enc. of Judaism Second (2005) edn. Leiden: Brill, s.v. 'Jerusalem in Judaism', by Mayer Gruber (2:1201-1211).

Enc. of Religion, Second (2005) edn. USA: Thompson Gale, s.v. 'Jerusalem' by Reuven Firestone.

Grolier Academic Enc., 1985 (11:399-401).

Illustrated World Enc. NY: Illustrated World Enc., Inc., 1969 (12:2903-05).

International Standard Bible Enc. (Version 1.0 © 1997). Albany, OR USA: AGES Software, s.v. 'Jerusalem' (6:180-250).

Jewish Enc. NY: KTAV Publishing House, INC., 1901 (7:118-57).

Merit Students Enc. USA: Crowell-Collier Educational Corporation, 1967 edn., s.v. 'Jerusalem' by Donald N. Wilber (10:158-162).

———Year Book 1973, s.v. 'Jerusalem' by Abba Eban (p. 46-55).

New Book of Knowledge, The Cildren's Enc. NY: Grolier Inc., 1970 (10:78-81).

New Caxton Enc. London: Caxton Pubg. Co., 1973, s.v. 'Jerusalem' (11:3420-22).

New Enc. Britannica, Macropaedia. Chicago: University of Chicago, 1982, s.v. 'Jerusalem' by Stewart Henry Perowne (10:138-44).

New Standard Enc. Chicago: Standard Educatioinal Corp., date etc. have been recorded in Vol. I only, which is not available (7:J-52 to J-55).

Universal World Reference Enc. Chicago, Illinois: Consolidated Book Publishers, 1964 (8:2709-10).

al-Suwaidān, Dr. Ṭāriq. *Falasṭīne, al-Tārīkh al-Muṣawwar.* al-Ibdā' al-Fikrī, Kuwait, 2004 (84-86).

Jerusalem. Keter Books, Israel Pocvket Library, 5 (1973).

Jamie Scott & Paul simpsom-Housley. *Sacred Places and Profane Spaces.* NY: Greenwood Press, 88 Post Road West, Westport, CT 06881, 1991.

Islamic Studies (Special. Issue on 'Jerusalem'), Vol. 40: Nos. 3,4 Autumn-Winter, 2001. Ed. Dr. Ẓafar Isḥāq Anṣārī, Guest ed. Salmā Khadrā Jayyūsī. Islamabad: Islāmic Research Institute, International Islāmic University.

Atlases

Oxford Bible Atlas. Ed. Herbert G. May. Oxford: Oxf. Univ. Press, 1984.

New Bible Atlas. Ed. J. J. Bimson and J. P. Kane. Leicester: I.V. Press, 1985.

Terrien, Samuel. *Lands of the Bible.* Wisconsin: Western Pblg. Co. Inc., 1957.

Magi, Giovanna. *Jerusalem.* Florence: Casa Editrice Bonechi, 1992.

Dictionaries, etc:

Fausset's Bible Dic. (Version 1.0 © 2000). Albany, OR USA: AGES Software, s.v. 'Jerusalem' (2:417-51).

Interpreter's Dic. of the Bible (2000). Nashville: Abingdon Press, s.v. 'Jerusalem' by M. Burrows (2:843-66).

McKenzie, John L. *Dic. of the Bible.* London: Geoffrey Chapman (1984), s.v. 'Jerusalem' (426-31).

Smith, William. *Dic. of the Bible.* Michigan: Regency Reference Library, Zondervan Pblg House, Grand Rapids (1967), s.v. 'Jerusalem' (292-305).

Illustrated Bible Dic. Inter-Varsity Press (1980). S.v. 'Jerusalem' by D.F. Payne, London Bible College, (2:752-60).

Bibliography

(a) The Bible,

Translations and Versions:

S. No	Name of the Book	Abbreviations
1.	*Authorized/ King James Version.*	AV=KJV
2.	*The Christian Community Bible.* Manila: Divine Word Publ., 1988.	CCB
3.	*Contemporary English Version.* NY: American Bible Society, 1995.	CEV
4.	*Easy-to-Read Version.* Texas: World Bible Trans. Center, Inc Fort Worth, 2000.	Easy-to-Read Version
5.	*Good News Bible* [*Today's Eng. Version*]. NY: American Bible Society, 1982.	GNB/TEV
6.	*Good News Bible* (Revised Edn.) Minto: The Bible Society in Australia Inc, NSW 2566, 1994.	GNB Rvd. Edn.
7.	*Greek New Testament.*	Greek.NT
8.	*The Holy Scriptures Heb. & English* (Hebrew OT with Eng. Tr.). Middlesex: The Society for Distributing Heb. Scriptures, nd.	Heb.OT
9.	*The Living B.* Illinois: Tyndale House Publrs., 1976.	LB
10.	James Moffatt *'A New Translation of the Bible'* (London: Hodder and Stoughton, Ltd. At St Paul's House, 1941	Moffatt
11.	*The Torah, The Masoretic Text.* Jewish Publication. Society of America.	MT

12. *New American B.*, Catholic Bibl. Association, 1991. NAB

13. *The New American Standard Bible*. Cambridge Univ. Press, 1977. NASB

14. *The New English Bible*. Oxford: Univ. Press, 1985. NEB

15. *New International Version*. London, 1984. NIV

16. *The New Jerusalem Bible*, Standard Edition. Bombay: St. Pauls, 1993. NJeruB

17. *The New King James Version*. The Gideons International,1985. NKJV

18. *New Living Translation: Award Bible*. Ed./Tr. A Huge Team of Tr. Illinois: Tyndale House Publishers, Inc. Wheaton, 1996. NLTr.

19. *The New Oxf. Annotated Bible, with Apocrypha.* Ed Bruce M. Metzger, R. E. Murphy. NY: Oxf. Univ Press, 1989. NOAB

20. *New Revd. Stand. Ver., Cath. Ed. for India*, 1993. NRSVC

21. *New World Translation of the Scriptures*. NY: Watchtower Bible and Tract Society, 1984. NWT

22. *The NT, Standard Edn*. Tr. Conor Murphy. Limuru. Kenya: Paulines Publications Africa, 1995. NTSEd

23. *The OT books of poetry 26 trans*. Ed. Curtis Vaughan. Michigan: Zondervan B Publi-shers, Grand Rapids, 1981. OT Poetry 26Tr

24. *The Tr. from Peshitta* (The Authorized B. of the Church of the East), 1957. Peshitta

25. *The Reader's Digest Bible*. London; The Reader's Digest Association Ltd, 1995. RDB

26.	*Revd Berkeley Version*. Gideon International, 1974.	RBV
27.	*Revd. Standard Version*. UK: The B.F.B.S., 1974.	RSV

(b) Commentaries of the Bible

Sr. No.	Name of the Book, Author, Publisher, etc.	Abbreviation
1.	*An American Com. on the NT*. Ed. Alvah Hovey. Phila-delphia: American Baptist Publication Society, 1886.	American NTC
2.	William Barclay. *The Daily Study B*. Bangalore: TPI,1995.	Barclay NTC
3.	William MacDonald. *Believers B C, (NT)*. Kansas: A & O Press, PO Box 8550, Wichita, 1989.	Believers Bible Com.
4.	*The B. Knowledge Com*. Ed. John F. Walvoord, Roy B. Zuck. Illinois: Victor Books, Wheaton, 1986. Com.	Bible Knowledge
5.	*Broadman B. Com*. Tennessee: Broadman Press, 1971.	Broadman B. Com.
6.	*The Collegeville BC (OT)*. Gen. Ed. Dianne Bergant. Minnesota: The Liturgical Press, Collegeville, 1992.	Collegeville Bible Com.
7.	*A Commentary on the Holy Bible*. Ed. J. R. Dummelow. The Macmillan Co., 1956.	Dumme-low Com. On Bible
8.	*The Expositor's Bible* (25 Vols). Ed. W. Robertson Nicoll. NY: A. C. Armstrong & Son, 3 & 5 West 18th Street, 1903.	Exposi-tor's Bible Com.
9.	John Fawcett, D.D. *The Devotional Family Bible.* London: Baldwin, New Bridge Str., 1811.	Fawcett, F. Bible Com.
10.	James Comper Gray and George M. Adams. *Bible Com*. Michigan: Zondervan Pblg. House, Grand Rapids, na.	Gray & Adams Bible Com.
11.	*The Pentateuch and Haftorahs*. Ed. Dr. J. H. Hertz. London: Soncino Press, 1979.	Hertz, J.H. Bible Com.

12.	*The International Bible Commentary.* Ed. William R. Farmer et al. Bangalore: TPI, 2004.	International Bible Com.
13.	Rev. S. R. Driver. *The International Critical Com.* (a Critical & Exegetical C. on Deu.). Edinburgh: T. & T. Clarke, 1895.	International

Critical Com.

14.	*The Interpreter's Bible*. Ed. George Arthur Buttrick. NY: Abingdon Cokisbury Press, Nashville, 1952.	Interpreter's Bible Com.
15.	Dr. I. W. Slotki. *Isaiah*, London: The Soncino Press, 1949.	Isaiah-Slotki
16.	*The Jerome Biblical Com*. Ed. Raymond E. Brown, Joseph A. Fitzmyer, Roland E. Murphy. Bangalore: TPI, 1987.	Jerome Bible Com.
17.	Ronald A. Knox. *The Holy Bible Tr. From Latin Vulgate*. London: Burns & Oates, Macmillan & Co Ltd, 1957.	Knox Vulgate
18.	Ronald A. Knox. *A NT Commentary for Eng. Readers*. London: Burns Oates & Washbourne Ltd, 1955.	Knox NTC
19.	*The Learning Bible*: *Contemporary English Version*. NY: American Bible Society, 2000.	Learning Bible
20.	Matthew Henry. *A Commentary on the Holy Bible*. London: Ward, Lock & Co., Warwick House, Salisbury Square, E.C.	Matt-Henry Com. On holy Bible
21.	W. Gunther Plaut, Bernard J. Bamberger. *The Torah, A Modern Com*. NY: Union of American Heb Congregations, 1981.	Mod.Torah Com.
22.	*Nelson Study Bible*. Ed Earl D Radmacher. Nashville: Thomas Nelson Pub, 1997.	Nelson Study Bible
23.	*The New Bible Com*. Ed. by F. Davidson etc. Michigan: W M. B. Eerdmans Publg. Co., Grand Rapids, 1953.	New Bible Com.
24.	D. Guthrie, J. A. Motyer, etc. *The New Bible Commentary Revised Edn*. London: Inter-Versity Press, 1972.	New Bible com. (Rvd)

25. *A New Catholic Com. on Holy Scripture*. Ed. Rev. Reginald C. Fuller. Surrey:Thomas Nelson & Sons Ltd, 1981.	New Catholic Com.
26. *A New Commentary on Holy Scripture*. Ed. Charles Gore, H. L. Goudge, Alf. Guillaume. London: Society for Promoting Christian Knowledge, 1928.	New Com. on

Holy Scriptures

27. *New Jerome Bible Com*. Ed. Raymond E. Brown, Joseph A. Fitzmyer, Roland E. Murphy. Bangalore: TPI, 1994.	New Jerome Bible Com.
28. *The NIV Study Bible*. Ed. Kenneth Barker etc. Grand Rapids: Zondervan Publishing. House, 1995.	NIV Study Bible
29. *The Open Bible* (Expanded Edn). Ed na. NY: Thomas Nelson Publishers, Nashville, 1985.	Open Bible
30. *Peake's Commentary on the Bible*. Ed, Matthew Black, H. H. Rowley. London: Thomas Nelson & Sons Ltd, 1967.	Peake's Com. on Bible
31. *Pocket Bibl Com*. William Neil. HarperSanFrancisco, 1975.	Pocket Bible Com.
32. *The Pulpit Commentary*. Ed. Rev. HDM Spence DD, Dean of Gloucester & Rev. Joseph S. Excell. London: Kegan Paul, Trench, Trubner & Co. Ltd, 1897.	Pulpit Bible Com.
33. Thomas Scott, Rector of the Aston Sanford, Bucks. *Scott's Bible*. Philadelphia: J. B. Lippincott & Co, 1857.	Scott's Bible Com.
34. *Seventh-day Adventist Bible Com*. Ed. Francis D. Nichol. Hagerstown: Review & Herald Pblg Association, 1978.	7th Day Adventist Bible Com.
35. *A Jewish Com. 'The Soncino Chumash'*. Ed. The Rev. Dr. A. Cohen. Surrey: The Soncino Press, Hindhead,1950.	Soncino Chumash
36. Dr. Frank Charles Thompson. *Thompson Chain Ref Bible* (5th Ed.). Bangalore: The Bible Society of India, 1988.	Thompson Bible

37.	Lawrence O. Richard. *Victor B Background Com. (NT)*. Colorado, 80918, USA: Victor Books/SP Publ., Inc., 2003.	Victor Bible (NT) Background Com.
38.	Marvin R. Vincent. *Word Studies in NT*. Michigan: WM. B. Eerdmans Pubg. Co, Grand Rapids, 1946.	Vincent's NT
39.	Warren W. Wiersbe. *Wiersbe's Expository Outlines on the NT*. Colorado 80918, USA: SP Pubns., Inc., Cook Communications Ministries, 2003.	Wiersbe's NT Expo Outlines
40.	*The Wycliffe Bible Com.* Ed. Charles F. Pfieffer (OT), Everett F. Harri-son (NT). Chicago: Moody Press, 1983.	Wycliffe Bible Com.

(c) Dictionaries, Encyclopedias, Concordances and Atlases

Sr.No	*Name, Author, Editor, Publisher, Year, etc.*	*Abbreviation*
1.	*Adv Learner's Enc. Dic*. Ed. Jonathan Crowther. Oxford Univ. Press, 1994.	AdvLrnrOxf Dic.
2.	*The Enc. Americana International Edn.* (in 30 Vols.). Connecticut: Grolier Incorporated, Danbury, 1987.	Americana
3.	*Arabic-English Dictionary.* Maan Zulfu Madina. NY: Pocket Books, 1973.	Arab-Eng-Dic. Zulfu
4.	*Enc. Biblica*. Ed. Rev. T.K. Cheyne. London: Watts & Co. 1899.	Biblica
5.	*Enc. Britannica* (15th Edn.). Chicago: the Univ of Chicago, 1988.	Britannica
6.	*The Chambers Dic*. Ed. Catherine Schwarz. Edinburgh: Chambers Harrap Pub. Ltd., 1995.	Chambers Dic
7.	*Chambers Essential English Dictionary*. 1998.	ChambEssDic
8.	F. L. Cross. *The Oxf. Dic. of the Christian Church*. London: Oxf Univ Press, 1974.	Christian ChurchDic
9.	*Colliers Enc*. (24 Vols.). NY, 1995.	Colliers Enc
10.	Rev. James L. Dow. *Collins Gem Dic. of Bible*. London & Glasgow: Collins, 1974	ColnGem Dic. of Bible

11. *Easton's 1897 B. Dic in "Power Bible"* CD. ROM Version.	Easton's B.Dic.
12. *Harper's B. Dic*. Ed. Paul J. Achtemeier. Bangalore: Theological Publications in India, 1994.	Harper's Bible Dic.
13. *A Dic. of the Bible*. Ed. James Hastings. Edinburgh: T. & T. Clark, 1904.	Hastings Dic.of Bible
14. *Dic. of B*. Ed. James Hastings, Rvd. Edn. By Frederick C. Grant & H. H. Rowley. NY: Charles Scribner's Sons, 1963.	Hastings Rvd Dic. of Bible
15. *Holman Concise Topical Concordance*. Tennessee, USA: Holman Bible Publishers, Nashville, 1998.	Holman Concise Topical Concord
16. *Holman Topical Concordance*. Philadelphia, USA: A. J. Holman Co., 1973.	Holman Topical Conc.
17. *The Illustrated Bible Dic*. Ed. J. D. Douglas, Rvn. Ed. N. Hillyer. Inter-Versity Press, 1980.	Illustrated BD
18. *International Standard Bible Encyclopedia*, OR USA: Books For The Ages, AGES Software, Versioin 1.0 © 1997	
19. *The Interpreter's Dic. of Bible*. (5 Vol). Ed. George Arthur Buttrick. NY: Abington Press, Nashville, 1962.	Interpreter's Dic. of Bible
20. *The Enc. of Islām* (New Edn.). Ed. E. Van Donzel, B. Lewis, C. E. Bosworth. Leiden: E. J. Brill, 1978.	Enc of Islām
New Edn	
21. *The Jewish Enc*. Ed. Dr Isidore Singer. NY: KTAV Pub House, Inc.,1901.	JewishEnc
22. *Enc. Judaica*-CD-ROM-Ed. Version 1.0, Copyright 1997. Judaica Multimedia (Israel) Ltd.	JudaicaEnc
23. E. W. Lane. Arabic-Eng. Lexicon. Cambridge: Isl. Texts Society UK, 1984.	Lane's Lexicon
24. *The Lion Handbook to the Bible*. Ed. David & Pat Alexander. Herts: Lion Publishing plc, England, 1986	Lion Handbook to Bible

25. *Longman Dic. of Eng. Language & Culture.* Essex: Longman Group UK Ltd, 1992 — Longman Dic. EngLngCultr

26. *Master Study Bible, NAS, Enc, Concordance, a Harmony of the Gospels, etc.* Nashville: Holman Bible Publishers, 1977. — Master Study Bible

27. *J L McKenzie's Dic. of Bible.* London: Geoffrey Chapman, 1984. — McKenzie DB

28. *A Dic. of Modern Written Arabic.* Ed. J. Milton Cowan. London: Macdonald & Evans Ltd, 1980. — ModW.ArbDic

29. *New Bible Dic.* (II Ed.). N. Hillyer (Revision Edn.). Leicestor: Inter-Varsity Press, Eng., 1986. — New Bible Dic.

30. *The New Shorter Oxford English Dic.*, 1993 — New Shorter

31. *The New Standard Enc & World Atlas* With an Introduction by The Rev. C.A. Alington, D.D., Hm of Eton. Prepared under the general editorship of J. M. Parrish, M.A. (Oxon), John R. Crossland, F.R.G.S., & A. W. Holland, managing ed. of the Enc. Britannica (13th Edn); with the specialist assistance of George Somerville, MD, DPM.; John S. Linnell, B.A. (Oxon); K. M. Gadd, M.A. (Oxon & London); C. H. Knowles, B.Sc. (London); the Rev. Eric Dixon, M.C., B.A., B.D. (Lond.); E. S. Roberts, B.A., and over 40 experts, learned societies and institutions. Odhams Press Ltd, London, W. C. 2, 1932. — New Standard Enc

32. *The New World Dic.-Concordance to the New American Bib.* Manila. Philippines: Daughters of St Paul, 1994. — N.W.Dic.-Conc

NAB

33. John R. Kohlenberger III. *NIV Compact Conc.* Manila, Philippines: OMF Literature Inc. PO Box 2217, 2002. — NIV Compact Concordance

34. J. D. Douglas & Merrill C. Tenney. *NIV Compact Dic. of the Bible* Michigan: The Zondervan Corp., Grand Rapids, 1989. — NIV Compact Dic. of Bible

35. *Oxf. Dic.& Thesaurus*. Melbourne: Oxf. Univ. Press, 1997.	Oxf. Dic.& Thes.
36. *Pictorial Biblical Enc*. Ed. Gaalyahu Cornfeld. NY: Macmillan Co., 1964.	Pictorial Bib Enc
37. *The Enc. of Religion*. NY: Macmillan Publishing Co., 1987.	Religion Enc
38. *Roget's II The New Thesaurus*. Ed. Fernando de Mello Vianna. Boston: Houghton Mifflin Co, 1980.	Roget's II Thesaurus
39. The Seventh-day Adventist Bible Dic. (Rvd Edn by R. H. Woolsley). Ed. Don F. Neufeld, Washington DC. Hagerstown: Review & Herald Publishing Association, 1978.	7th Day Bible Dic.
40. H.A.R. Gibb, J. H. Kramer. *Concise Enc. of Islam*. Leiden: Brill Academic Publishers, Inc. 2001.	Concise Enc. of Islam
41. W. Smith. *A Dic. of Bible* (Revd. Ed. F.N., M.A. Peloubet). Michigan: Regency Ref. Lib. Grand Rapids, 1984.	Smith's

Dic. of Bible

42. *The Standard Jewish Enc*. Ed. Dr. Cecil Roth. London: W. H. Allen, 1959.	Standard Jewish Enc.
43. James Strong. *Strong's Exhaustive Concordance*. Michigan: Baker Book House, Grand Rapids, 1984.	Strongs

Conc.

44. James Strong. *A Concise Dic. of the Words in The Hebrew Bible*. NY, Cincinnati: The Methodist Book Concern, 1890.	Strongs

Heb B. Dic.

45. W. E. Vine, Merrill F. Unger, William White Jr. *Vine's Complete Expository Dictionary of O & NT Words with Topical Index*. Nashville, USA: Thomas Nelson, Inc., 1996.	Vine's Complete Expo. Dic. of O & NT Words
46. *Webster's Dic. of Eng. Usage*. Ed. E. Ward Gilman. Massachusetts: Merriam-Webster Inc., Springfield, 1989.	Webster Dic. of Eng. Usage

47. *Webster's New Dic. of Synonyms*. Ed. Philip B. Grove. Massachusetts: G.&C. Merriam Co, Springfield, 1978. — Webster New Dic. of Syn.

48. *Webster's New World College Dic*. 3rd Edn. Ed. Victoria Neufeldt. NY, USA: Macmillan, 1997. — Webster N.W. College Dic.

49. Aḥmad bin Fāriṣ. *Mu'jam Maqāyīs al-Lughah*. Beirūt: Dār Iḥyā al-turāth al-'Arabī, 2001. — Maqā'īs al-Lugha

50. Ismāīl ibn Ḥammād al-Jawharī. *Tāj al-Lughat wa Ṣiḥāḥ al-'Arabiyyah*. Beirūt: Dār al-'Ilm lil Malāyīn, 1984. — Ṣiḥāḥ al- Jawharī

51. Al-Ustādh al-Ṭāhir Aḥmad al-zāvī, *Tartīb al-Qāmūs al-Muḥīt 'ala Ṭariqah al-Miṣbāḥ al- Munīr*, 1979. — Tartīb al-Qāmūs

52. *Mu'jam al-Wasīt*. Beirūt: Dār Iḥyā al-turāth al-'Arabī, 1972, — Mu'jam al-Wasīt

53. Ibn Manẓūr. *Lisān al-'Arab*. Beirūt: Dār Ṣādir, 1300 AH, — Lisān al-'Arab

54. Mu'allim Buṭrus al-Bustānī. *Muḥīt al-Muḥīt*. Beirūt: Maktabah Lubnān Nāshirūn, 1993 — Muḥīt al-Muḥīt

(d) Miscellaneous

Sr No	*Name of the Book, Author, Editor, Publisher, Year, etc.*	*Abbreviation*
1.	Al-Imām Abī 'Abd Allāh Muḥammad bin Isḥāq al-Fākihī, *Akhbār Makkah fi Qadīm al-Dahr wa Ḥadīthihi'*. Makkah: Maktabah al-Nahḍat al-Ḥadīthah, 1987.	Akhbār Makkah
2.	Dr. Muḥammad Muḥsin Khān. *Tr. of the Meanings of Saḥiḥ Al-Bukhārī*. Riyādh: Dār al-Salām, S.A., PO Box 22743, 1997.	Al-Bukhārī
3.	Ḥamīd al-Dīn Farāhī. *al-Ra'y al-Ṣaḥīḥ fī man Huwa al-Dhabīḥ*. Damascus: Dār al-Qalam, 1999.	Al-Dhabīḥ~?
4.	George Sale, 'The Preliminary discourse' to the *Alkoran of Mohammed*. London: Frederick Warne & Co., na.	Al-KORAN, Tr. G. Sale

5. *The Koran*, Tr. N. J. Dawood, India: Penguin Books, 1994.
N. J. Dāwūd

6. N. J. Dawood, Revised Dr. Zayid. *The Quran, An Eng Trans*. Beirut: Dar Al-Choura, 1980.
The Quran, Daral-Choura

7. *The QUR'ĀN*. Tr. E. H. Palmer. Delhi: Motilal Banarsidass, 1988.
The QUR'ĀN Tr. Palmer

8. Geddes MacGregor. *The Bible in the Making*. London: John Murray, 1961.
Bible in the Making

9. Raymond E. Brown. *An Introduction to the NT*. Bangalore: Theological Pub in India (TPI), 2000.
Brown's NT Introduction

10. *The Cambridge History of the Bible*. Ed. P. R. Ackroyd & C. F. Evans. Cambridge: at the University Press, 1970.
Cambridge Hist Of Bible

11. Paul Johnson. *A History of Christianity*. NY: Simon & Schuster, 1995.
History of Christianity

12. Rheme Perkins. *NT Introduction*. Bombay: St Paul Publications, Bandra, 1992.
Introduction NT

13. Werner H Schmidt. *OT Introduction*, Tr. by Matthew J. O'Connell, Bombay: St Paul Publications, Bandra, 1992.
Introduction OT

14. *The Works of Flavius Josephus*. Tr. by W. Whiston. Boston: D Lothrop & Co., na.
Josephus, Woks of

15. *The Book of the Jubilees, in 'The Apocrypha and Pseudepigrapha of the OT in Eng.'* Ed. R. H. Charles. Oxford: The Clarendon Press, 1968.
Jubilees,

Book of

16. *A Lion Handbook: the World's Religions*. Ed. R. Pierce Beaver, etc. England: The Lion Publishing, Herts, 1984
Lion Handbook World's Rlgns

17. Raymond E. Brown, Joseph A. Fitzmyer, and Roland E. Murphy. *The New Jerome Bible Handbook*. Minnesota: The Liturgical Press, Collegeville, 1993.
New Jerome Bible Handbook

18. *The NT Background*. Ed. C. K. Barret. HarperSanFrancsco, 1995.
NT Background

No.	Reference	Abbreviation
19.	Bruce M. Metzger. *The Text of the NT*. Oxford: at the Clarendon Press, 1964.	NT Text
20.	F. F. Bruce. *Places Abraham Knew*. London: Scrip-ture Union, City Road, ECIVZNJ, 1984.	Places Abra-ham Knew
21.	Rev. Joseph Kudasiewicz. *The Synoptic Gospels Today*. Manila: T Pauls, Makati City, Philippines, 1996	Synoptic Gospels Today
22.	Mawlānā Amīn Aḥsan Iṣlāḥī. *Tadabbur-e-Qur'ān*. (Lahore: Faran Foundation, 1977), 5:485. (al-Qur'ān 37:107)	Tadabbur-e-Qur'ān
23.	Ken Anderson. *Where to Find It in the Bible*. Nashville, USA: Thomas Nelson Publ, 1996.	Where to Find It in Bible

Index

T